Divided We Fall

Bryce Christensen

Divided We Fall

Family Discord
and the
Fracturing of America

Transaction Publishers
New Brunswick (U.S.A.) and London (U.K.)

New material this edition copyright © 2006 by Transaction Publishers, New Brunswick, New Jersey.

This book is printed on acid-free paper that meets the American National Standard for Permanence of Paper for Printed Library Materials.

Library of Congress Catalog Number: 2005054944
ISBN: 0-7658-0316-X
Printed in the United States of America

Library of Congress Cataloging-in-Publication Data

Christensen, Bryce J.
    Divided we fall : family discord and the fracturing of America / by Bryce J. Christensen.
        p. cm.
    Includes bibliographical references and index.
    ISBN 0-7658-0316-X (alk. paper)
    1. Problem families—United States. 2. Social problems—United States.
    3. United States—Social conditions—1980- I. Title.

HV699.C47 2005
362.820973—dc22   2005054944

Contents

to Mary

Acknowledgements

This book began in conversations with Dr. Allan Carlson, the President of the Howard Center. Recognizing important continuities of theme in a number of essays I had published in *The Family in America* (which he edits), Dr. Carlson urged me to revise and combine them into a book. In the revision process, as in the writing of the original essays, Dr. Carlson has provided both insight and inspiration.

I drew encouragement to act on Dr. Carlson's suggestion when the editors of *Society*, of *The Sutherland Journal of Law and Public Policy*, and of *Touchstone* here in the United States; of *Endeavour Forum* in Australia; and of *G³os Dla Zycia* in Poland asked for rights to reprint versions *Family in America* essays that have here become Chapters Two, Three, Six, and Eight.

My special thanks also go to Dr. Irving Louis Horowitz, Chairman of the Board and Editorial Director for Transaction Books. He has been both patient and perceptive in guiding me through repeated revisions of the original manuscript. My editor at Transaction, Anne Schneider, has also been most helpful in handling the manuscript.

I further wish to thank my department chair here at Southern Utah University, Dr. Kay Cook, whose understanding and cooperation have given me favorable circumstances for writing.

Finally, I wish to thank my wife and sons, whose love and loyalty have informed everything worthwhile I have ever written about family matters.

To these individuals I acknowledge that I owe much for any of this book's merits. For any of its remaining deficiencies, I take personal responsibility.

Introduction

In the weeks that followed the horror of September 11, 2001, politicians of both major parties resolutely asserted America's national unity. Unfortunately, as the months passed, reality strained the rhetoric of unity. Deep divisions often tear the national fabric—or at least pull it very taut with tension. For those Americans slow to recognize the national divisions, the ubiquitous media graphics for the 2004 presidential election (remarkably similar to those for the 2000 election) fixed Red and Blue in the national consciousness as contrasting colors symbolic of a remarkable gulf in American political life.[1] Eager to invest this electoral divide with deep cultural significance, pundits have identified a number of supposedly fundamental red-blue contrasts—farmers vs. city dwellers, tax cutters vs. tax raisers, gun owners vs. gun controllers, developers vs. environmentalists.

Some analysts have asserted that the Red-Blue gulf yawns particularly wide on family issues. Because Red politicians (including George Bush) typically characterize themselves as defenders of the traditional family, and because Blue politicians (including Al Gore and John Kerry) have drawn strong support from feminist and homosexual groups indifferent or hostile to the traditional family, Red Americans and Blue Americans do indeed appear deeply divided on family issues. The reality—explored in this book—is far more complex, resistant to a simple collision between Red and Blue perspectives. Although high-visibility family issues such as gay marriage and abortion can significantly affect Red-Blue politics, a candid and searching examination of the whole gamut of family issues (including divorce, cohabitation, foster care, child support, and day care) reveals a bewildering array of cross-cutting tensions and ambiguities.

In some ways, the shrill rhetoric of election years exaggerates partisan differences on family issues. After all, regardless of which levers they pull on Election Day, most Americans still deeply value marriage, regard divorce as harmful, and believe strongly in parental commitment. Though this broad American consensus on family questions receives less attention than it deserves, it ought to blind no one to the ways that family issues do indeed divide America. The divisions, in fact, run far deeper than Red vs. Blue, deeper than Republican vs. Democrat, deeper than conservative vs. liberal. An honest and searching assessment of the way family issues are dividing America will reveal not a neat map of Red bloc vs. Blue bloc but a confusing kaleidoscope of social shards, not a tidy contrast between Republican family policies vs. Democratic family policies but a tangle of often-ignored cultural pathologies.

An honest analysis of how family issues are fracturing America must begin with a candid acknowledgement of just how many fissures recent changes in family life have opened in the nation's social life and just how deeply these fissures now run. Many Americans still passionately adhere to the two-parent family as a social ideal and regard with dismay the growing incidence of divorce, cohabitation, out-of-wedlock childbearing, and abortion. For many of those who affirm this ideal, family commitments reflect religious convictions and inherited moral traditions. These convictions and traditions transcend political affiliation; indeed, many Americans regard their family commitments as pre-political givens, not open to intellectual or political debate.

However, some Americans—especially some political opportunists, Republican and Democratic—have made family issues the very basis for ideological posturing. Some of the ideologues who set the agenda for Blue America celebrate diversity in family forms and attack as judgmental those who decry divorce, cohabitation, out-of-wedlock childbearing, and abortion. For these ideologues, to hold the two-parent family up as the ideal is to succumb to outdated stereotypes. On the other hand, some of the ideologues for Red America see electoral advantage in "wedge issues" such as gay marriage and abortion rights. As vocally as they might decry gay marriage and elective abortion, they are quietly very happy for issues that help them troll for votes among socially conservative Hispanics and African-Americans. The very illusion that the nation's family discontents will yield to political solutions—liberal or conservative, Democratic or Republican—helps intensify those discontents, even as it serves the interests of politicians of diverse affiliations.

Anyone willing to look past the slogans and the photo-ops will begin to glimpse the deeper complexities affecting family issues. The family lives of some conservative Republican politicians who have carried the pro-family banner in recent decades (Reagan, Gingrich, Dole) look more like the problem than the solution. On the other hand, some liberal Democratic politicians who have promulgated the rhetoric of family diversity (Gore, Boxer, Dean) have worked hard to preserve in their own lives the very marital institution that their rhetoric and public policies have sometimes tended to devalue. When it affords them no electoral advantage, politicians of both parties have too often turned a blind eye to the social pressures undermining family life—have even heedlessly collaborated (in bipartisan fashion) in intensifying these pressures.

But the conflict over family life is a conflict over more than ideology, more than political positions. It is a deeply personal conflict, affecting—and affected by—our most intimate relationships. After marriages end in divorce, after children are split from a parent and perhaps from other siblings, profound personal animosities poison lives for decades. Such bitter experiences color life much more deeply than does the typical profession of any political view, Republican or Democratic. And, of course, such bitterness affects far too many people and affects them in ways far too complicated to ever be captured in any two-tone Red-Blue political map. Just as the internecine brother-against-brother combat of 1861-1865 defies reduction to simple blue-gray maps, so too, the fracturing of millions of American marriages and families in recent decades resists the caricatures of blue-red cartography.

But as impossible as it is to represent schematically, the conflict surrounding family issues is terribly real, so real that it constitutes a new kind of civil war. Americans are now seeing unprecedented conflict not only of brother against brother, but former wife against former husband, grandparent against former daughter- or son-in-law, parent against child, and so on in all the ugly possible permutations. This new American Civil War defines the focus for chapter 1. And this war rages on with unabated ferocity on both the personal and political levels.

The terrorist attacks of 9/11 signaled the nightmarish beginning of a quite different war. For a brief period, the outpouring of patriotic sentiment occasioned by the attacks seemed to signal an end to the pre-9/11 divisions in American life. But Americans could not really hope to heal the country's deep divisions—especially those created by four decades of increasingly fractious family life—with flag ceremonies or anthems. To the degree that Americans ever believed that patriotic displays alone would heal the rents in our national social life, to that degree they were manifesting a pervasive cultural weakness that made America peculiarly vulnerable both to terrorist assault and to family disintegration in the first place. The object of repeated unfavorable comment by perceptive foreign critics, a jejune national optimism runs through far too much of American life. For too long, this facile national optimism had crowded out of view the ugly international realities that intruded on 9/11. And for too long, this same shallow optimism had inhibited the development of the moral sobriety necessary to make enduring marital and family commitments.

For many Americans, a puerile optimism flows from an unbounded faith in free-market capitalism. That unfettered capitalism can foster greed and egotism in ways subversive of the family ideals they profess seems not to have occurred to some cheery-minded Americans. But while some Americans appear blissfully myopic in their championing both the traditional family and an untethered consumer capitalism, an influential few American ideologues seem deliriously intoxicated in their deliberate assault upon the family. Indeed, some New Left and feminist ideologues optimistically regard the dismembering of the traditional family—however painful at first—as part of a joyous march toward a radiant post-familial, post-gendered utopian future. These ideologues thus claim radiant hopes for the future as their political property and denigrate their own stubborn attachments to traditional family life as the waning effects of nostalgia. The shock of 9/11, however, exposed many of the diverse forms of American optimism as giddiness.

When President Bush responded to the 9/11 attacks with a war against terror, most Americans initially supported him. But as chapter 2 shows, a nation deeply divided in peace can hardly be expected to maintain a united front in war. Quite aside from the real reservations of some of Bush's conservative allies about the invasion of Iraq and the subsequent attempts at the very kind of nation-building he had previously eschewed when the theater was Kosovo, personal and ideological rifts in family life soon translated into conflicting attitudes toward the war, especially as the war dragged on and became a focal point for 2004's election-year debates. On a personal level, marital and family strife inevitably weakened the morale of troops whose lives had been poisoned by such strife. Traditionally, American soldiers have fought to defend their wives and children (as is discussed in chapter 7). But how hard does a divorced enlisted man—all too common in today's Army—fight for an embittered ex-wife or even for children whom he has rarely seen and who have been alienated from his affections? How hard does a divorced woman—also all too common in today's Army—fight if she has enlisted only because her marriage has failed and she can find no better financial option?

On an ideological level, 2004 election-year politics emboldened some opponents of the Bush Administration to look for targets of political opportunity in the war against terror. Thus, some of the ideological radicals whose reflexive opposition to conservative social ideals made them—at least temporarily—part of the "Blue" coalition were very vocal in criticizing the Bush administration's war policy *except* whenever it coincided with their own domestic offensive against traditional family life. Thus, some left-leaning commentators stopped criticizing and started cheering whenever those doing the fighting and dying in the War Against Terror were non-traditional female soldiers, especially single mothers. Thus, while most Americans supported the war against terror as necessary to protect American families, some ideological critics supported that war only when it offered chances to engineer new kinds of American families. Such divided aims could hardly foster constancy or firmness in martial purpose.

At home, far from Afghanistan and Iraq, personal and ideological family conflict have helped dissipate the national heritage America's soldiers are trying to defend abroad. Chapter 3 looks, for instance, at how conservative and liberal politicians have together dealt with the aftermath of divorce and illegitimacy by building a dubious new bureaucracy for collecting child support—often in highly intrusive and arbitrary ways—from non-custodial parents (overwhelmingly fathers). Although some have realized financial or political advantages (discussed in chapter 8) through the building of this bureaucracy, most of those involved see themselves simply as problem-solvers and pragmatists. Too few seem willing to acknowledge how basic legal rights are being abridged in the process or how the new bureaucracy actually masks rather than cures the fundamental social problems created by family failure.

The same kind of short-sighted pragmatism shows up among those overseeing the government agencies providing foster care for abused children and shelter to the homeless. Without question, the public officials involved (Republicans and Democrats) have worked hard to meet the real needs of abused children and homeless individuals. But few have given much attention to the chain of pathologies linking child abuse and homelessness to family failures; fewer still scrutinize the cultural forces that cause such family failures. Chapter 4, however, exposes the ultimate futility of enlarging the foster-care system without reversing the family- and marriage-destroying social trends that render ever more children vulnerable to abuse and neglect. Chapter 5 indicts both the consumerism that conservatives insouciantly accept and the ideology that leftists promote as curiously interwoven causes of both the physical homelessness that media commentators lament and the emotional homelessness the media usually ignore.

Growing numbers of children in foster care and growing numbers of homeless people on the streets are not the only consequences of anti-family trends in law and culture. Though not always recognized as such—not even by its most vocal advocates—gay marriage is the entirely predictable and even inevitable culmination of decades of change in heterosexual attitudes toward marriage, divorce, and sexuality. Chapter 6 provides much-needed historical context for the gay-marriage debate, showing that renewing American family life requires much more than electoral referenda defining marriage as a male-female institution.

And whether they are looking at homosexual couples or heterosexual couples, when Americans begin debating what government officials can or should do for households, they too often unthinkingly envision a one-way relationship in which the state confers benefits upon individuals and households. The state's very real dependence upon its citizens' patriotic impulses and upon the family patterns that foster such impulses often disappears. Chapter 7 looks at the dangerous disappearance of patriotism and civic self-sacrifice in a world in which fewer and fewer families can serve as the "seedbed of the state" (Cicero's apt phrase). The problem is hardly that contemporary Americans have cut themselves loose from the state. No. The perilous reality, explored in chapter 8, is worse than that. Instead of making personal sacrifices to support a state that, in turn, defends and protects their families, Americans are increasingly looking to the surrogate-family state as a source of benefits—income, employment, therapy. Fewer and fewer Americans maintain ties of selfless civic loyalty *to* the state and more and more Americans seek ties of opportunistic advantage *from* the state. That is a fatal shift in political culture entirely predictable when marriages and families grow weak.

As chapter 9 shows, the horrors of 9/11 did at least briefly turn many Americans toward a more sober perspective on life by shattering optimistic illusions and ideologies while validating the enduring strengths of traditional family ties. When calamity strikes, Americans do instinctively turn to parents, siblings, and spouse. Despite the ebullience of their promises, both advertising executives and political activists seem far less reliable than family members when buildings start to fall.

But many of those morally sobered by the tragedy of 9/11 have found relatively few settings in which they can meaningfully explore their deep concerns about the nation's family life. In part, that difficulty reflects the strange reticence of the national media to acknowledge fully the malign consequences—political, social, economic—of family disintegration. But the bigger problem may be that even when these family-related malignancies have forced their way into public attention, many commentators have aborted the much-needed dialogue about how to restore social health with a paralyzing metaphor. "You cannot," these commentators assert, "turn back the clock." Chapter 10 challenges the assumptions behind this defeatist metaphor by surveying a range of historical perspectives offering real hope for social renewal. When commentators try to terminate much-needed discussion of harmful family trends with their clock metaphor, Americans should remember the much more helpful metaphor of the Doomsday clock initially developed in the Sixties and Seventies by the editors of *The Bulletin of Atomic Scientists* at the University of Chicago. On this metaphorical clock, midnight represented nuclear apocalypse. Periodically, the *BAS* editors would provide an updated reading of the clock, moving forward—toward midnight—when nuclear weapons spread or acquired new lethality and moving backward when countries signed new arms agreements or destroyed nuclear weaponry. On family issues, the hour is indeed late. But it is not yet midnight. And we can—we *must*—turn back the clock.

Note

1.   Cf. Robert J. Venderbei, "Election 2004 Results," Princeton University, 21 Jan 2005 <http://www.princeton.edu~rvdb/JAVA/election2004>; "Election 2000: Latest Vote, County by County," USA Today 20 Nov. 2000, 21 Jan. 2005 <http://www.usatoday.com/news/vote2000/cbc/map.htm>.

1

Divided We Fall: Family Strife in America's Second Civil War

From bumper stickers and billboards to political speeches and church sermons, few themes received more attention in post-9/11 America in the weeks immediately after the terrorist attacks than the need for national unity in the face of ominous external threats. "United We Stand" sufficed for the bumper stickers and T-shirts, but clerics, journalists, and academics expatiated on the theme of national unity at much greater length. Columbia University sociologist Todd Gitlin, for instance, declared, "One deep truth about September 11 is that a community was attacked, not an assortment of individuals." Within this community, Gitlin further explained that in post-9/11 America, "You are in solidarity with strangers: their losses are your own." This national solidarity summoned all Americans to "commonality and sacrifice," expressed through a "patriotism of mutual aid, not just symbolic displays."[1] In the same vein, the Episcopalian cleric Richard H. Downes saw in the tragic events of 9/11 a forceful reminder that "church and nation both require a strong sense of collective affirmation to bring out the meanings each embodies." In the aftermath of the terrorist attacks, Americans needed again "to ponder who we are and how we are obligated to each other."[2] Speaking in a similar tone, author and commentator George Packer identified 9/11 as an event exposing the fatuity of the divisive modern politics that have "balkanized" and "fragmented" American public life. Though he suspected that "That day changed America less than most people anticipated," Packer nonetheless believed that 9/11 occasioned a shift in public mood, as Americans "looked at one another differently." For the first time in many years, Americans again realized that "they were not merely individuals with private ends but rather fellow citizens, alive to the sentiments once expressed by the poet

1

Walt Whitman: "'What is more subtle than this which ties me to the woman or man that looks in my face?'" Because it made Americans newly cognizant of their ties to their fellow Americans, Packer asserted that 9/11 "made Americans think about change—not just as individuals, but as a country."[3]

The pervasive rhetoric of national unity perhaps served its purpose. It reassured a people unnerved by the unexpected and stunningly successful terrorist attacks of 9/11 and rattled by the prospect of other such attacks, perhaps by extremists armed with devastating nuclear, biological, or chemical weaponry. Indeed, this rhetoric of unity may even have done its work too well. For the rhetoric of unity obscured the sad reality of a nation deeply divided. In one way, those divisions emerged in 2004 as Red Americans and Blue Americans lined up on opposite sides of an overheated presidential election. Though real, that Red-Blue division unfortunately obscured a real unity still defined by shared social hopes. Even when they differ as to their political prescriptions for realizing these hopes, Red Republicans and Blue Democrats alike share recognizably similar hopes for happy and lasting marriages, for fulfilling and harmonious family lives. But even before the divisive election-year rhetoric heated up, millions of Americans (Red and Blue) were divided from their fellow citizens by the life-scarring experience of family failures. Even without the dubious labors of Red and Blue sloganeers, America has become a nation more deeply divided than it has ever been, a nation whose citizens have been pulled apart—personally, socially, morally, economically, ideologically, and politically—by the unprecedented disintegration of the nation's marital and family life. The post-9/11 belief that such divisions could be healed through patriotic rhetoric and gestures (Republican or Democratic) was a cruel illusion.

In the more than two centuries of their country's existence, Americans have never before seen more fragmentation and disarray in marital and family life than we currently see. Though the divorce rate has declined slightly since the early 1980s, it still remains more than 30 percent higher than it was in 1970, when it was already high by historical standards. Meanwhile, the national marriage rate has plummeted to an all-time low, dropping almost 40 percent just since 1970, a drop that helps to account for an illegitimacy rate that has skyrocketed from just 5 percent in 1960 to 33 percent in 1998. Just as dramatic has been the multiplication of the number of couples repudiating wedlock in favor of non-marital cohabitation: the Census Bureau counted 4.5 million such couples in 1999, compared to just 1.6 million in 1980. Also on the rise, the number of female-headed households with children has risen from 3.0 million in 1970 to 7.8 million in 1999. And while the number of married-couple households with children has remained relatively stable, declining from 25.5 million in 1970 to 25.0 million in 1999, it must be remembered that the population as a whole grew by almost 30 percent (about 60 million) during this period.[4] It must also be remembered that among children who live with married parents, only a little over half live with both biological parents; almost as many live with a remarried biological parent and a stepparent.[5] Problematic surrogate parents of a different sort have likewise insinuated themselves into the lives of a growing number—now over a million—of pre-school children whose employed mothers daily leave them in the care of day-care workers.

For a time, a post-9/11 upsurge in marriages and engagements encouraged some to hope that perhaps the harrowing shock of the terrorist attacks had renewed the country's commitment to wedlock and family life. However, subsequent research into national attitudes suggests that the shift in family attitudes may have been "a mere blip" and that, overall, "attitudes of average Americans have not changed much since the September 11 attacks."[6] The moral challenge of having to fight Osama Bin Laden and his followers may have sobered some Americans, but it has not yet decisively reversed the country's worrisome retreat from family life.

Nor can any sober commentator on the nation's social life plausibly interpret the astounding national retreat from wedlock and family life as merely an innocuous shift in personal lifestyles. This retreat from marriage and family has seriously harmed our national public life, creating grievous tears in our national social fabric, profoundly dis-unifying the nation. Until Americans face that grim reality, even the most inspired talk about national unity will amount to no more than whistling-in-the-dark self-delusion.

To understand how deeply family disintegration has divided America, it may be helpful to contrast the country's state of disunion in the early twenty-first century with the most often-invoked example of national disunion: the Civil War of 1861 to 1865. In trying to convey the horribly internecine character of the great national struggle of the 1860s, historians have often described it as a conflict of "brother against brother." To be sure, in a significant number of cases, brothers did fight on opposite sides in this terrible bloodletting. General George H. Thomas—one of the Union heroes of Chattanooga—was a Virginian fighting against other Virginians. An entire Confederate Unit (the Shiver Grays) was recruited from a single town (Wheeling) in the Union State of West Virginia. The border state of Kentucky sent tens of thousands of soldiers to both sides of the conflict.[7] Still, the war that Southern partisans referred to as the War Between the States was largely defined by regional allegiances: brothers who lived in the same state usually fought on the same side, and the tragedy of brother taking up arms against brother was largely limited to border states. Even in border states, the lines of conflict more frequently ran between families than between brothers. In the current civil war which is tearing American families apart, the lines of division run right through millions of disintegrating homes.

Indeed, when future historians try to describe the ubiquitous social conflict that has rent America since the late 1960s, they may well invoke the phrase "brother against brother"—as well as many other similar phrases ("sister against sister," "former husband against former wife," "parent against child," " grandparent against former daughter-in-law," and so on)—to describe a genuinely internecine countrywide conflict fought out not on clearly defined battlefields such as Gettysburg and Cold Harbor but rather in tens of thousands of bitter and interminable domestic conflicts. For the social tragedy of family disintegration that now plays itself out hundreds of thousands of times each year in the United States pits husband against wife (or cohabiting lover vs. cohabiting lover), sibling against sibling, parent against child, grandparent against former daughter-in-law, and stepparent against former parent. With good reason, the literary critic Alvin Kernan has remarked that in the firestorm of recent social change in America, "the family is probably the most desperate battlefield."[8]

Domestic Battlegrounds

The conflict on these domestic battlefields has grown cruel and vicious as family life has decayed. In two studies at the University of New Hampshire, progressive-thinking sociologists who were not initially inclined to regard marriage as superior to non-marital cohabitation learned—to their astonishment—that cohabiting women are almost five times as likely as married peers to suffer "extreme violence" in their homes.[9] In the violent domestic conflict increasingly wracking American society, children suffer as well as women. Researchers on child abuse have discerned a clear "association between physical abuse of children and deviance from normative family structure," with careful investigation revealing that "battered babies are likely to be reared in broken homes" and that premarital pregnancy, illegitimacy, and absence of the child's father are among the most common "precursors of baby battering."[10] Columbia University researchers have determined from available child-abuse data that children living in single-parent families are more than twice as likely to experience physical abuse (Odds Ratio of 2.26) than peers in two-parent homes.[11] And researchers from Ohio State University have established that domestic violence harmful to women and children is especially likely to erupt in "disadvantaged neighborhoods" in which 42 percent or more of the households are headed by single females.[12]

But besides fostering domestic abuse, the fragmentation of the family sets the stage for socially divisive custody fights that traumatize children and embitter and impoverish adults. When husbands or wives decide to file for divorce, they find that no-fault divorce laws have made it easy to sever the ties to an unwanted spouse. Those laws, however, have not simplified the legal adjudication of child custody. Indeed, legal scholar Lynn D. Wardle identifies an increasing number of acrimonious custody disputes as a prime indicator that the nationwide adoption of no-fault divorce statutes has not led to the reduction in adversarial litigation promised by no-fault advocates. Thus, while "there unquestionably is less hostile litigation regarding the grounds for divorce," since the adoption of no-fault divorce laws, "it appears that this has been due primarily to a transfer of hostility into other facets of the divorce proceeding," including especially those governing child custody.[13] In the absence of a finding of fault as the justification for the divorce, the judges who weigh the competing claims of divorcing parents often split siblings—even identical twins—leaving them lost, disoriented, and dismayed at the sudden and unexpected sundering of their ties to brothers and sisters.[14] When America's Civil War of the 1860s split siblings, it split adults who freely—though tragically—decided on their opposing fates. But the siblings split by America's domestic civil war of the late twentieth and early twenty-first centuries are bewildered children with no control over what happens to them.

Even if custody disputes do not split siblings, they do separate children from parents. Psychologists have found that the children affected by this fissuring of the family typically have "expressed the wish that their parents were reunited." Many of these children are "confused about which parent they 'loved' most and wishing that their parents 'would stop saying unkind things about each other.'"[15] Even after the pronouncement of the divorce decree, children thus find themselves pinned down in the ugly house-to-house combat that continues between the former spouses.

The hostility in child custody disputes has grown so intense that "the practice of one parent falsely accusing the other parent of child abuse, especially child sexual abuse, appears to have increased since the adoption of no-fault divorce grounds."[16] Such tactics naturally prolong the court proceedings necessary to adjudicate child custody and inflate their costs: the legal bills for one highly visible child-custody fight reached $4 million.[17] And when the courts have finally reached a custody decision—a decision inevitably unfavorable to one of the legal combatants—not a few determined parents are now resorting to the desperate expedient of kidnapping their own children. As the nation's leading authorities on missing children have explained, "Most U.S. kidnappings are carried out by family members, often parents," and "usually during custody disputes."[18] As Ben Ermi of the National Center for Missing and Exploited Children has acknowledged, of the nearly 700,000 children reported missing each year, "the second highest number [after runaway cases] involve family abductions."[19] In 1999, of the thousands of children kidnapped in the United States, only 134 were cases of stranger abduction.[20] Although most family abductions are non-violent local affairs, some involve weapons, and hundreds of cases each year develop into international sagas.[21]

Even if they never resort to handguns or passports, many divorced parents wage custodial war with their former spouses for a long time. In a recent national study, fully one-third of all divorced parents surveyed reported "continued conflict over custody and visitation issues."[22]

But when family failure splits society into criminals and victims, kidnappers and hostages, prosecutors and defendants, the immediate members of the families are not the only ones exposed to often dangerous conflict. Failure in the home all too frequently translates into crime in the street. As historian David T. Courtwright has argued in *Violent Land*, the disintegration of urban family life has produced the same kind of social disorder in the modern city as America once saw on its Wild West fringe in Dodge City or Abilene—and for the same reason: the disappearance of the marital and family ties that restrain male aggression. Courtwright explains that because "the total amount of violence and disorder in society is negatively related to the percentage of males in intact families of origin or procreation," the upsurge in illegitimacy and divorce in the inner-city has created "artificial and unusually violent frontier societies—vice-ridden combat zones in which groups of armed, unparented, and reputation-conscious young bachelors ... menace one another and the local citizenry."[23] It is no surprise, then, that University of Washington criminologists recently concluded that, compared to males born to married mothers, "males born to unmarried mothers were 1.7-fold more likely to become an offender [as a juvenile] and 2.1 times more likely to become a chronic offender."[24] Just as predictably, researchers at the University of Missouri-Columbia have found that the typical adolescent killer is a young man whose "parents were never married or are divorced, and [who] lives with his mother."[25] No wonder that criminologists at the University of Florida find that—at least among the nation's white majority—as urban family forms become more diverse, the toll of urban murders rises.[26]

And while today's researchers trace street crime to divorce and illegitimacy, tomorrow's researchers will likely be tracing such crime to maternal employment and day care. Already child psychologists are reporting that time in day care predicts elevated levels of "problem behavior, as well as assertiveness, disobedience, and aggression."[27] More specifically, time in day care has emerged as a precursor to hitting, kicking, pushing, threatening, swearing, teasing, and arguing.[28] It takes no unusual prescience to predict what crimes a bullying, slugging day-school preschooler will be committing in his adolescence and young adulthood.

But the divisive dynamics of family disintegration pull the country apart even when the behavior it produces remains within the limits of legality. For without question, the retreat from family life has polarized and poisoned American politics. Gender politics, for instance, have become much more contentious as divorce rates have climbed and marriage rates have fallen. For while political scientists find that "women vote like men" in married-couple households, they see a yawning gender gap among single and divorced individuals.

In the 1980 presidential election, for instance, the gender gap was a miniscule 2 percent in "two-adult households" (overwhelmingly married-couple households), compared with a remarkable 11 percent in "other households."[29] The inference that marriage conduces to political harmony between men and women while marital failure leads to political conflict between the sexes grows to something close to certainty in light of recent research. That research shows conclusively that "divorced women are significantly more feminist than married women," thus identifying women's marital status as one of the nation's clearest "lines of political cleavage."[30]

Like divorce, out-of-wedlock childbearing has heightened ideological gender tension and conflict in American politics. A 1987 study showed that while marital childbearing made women "more traditional" in their social attitudes, non-marital childbearing had the opposite effect, making women "less traditional," more feminist.[31]

Even abandonment of the home in favor of paid employment pushes women in the same socially dis-unifying feminist direction. Sociologist Jennifer Glass has documented a "rapidly growing" divergence in moral attitudes separating full-time career women from women who are full-time homemakers or who are employed only part-time. In this divergence, Glass sees social and political "implications of polarization in women's interests [that] may become profound."[32]

But the retreat from family life is dis-unifying the nation along axes other than those defined by gender ideology. Family disintegration is also creating increasingly impassable chasms between America's poor and America's rich. Because Americans generally shared in the benefits of the nation's twentieth-century economic development, statistical indices of economic inequality dropped steadily through most of the century as the gap separating America's rich from the poor shrank. However, since 1970 these indices have reversed direction, indicative of a widening economic division between the haves and the have-nots. Economists who have examined these trends closely have concluded that the rising number of female-headed households had "a strongly significant positive effect on income inequality in 1970 and its effect increase[d] in both magnitude and significance in 1980 and 1990." In the widening rich-poor chasms that family disintegration has created, economists see "disturbing consequences" ahead.[33]

Intergenerational Conflicts

Disturbing also are the new political and economic fissures that separate generations disparately affected by the national decline in family life. Because fewer and less stable marriages have helped cause what analyst Ben Wattenberg has called "the Birth Dearth," policymakers are deeply worried about the future tax base for programs such as Social Security, Medicare, and Medicaid.[34] With nursing-home care already consuming over 40 percent of the nation's runaway Medicaid budget, a high rate for divorce and a low rate for fertility greatly worry policymakers aware that in future decades "the care spouses traditionally have provided each other in old age will be far less available" and that aging baby-boomers will have "few adult children to fill the role of caregiver, because they have produced so few offspring."[35] What do analysts who track these trends see ahead? They see yet more combat in America's ongoing domestic civil war—the ugly combat of "intergenerational conflict" over unsustainable health-care burdens.[36]

Though it has not created the same kind of region-against-region warfare seen in the Civil War of the 1860s, the current domestic civil war has exacerbated the social and cultural tensions between the nation's rural areas and its urban centers. The relatively high concentration of separated and divorced individuals in urban areas that sociologists found in a 1992 study helps make these areas decidedly more non-traditional than rural areas, where separated and divorced individuals constitute a smaller fraction of the population.[37]

The growing cultural rift that family decay has helped to effect between rural and urban areas only underscores the importance of what political scientist Clem Brooks has called "the emergence of a new cleavage in U.S. politics," as a growing number of voters nationwide base their social and political orientation on their anxieties over the parlous state of the American family. While less than 2 percent identified "family decline" as the nation's most serious social problem from 1974 through 1984, by 1996 fully "one out of ten adult Americans ranked family decline as the most important social problem."[38]

A sober observer need wonder very little about the reasons that more and more voters regard family decay as the nation's number one social problem, no farther indeed than a sober observer in the late 1850s needed to wonder about why more and more Americans at that time regarded slavery as the nation's number one political problem. For in the disintegration of the family, Americans are seeing a type of social secession more radical and far-reaching than anything every contemplated by John Calhoun or Jefferson Davis. In severing their ties to spouse and family, Americans are not only seceding from their family union, but they are also typically seceding from their neighborhood, their community, their state, and their country. The result has been a frightening loss of civic and national unity and an equally alarming rise in civic and national conflict. For although some Sixties activists and their epigones have thought that repudiating the family would liberate the individual and so usher in a harmonious new Age of Aquarius, family decay has actually created a brutal and divisive individualism that resembles none of the beguiling fantasies of Woodstock but instead looks very like Hobbes's grim state of   nature: the war of each against all. Even the movements that have helped to destroy family ties find themselves, in turn, being torn apart by the unlimited Hobbesian individualism they have set loose: we now hear prominent feminist commentators lamenting that feminism is "falling victim to individualism" as "independent-minded women ensconced on the fast track to fame and fortune" refuse to make sacrifices for their ideological sisters.[39]

Hobbes had his own solution for the problem of each-against-all individualism: the powerful and coercive government machinery he called Leviathan. And something very like Hobbes's Leviathan looms ever larger in an America where family disintegration has helped swell the size of the nation's prisons and police forces, where divorce courts have multiplied in size and power, and where government officials who collect child support have acquired unprecedented powers to monitor and control the lives of citizens.[40]

A powerful and intrusive government bureaucracy can to some degree overcome social disorder by forcefully effecting a kind of national unity: those dependent on government bureaucracy for benefits or for employment thus cling to the state for personal advantage; those compelled to pay for benefits yield to its irresistible force. Thus we see, for instance, a growing number of divorced and never-married women relying on the state for child-support payments, a growing army of state officials finding their employment in collecting those payments, and a burgeoning population of men under coercive government supervision to ensure compliance in making those payments. But as is discussed in chapter 7, the national unity effected by coercive state machinery partakes of no selflessness and springs from no civic virtue. Brittle and superficial, such national unity is light years away from the national unity called for by America's most prominent commentators in the months after 9/11.

But those who hope for selflessness and civic virtue in a nation of broken marriages and fractured families are hoping for what never has been and never can be. No human movement or institution will ever replace the family in inspiring a willingness to sacrifice. As sociologists Howard M. Bahr and Kathleen S. Bahr have pointed out, the family has always inculcated self-sacrifice as "the essential glue of a moral society." However, as family life decays, in part because of the ideological triumph of self-interest and of individualism in both therapeutic and utilitarian varieties, Americans are witnessing the rise of "an ethic that denies the legitimacy of self-sacrifice in general."[41]

Given the importance of marital and family ties in inculcating civic selflessness, it comes as no surprise that sociologists find that high divorce rates are linked not only to a high crime rate but also to "low rates of participation in community politics, recreation (e.g., YMCA), and educational activities." Overall, "married persons are likelier to participate in formal organizations than are divorced and unmarried people."[42] After decades of high rates for divorce and low rates for marriage, it was almost inevitable that a leading sociologist would adduce strong evidence of a decline in "social civility—as evidenced in lower rates of "volunteering, civic association membership, voting, and religious participation"—resulting in a clear and troubling erosion in civic involvement between the middle of the twentieth century and the close of that century. Such social civility as this sociologist did find still persisting in American society, he found disproportionately among married citizens.[43]

Compared to married peers, Americans with no intact marital ties typically evince little of the civic virtue necessary to forge meaningful national union. For even if they have avoided criminal behavior, even if they have avoided bitter conflict with a former spouse, and even if they have opted out of the divisive ideological crusades polarizing political life, Americans without family ties typically lack the psychological and moral strength to make selfless sacrifices on behalf of national civic life. Millions of Americans who would sincerely like to contribute to a healthy nation simply lack the inner reserves to do so because family failure has plunged them into pathological self-absorption. Psychologists find that, compared to married peers, unmarried mothers are "almost three times more likely to have experienced a major depressive disorder."[44] Characterized by some researchers as "moody, sad, and nervous," children of single-parent families account for between 50 and 80 percent of the patients in many mental-health institutions.[45] Nor does the psychological distress induced by family failure quickly dissipate from children's lives: researchers find that parental divorce often puts children into "negative life trajectories through adolescence into adulthood."[46]

Americans can hardly look for the exemplary civic life that unites a nation from men and women burdened by psychological distress. In far too many cases, Americans do not see prolonged life of any kind among those overwhelmed by psychological distress: the offspring of single-parent and step-parent families have accounted for a disproportionate fraction of the growing number of adolescent suicides in recent decades. A statewide 1988 study in California found that over half (52 percent) of adolescent suicides were from homes in which the decedent's parents were divorced or separated.[47]

In the Civil War of the 1860s, Americans on both sides honored the fallen as soldiers who bravely gave all to defend either the national union or at least their region and state. In today's ongoing second civil war, how will Americans honor the thousands who in despair take their own lives as the casualties of the social warfare that has been tearing apart their very homes? There will be no 21-gun salutes in today's horrid civil war. The alienated parents and divided siblings of the deceased often won't even stand together at the graveside.

But family disintegration not only unfits those directly affected for public life by making them contentious or depressed; it also undermines the positive, potentially unifying civic labors of Americans still living in intact marriages and families. Even if a couple do marry and their union does survive, their home cannot function very well as "the seedbed of the state" (Cicero's apt phrase) if the family members live much of their lives in the shadow of nearby family failure. As anyone who has known divorcing couples well knows, in the months leading up to and immediately following the rupture both husband and wife typically marshal a small army of partisans—friends, extended family members, neighbors, co-workers—to uphold their version of events and to join in echoing ritual denunciations of the other side. Because of the frequency of divorce in today's ongoing civil war, many social gatherings have become veritable minefields of conflicting loyalties and animosities created by failed marriages.

Furthermore, a single divorce in the neighborhood can cast a chilling shadow of doubt and fear on all the households around. Husbands and wives who have not previously considered separating look at spouses with new concern, anxious about dark possibilities made more real and disturbing by their neighbors' rupture. Children whose playground peers have just seen their parents divorce begin to lose sleep over the previously-unthought-of possibility that their parents, too, may part. It is no wonder that long-term survey data show a decline in overall marital happiness during decades when advocates of liberalized divorce laws pushed through statutes that (in their view) should have made it easy for unhappy couples to move out of unhappy unions into happy ones. For, as sociologist Norval Glenn has plausibly argued, the ubiquity of divorce has made many husbands and wives hesitant to commit themselves fully to a union they fear might fail.[48] Such hesitance not only reduces marital and family happiness but also diminishes the strength and staying power of the civic impulses of the Americans most capable of unifying our nation.

Unfortunately, as family disintegration reduces the number and well-being of Americans fighting to unite the country, it also swells the ranks of the religious terrorists plotting against its very existence. According to the best scholars on the questions, religious terrorists want to attack America not simply to snuff out democracy and free-market economics. These religious extremists typically want to attack America in part because they regard the disintegration of traditional family life in America as a contagion of immorality that must be checked.[49] When Abraham Lincoln took a firm stand against slavery in the territories, the consequent secession of the slave states started America's first Civil War. But at least Lincoln's firm moral position did not swell the Confederate armies with pro-slavery volunteers from other countries, nor did it at all reduce the size or resolve of the pro-union armies in blue.

America's first Civil War finally ended when the forces of disunion were decisively defeated by Union forces on the battlefields around Richmond. Unfortunately, despite the horrifying casualty tolls—evident in the sky-high rates for child poverty and adolescent suicide, in the multiplication of psychiatric clinics and prisons—

today's American civil war of family disintegration rages on. And until the nation's cultural and political leaders can bring the family's numerous and often un-identified ideological and cultural enemies to some Virginia courthouse to sign surrender terms, the casualties will continue to mount—even as Bin Laden and his allies plan future attacks against a country in which national unity is increasingly just a rhetorical slogan politicians use to reassure a deeply riven people.

Notes

1.   Todd Gitlin, "Varieties of Patriotic Experience," in *The Fight is for Democracy: Winning the War of Ideas in America and the World*, ed. George Packer (New York: Perennial, 2003), 107-136.

2.   See Alan Wolfe, *The Transformation of American Religion: How We Actually Live Our Faith* (New York: Free Press, 2003), 7-8.

3.   George Packer, Introduction, *The Fight is for Democracy*, 4-11.

4.   *Statistical Abstract of the United States, 2000*, Tables, 57, 60, 62, 86, U.S. Bureau of the Census, 2 September 2003 www.census.gov.

5.   See quotations from Bahira Sherif in Theresa Gawlas Medoff, *UD Messenger*, Vol. 9, Number 4, 2000, University of Delaware, 2 September 2003, http://www.udel.edu.

6.   See Mark Hertsgaard, *The Eagle's Shadow: Why America Fascinates and Infuriates the World* (New York: Farrar, Straus, and Giroux, 2002), 14, 202.

7.   See "The Civil War," in *Encyclopaedia of USA History*, 2 September 2003 http://www.spartacus.schoolnet.co.uk/USA.htm; see also West Virginia in the Civil War, 2 September 2003 http://www.wvcivil war.com; see also Union Troops and Confederate Troops in Kentucky Civil War, 2 September 2003 http://www.roots web.com/~kymilcv.

8.   See Alvin Kernan, *The Death of Literature* (New York: Yale University Press, 1990), 8.

9.   Kersti Yllo and Murray A. Straus, "Interpersonal Violence Among Married and Cohabiting Couples," *Family Relations* 30(1981): 339-347; see also Jan E. Stets and Murray A. Straus, "The Marriage License as a Hitting License: A Comparison of Assaults in Dating, Cohabiting, and Married Couples," Paper presented at the 1988 meeting of the American Sociological Association, 8 July 1988.

10. See Selsyn M. Smith, Ruth Hanson, and Sheila Noble, "Social Aspects of the Battered Baby Syndrome," in *Child Abuse: Commission and Omission*, eds. Joanne V. Cook and Roy T. Bowles (Toronto: Butterworths, 1980), 217-220.

11. See Jocelyn Brown et al., "A Longitudinal Analysis of Risk Factors for Child Maltreatment: Findings of a 17-Year Prospective Study of Officially Recorded and Self-Reported Child Abuse and Neglect," *Child Abuse & Neglect* 22 (1998): 1065-1078.

12. See Lauren J. Krivo and Ruth D. Peterson, "Extremely Disadvantaged Neighborhoods and Urban Crime," *Social Forces* 75 (1996): 619-650.

13. Lynn D. Wardle, "No-Fault Divorce and the Divorce Conundrum," *Brigham Young University Law Review* 1 (1991): 79-142.

14. See, for example, David O'Reilly, "Double or Nothing: Other Twins are Appalled When a Judge Splits Custody of Identical Twins," *Chicago Tribune* 23 April 1995: 9.

15.   See R. Holroyd and A. Sheppard, "Parental Separation: Effects on Children; Implications for Services," *Child: Care, Health and Development* 23(1997): 369-378.

16.   See Wardle, op. cit.

17.   See Anne Gearan, "Families Still Consumed by Bitter Custody Fight," *Las Vegas Review-Journal* 6 July 1992: 3C.

18.   See Scan Kelly and Marilyn Robinson, "Lost in Thin Air: Missing-Person Rate High for No Clear Reason," *Denver Post* 30 March 2003: B01.

19.   Quoted in Ray Sanchez, "Few Strangers Behind Missing," *Newsday* 10 March 2001: A3.

20.   See "Exploiting Parents' Fears," Editorial, *Denver Post* 9 August 2002: B6.

21.   See Scott Gold, Tina Dirmann, and Jack Leonard, "2 Armed Men Seize Boy, 9, in Violent Abduction; Kidnapping: Child Was at Center of a Bitter Custody Fight," *Los Angeles Times* 29 August 2002: B1; see also "International Custody: Fights and Flights," *Family Law Advisor* March 1996, http://www.divorcenet.com/fla011.html#6.

22.   See The American Academy of Pediatrics Task Force on the Family, "Family Pediatrics," *Pediatrics* 111 Supplement (2003): 1549.

23.   David T. Courtwright, *Violent Land: Single Men and Social Disorder from the Frontier to the Inner City* (Cambridge, MA: Harvard University Press, 1996), 5-7, 270-280.

24.   See Amy Conseur et al., "Maternal and Perinatal Risk Factors for Later Delinquency," *Pediatrics* 99 (1997): 785-790.

25.   See Patrick J. Darby et al., "Analysis of 112 Juveniles Who Committed Homicide: Characteristics and a Closer Look at Family Abuse," *Journal of Family Violence* 13 (1998): 365-374.

26.   See Karen F. Parker and Tracy Johns, "Urban Disadvantage and Types of Race-Specific Homicide: Assessing the Diversity in Family Structures in the Urban Context," *Journal of Research in Crime and Delinquency* 39 (2002): 277-303.

27.   See National Institute of Child Health and Human Development / Early Child Care Research Network, "Does Amount of Time Spent in Child Care Predict Socioemotional Adjustment During the Transition to Kindergarten?" *Child Development* 74 (2003): 976-1005.

28.   See Ron Haskins, "Public School Aggression among Children with Varying Day Care Experience," *Child Development* 56 (1985): 694-702.

29.   See Kathleen A. Frankovic, "Sex and Politics—New Alignments, Old Issues," *PS* 15(1982): 444.

30.   See Eric Plutzer, "Work Life, Family Life, and Women's Support of Feminism," *American Sociological Review* 53 (1988): 640-649.

31.   See S. Philip Morgan and Linda J. Waite, "Parenthood and the Attitudes of Young Adults," *American Sociological Review* 52 (1987): 541-547.

32.   Jennifer Glass, "Housewives and Employed Wives: Demographic and Attitudinal Change, 1972-1986," *Journal of Marriage and the Family* 54 (1992): 559-569.

33.   See Francois Nielsen and Arthur S. Alderson, "The Kuznets Curve and the Great U-Turn: Income Inequality in U.S. Counties, 1970 to 1990," *American Sociological Review* 62 (1997): 12-33.

34.   See Ben Wattenberg, *The Birth Dearth* (New York: Pharos Books, 1987), 68-70.

35.   See Peter A. Morrison, "The Current Demographic Context of Federal Social Programs," N-2785-HHS/NICHD, The RAND Corporation, September 1988, 9-12.

36.   Wayne A. Ray et al., "Impact of Growing Numbers of the Very Old on Medicaid Expenditures for Nursing Homes: A Multi-State, Population-Based Analysis," *American Journal of Public Health* 77 (1987): 699-703.

37.   See Sung Joon Jang and Richard C. Alba, "Urbanism and Nontraditional Opinion: A Test of Fisher's Subcultural Theory," *Social Science Quarterly* 73 (1992): 596-608.
38.   Clem Brooks, "Religious Influence and the Politics of Family Decline: Trends, Sources, and U.S. Political Behavior," *American Sociological Review* 67 (2002): 191-211.
39.   See Pat Swift, "Is Feminism Falling Victim to Individualism?" *Buffalo News* 10 June 1995: 7C.
40.   See Bryce Christensen, "The Family vs. the State," *Essays in Political Economy* (The Ludwig von Mises Institute, Auburn University), May 1992, 6-9.
41.   See Howard M. Bahr and Kathleen S. Bahr, "Families and Self-Sacrifice: Alternative Models and Meanings for Family Theory," *Social Forces* 79 (2001): 1231-1258.
42.   See Robert J. Sampson, "Crime in Cities: The Effects of Formal and Informal Social Control," in *Communities and Crime*, eds. Albert J. Reiss, Jr. and Michael Tonry, Vol. 8 in *Crime and Justice*, eds. Michael Tonry and Norvel Morris (Chicago: University of Chicago Press, 1987), 271-307.
43.   See Corey L.M. Keyes, "Social Civility in the United States," *Sociological Inquiry* 72 (2002): 393-408.
44.   See Lorraine Davies, William R. Avison, and Donna D. McAlpine, "Significant Life Experiences and Depression Among Single and Married Mothers," *Journal of Marriage and the Family* 59 (1997): 294-308.
45.   See Gong-Soong Hong and Shelley I. White-Means, "Do Working Mothers Have Healthy Children?" *Journal of Family and Economic Issues* 14 (1993): 163-181; see also Helen S. Merskey and G.T. Swart, "Family Background and Physical Health of Adolescents Admitted to an Inpatient Psychiatric Unit: I, Principal Caregivers," *Canadian Journal of Psychiatry* 34 (1989): 79-83.
46.   See P. Lindsay Chase-Lansdale, Andrew J. Cherlin, and Kathleen E. Kiernan, "The Long-Term Effects of Parental Divorce on the Mental Health of Young Adults: A Developmental Perspective," *Child Development* 66 (1995): 1614-1634.
47.   Franklyn L. Nelson, "Youth Suicide in California: A Study of Perceived Causes and Interventions," *Community Mental Health* 24 (1988): 31-42.
48.   Norval D. Glenn, "The Recent Trend in Marital Success in the United States," *Journal of Marriage and the Family* 53 (1991): 261-270.
49.   See Jessica Stern, *Terror in the Name of God: Why Religious Militants Kill* (New York: ecco/HarperCollins, 2003), xix, 56-57, 99-125.

2

Friendly Fire in the War on Terror?
The Bewildering Tactics of America's
Anti-Family Ideologues

A nation deeply divided in peace will inevitably find it difficult to maintain a unified front in war. Predictably, then, a United States deeply fissured by family conflicts has found that those conflicts have compromised its unity in the war against terrorism. The loss of martial unity manifests itself in one way when individual soldiers lose their fighting spirit because their personal experiences in marriage and family have been bitter ones. The soldier who is fighting for a wife and children back home is almost certainly more highly motivated than the soldier who has rarely seen his ex-wife or their children since the divorce that broke up their family. Nor is it easy to conceptualize as an ideal soldier a woman who has enlisted only to alleviate the impoverishment into which divorce has plunged her. Unfortunately, in today's army thousands of America's soldiers are living precisely these post-family, post-wedlock scripts.

Family conflict, however, has compromised the nation's martial unity on another level as well. A careful study of the media coverage of the war against terror strongly implicates family-centered ideological disputes in some troubling and divisive distortions of that media coverage.

Upon their return from a fact-finding mission to Iraq late in 2003, members of a Congressional delegation expressed keen dismay at what they perceived as excessively negative media coverage of American involvement there. "I'm afraid," said Representative Jim Marshall (D-GA), "the news media are hurting our chances [of success]; they are dwelling upon the mistakes, the ambushes, the soldiers killed. . . . The falsely bleak picture weakens our national resolve, discourages Iraqi cooperation, and emboldens our enemy."

One of Marshall's companions, Rep. Todd Tiahart (R-KS), spoke in the same vein, decrying the media reports of "chaos in the streets" of Iraq and of "Iraqis resent[ing] our presence" as "totally false." [2]

Other commentators later echoed Marshall and Tiahart's complaints. Editorialist John Leo characterized media coverage of the Iraq war as "skewed," asserting that there is "not much room for good news in [the] media's view of Iraq." [3] And journalist Rod Blum deplored the way the mainstream media have become so negative in their coverage of the war that they have been "ignoring the positive and dramatic changes occurring in Iraq." [4]

Why have the media depicted American involvement in Iraq in such a negative light? One thing seems certain: in depicting the war in Iraq unfavorably, the mainstream media were rarely taking their cues from "anti-war conservatives." Yes, not a few self-identified conservatives argued that invading Iraq was imprudent and wonder why President Bush ever abandoned the conservative principles he espoused in 2000 when attacking the Clinton administration for "extending our troops all around the world in nation-building missions."[5] But it was neither anti-war conservatives nor pro-war conservatives who set the agenda for media coverage of the war in Iraq. Nationally syndicated columnist Joseph Perkins clearly identified just who set the media agenda when he asserted that those governing "much of the U.S. media . . . [were] blinded by their contempt for President Bush." [6]

Perkins indeed linked the negative portrayal of the war in Iraq to the much more pervasive bias which at least temporarily set much of the national media against the Bush Administration. Predictably, media bias against Bush and his war policy translated during the run up to the November 2004 election into media support for Senator John Kerry and his opposition to the Bush war policy. Writing in October of 2004, Perkins remarked, "The mainstream media have chosen sides in the presidential election. The news networks, the major newspapers (and magazines) overwhelmingly favor Kerry."[7] Of course, Bush enjoyed the support of many in the media, and, of course, Kerry came under fire from more than a few journalists. But especially with regard to the most prestigious media forums, Perkins was probably right in positing an anti-Bush bias (and therefore a pro-Kerry bias). And because Bush advocated the invasion of Iraq as essential to the war on terror while Kerry withdrew his initial support, accusing the President of having used misleading justifications for sending U.S. forces to Iraq, negative coverage of the Iraq war fitted quite naturally into a broader effort to elect Kerry and to discredit Bush.[8]

Anti-Bush bias in the media (and the pro-Kerry bias that grew from it) sprang from many sources, from hostility to Bush's repeated tax cuts for the rich to dismay at Bush's periodic assaults on English syntax. Many journalists—like many average Americans—were simply put off by Bush's brash and unvarnished personal style. But in turning against Bush (and toward Kerry), more than a few journalists were acting on ideological impulses. In a remarkably candid essay, Kerry partisan Bob Levin identified opposition to the "senseless march to Baghdad" as part of a Blue ideological package for certain urban media types like him, people who were less religious, more liberal and Democratic, and more favorable to gay marriage and elective abortion than were the Red-thinking supporters of President Bush.[9]

In part, the Blue ideological package Levin described was an ephemeral election-year illusion. Many Blue Americans who voted for Kerry were religiously devout moderates (not liberals), who opposed gay marriage and who wanted to see the number of abortions fall (even if that fall were not effected by legal prohibition). What is more, some who have examined the Blue coalition closely have detected much less ideology than simple self-interest, as "tax-eaters" who receive public moneys through government employment or through government benefit programs supported the candidate they thought would best protect their income source.[10] (It should be acknowledged, however, that such self-interest can harm family life without rising to the level of ideological consciousness, as chapter 8 will show). In any case, much of the Red-Blue ideological posturing ceased after the votes were counted.

However, careful scrutiny of the pre-election media coverage of the war reveals that among the urban media colleagues Levin regarded as his natural allies, some who shared his ideological social commitments did in fact adhere strongly to an anti-traditional social vision, more strongly even than they adhered to their electoral-cycle anti-war activism. And although some employed in the media are distinctively conservative and many more profess no ideology whatever, Americans have witnessed in recent decades the emergence of what one observer has aptly characterized as "clear liberal domination of what we call the elite media."[11] In documenting this liberal domination of the media, researchers from UCLA and the University of Chicago found in study findings first released in 2004 that "the liberal inclination [in the media] is pronounced." Characterizing this bias as very pronounced in such mainstream media outlets as *Newsweek, The New York Times, Time, CBS Evening News,* and *NBC Nightly News,* the UCLA and Chicago scholars concluded that "the media are skewed substantially to the left of the typical member of Congress." [12] This strongly leftist bias has decidedly affected the way the media have reported and commented on the remarkable retreat from traditional family life in recent decades: left-leaning journalists have glamorized the single life, advocated maternal employment, justified elective abortion, and minimized the risks of non-parental childcare while saying little about the social harm caused by divorce, illegitimacy, or non-marital cohabitation.

While their liberal-left bias has unquestionably tilted the media toward Democrats (including Gore in the 2000 election and Kerry in the 2004 election) and away from Republicans (including Bush in both 2000 and 2004), media liberals have often espoused social positions more radical and extreme than have the political candidates they have endorsed. Electoral accountability brings centrist pressures to bear on even the most liberal politicians (Kennedy, Kerry, Feinstein), who usually try to engage in civil and ongoing dialogue with social conservatives. Little restrains media ideologues. (Note, in this context, that despite the popularity of the idea among liberal media commentators who endorsed him, Senator Kerry rejected homosexual marriage). Because controversy actually attracts viewers and sells papers, media ideologues can with impunity push social agendas very far to the left of the American mainstream.

Just how far some ideologically motivated journalists were willing to go became all too apparent in 2004 coverage of the War on Terror. Because media ideologues generally regarded President Bush as a defender of the traditional family and viewed Senator Kerry as a voice for at least marginally more progressive social views, they could for a time advance their overall social agenda by opposing Bush's war policy in ways that reduced the likelihood of his re-election. However, the media's deeper cultural attachments showed through whenever the focus shifted away from the anti-terrorist actions of the American military in general or the decisions of the Commander in Chief in particular and toward the non-traditional activities of female soldiers in Iraq (or Afghanistan or Guantanamo Bay).

Even at the height of the election campaign, many media ideologues suspended their attacks on Bush's war policies whenever they could advance their social agenda more directly by focusing—quite affirmatively—on a woman soldier who had rejected the traditional at-home roles of wife or mother in order to fly an attack helicopter or drive a Humvee in Baghdad.

Boos for the War, Cheers for the Female Soldiers

In the astonishing way media ideologues shifted their views whenever female soldiers came into view, Americans glimpsed something profoundly alien in these ideologues' perspective on the war. Most Americans—including anti-war conservatives and millions of Kerry voters in Blue America—cherish America's family-centered cultural and social traditions and will defend them against the violent threat of terrorism. But an influential minority, with a disproportionately loud voice in the media, disdain every American cultural norm or social tradition that reinforces family life and would rather attack than defend such norms and traditions.

Most Americans are willing to wage a military war to defend America as the family-centered country it has been since its founding. A small but potent minority of ideologically radicalized Americans, however, will support a military war only insofar as it coincides with their cultural war to abolish or re-engineer every traditional family practice that impedes the march toward a Brave New World of trans-gendered and post-familial lifestyle freedom. So while most Americans (Red and Blue, Republican and Democratic) recognize in Osama Bin-Laden and his allies a terrible threat to what America is and has always been, an ideologically motivated minority fear these terrorists principally because they threaten to interrupt their own project of remaking America into a post-familial society it has never been before.

Even as they criticize the Bush administration for a costly military neo-imperialism that turns foreign countries into dependents or into captive markets, this radicalized minority quietly enlarges an even more costly bureaucratic empire at home that turns ever more socially rootless citizens into captive clients of a burgeoning government apparatus for social engineering. Most Americans support the use of tanks and smart bombs to destroy al-Qaida and the remnants of the Afghan Taliban and the Iraqi Republican Guard. But a determined minority is less interested in deploying weaponry that *pro-*

tects America than in advancing policies (created by judicial fiat when necessary) and in building powerful new bureaucracies that will *change* America. Though such will undoubtedly affect the military's uniformed divisions and regiments (by bringing more divorced men and women into the ranks, for instance), their most decisive effect will be on the most fundamental of what Edmund Burke aptly called "the little platoons" of society, namely the family.[13]

Given the remarkable influence of radical feminists on the media, it should come as no real surprise that reporters periodically interrupted their generally negative coverage of the war in Iraq to laud and praise the female soldiers in the theater. Looking specifically at media coverage of the Iraq War, a *Chicago Sun-Times* reporter acknowledged a clear pattern: "The news is different when women are involved." [14] And behind that difference Americans could see ideological enthusiasm for women in non-domestic, non-familial roles. "They buckle themselves into B-52s," wrote one typically feminist journalist. "They deploy bombs by the ton. They launch missiles. They question suspicious Iraqis. More than ever, women are involved in combat. Women are being taken prisoner—and proving their heroism—on ever murkier battlefields where nearly everyone is at risk, whether on the front lines or ferrying food or supplies." In all of this expanded female militarism, the ideologically oriented writer saw "women gain[ing] ground," as their exploits provided new opportunities "to smash barriers" that had limited women in the past.[15]

In the same feminist spirit, another media representative hailed the fight for Iraq as "a historic moment for American women on the fields of war. More women are fighting—and dying—in military combat zones now than at any time in the past 50 years, and maybe ever." To drive home the ideological point, she quoted a female sergeant in the Military Police in Iraq: "This is not [just] a man's job anymore."[16] The gender egalitarianism of feminist doctrine likewise wove itself through the commentary of a reporter thrilled that "the war in Iraq has placed women in harm's way as never before ... [as] their [military] roles have greatly expanded." This overawed reporter listened with rapture to a female pilot of an attack helicopter, who "sounded as gung-ho as any of her male colleagues, whose ships took heavy fire. 'It made me a little bit mad to think I didn't even get a bullet,' she said." The reporter's ideological focus could almost make readers forget that the war was between Americans and Iraqi Baathists, not between women and their patriarchal oppressors: "In the war zone . . ." he wrote, "the women have won." So confident was he in the prowess of the new generation of G.I. Janes that the reporter turned fears about their security into a bravado warning to their foes: "The enemy isn't safe from the women of the U.S. military, either."[17]

A choir of usually anti-war media ideologues still could not help but see portents of social progress in female soldiers' involvement in Iraq. As part of that choir, another journalist delighted that "American women have participated more extensively in combat in Iraq than in any previous war in U.S. history. They've taken roles nearly inconceivable just a decade or two ago—flying fighter jets and attack helicopters, patrolling streets armed with machine guns and commanding units of mostly male soldiers."[18]

When the ideologically biased media were reporting on female soldiers, reporters often explicitly underscored the feminist social objectives that justified the temporary abandonment of their generally anti-war posture. One commentator thus drew "a lesson on gender equality" from the death of a female civil-affairs specialist killed in Iraq by a roadside bomb: "Women should be respected more than what they are. They are doing this tremendous duty for us. . . . [I]t takes courage for women to do that. It does. Women are out there on the battlefields. Fighting for us, for our freedom. Just like a man." The ideological transformation of female soldiers into creatures "just like a man" required, as intended, the repudiation of traditional femininity: the reporter stressed that the civil-affairs specialist killed by the roadside bomb had left behind a world in which she was "so girly-like" that she "could spend hours piling her curly hair atop her head" and would pick "a new dress for every dance."[19]

For most ideologically motivated commentators, however, the abandonment of dresses and curly hair was secondary to the cutting of female soldiers' ties to women's traditional family roles. That female soldiers have so completely severed these ties that they are indistinguishable from males sends some reporters into ideological raptures. "A single mother Army cook," one such reporter rhapsodized, " . . . faces death or captivity [just] like [her] male counterparts."[20] Another reporter handed the microphone to one of the forward-thinking female soldiers who had left children behind to become just like the men on the battlefields of Iraq: "I would love to be at home with my kids, but I'm doing this for them. I wouldn't want to do anything else."[21]

Because media excitement over female soldiers as post-family gender pioneers sprang from feminist ideology, reporters particularly relished the way these soldiers were defying the traditional patriarchy of the lands where they found themselves deployed. What could be sweeter than the "delicious irony" of female soldiers deployed in Afghanistan, "the birthplace of the Taliban, the hard-line Islamist regime that forced women to quit their jobs and wear head-to-toe veils." "Afghan men," the reporter rejoiced, "are getting an object lesson in women's empowerment." [22] The object lessons were even more pointed at the prison at Guantanamo Bay, where the media took keen delight in the spectacle of "Taliban fighters who wouldn't allow women to study in Afghanistan and punished them if a veil slipped or ankle showed are now getting orders from women guards." "In their culture," one of Guantanamo's female guards asserted, "they [the detainees] get to tell the females what to do. Well, they are now in a new culture, and I get to tell them what to do." "I believe everything should be 50/50," one of the glamorized guards explained. "If a woman does dishes, a man should too. I'm sure they (the detainees) don't feel that way."[23]

Nor did feminist commentators take pleasure just in what America's female soldiers were doing to Moslem males; they were also thrilled that the deployment of America's female soldiers to their country helped inspire 47 Saudi women to take an illegal joy ride in Riyadh to protest Saudi Arabia's ban on female drivers.[24]

Female Abusers, Female Heroes

The very visible involvement of a female soldier (Pfc. Lynndie England) in the abuse of Iraqi prisoners at Abu Ghraib amounted to nothing more than a piquant novelty for non-ideological reporters. A few conservative commentators, it is true, regarded the images of a female soldier leading a naked Iraqi prisoner as particularly "damaging" because they provided "a symbolic representation of the Islamist warning about where Western freedom ultimately leads" and corroborated jihadists' fears about the consequences of "equality and sexual liberation" by illustrating an ugly episode that unfolded "exactly as Osama bin Laden would have scripted it."[25] Some conservatives even criticized the "politically correct" military policies that had "place[d] women in positions of power over male [Iraqi] prisoners."[26]

For ideological leftists in the media (who far outnumbered their conservative colleagues), the episode did momentarily create awkward tensions. Most media ideologues dealt with these tensions by temporarily soft-pedaling their feminist themes and amplifying their anti-war and anti-Bush motifs. Bush Administration policies were to blame for the female guard and her leash, not the woman herself.[27] The more galvanized media ideologues went on the offensive, aggressively attacking the "women don't belong" mindset of conservative critics who were advancing a malign "political agenda" by unfairly "interpret[ing] Pfc. England as a 'gender representative.'"[28] These conservative critics, the ideologues asserted, were "sexists" guilty of "mocking [as a] 'she-man'" a female soldier no worse than the males involved in the same abuse.[29]

In any case, for feminist ideologues, the femaleness of the guard leading a naked Iraqi prisoner by a leash simply counted for much less than did the femaleness of non-traditional women soldiers dropping bombs and killing enemies on the battlefield. From an ideological perspective, these Amazon heroics more than compensated for female misdeeds at Abu Ghraib because they matched or eclipsed the battlefield deeds of the men traditional family-oriented women relied on to protect them. So eager were media ideologues to celebrate departures from the family-centered gender roles that they helped make a single woman (Jessica Lynch) "the Iraq War's most famous soldier" on the basis of wildly inaccurate and irresponsible journalism.[30] It was Lynch, not England, that media ideologues were determined to make "a gender representative." In a front-page story published in April 2003, the prestigious *Washington Post* reported that Lynch, who had just been rescued from an Iraqi hospital by an (ironically) all-male special operations team, was initially captured "fighting to the death." The breathless *Washington Post* reporters asserted that Lynch had "fought fiercely and shot several enemy soldiers," that she had continued "firing her weapon until she ran out of ammunition," that she "didn't want to be taken alive," and that she had been both shot and stabbed before being taken captive.[31]

This inspiring story quickly went out over the wires and was loudly amplified by the media throughout the country. Very quickly, Lynch found herself one of *Glamour* magazine's Women of the Year, received an offer from CBS for the rights for her story for a made-for-TV movie, and became the subject of a laudatory book written by a Pulitzer Prize winner (to whom the publisher—Alfred A. Knopf—paid a large advance), and received invitations to join the nation's glitterati at Golden Globe parties.[32] At last, ideologues had found the heroic post-family Amazon they had been seeking.

Unfortunately, later investigation revealed "the coverage about Lynch [to be], in nearly every particular, inaccurate."[33] Far from fighting ferociously until her ammunition ran out at the time of her capture, Lynch did not fire a single shot and "spent much of the firefight curled up in a foetal position." And contrary to the early reports, Lynch sustained not even one gunshot or knife wound from her captors: her injuries (which were indeed serious) resulted from the crash of the vehicle she was riding in. Military officers issued a 15-page report thoroughly discrediting the media reporting that had turned Lynch into "Barbie Army," and the *Washington Post* was compelled to retract its original story of her capture after its own ombudsman sharply criticized that story as "wrong in its most compelling aspects."[34]

Of course, the media handled the retraction of the Lynch-as-hero story quietly enough that most Americans never even realized how erroneous the initial hype had been. Certainly, media ideologues were less than eager to acknowledge that "the Iraq War's most famous soldier," the female warrior on whose shoulders "a nation's expectations r[o]de," had behaved like "a terrified little girl" during the firefight preceding her capture and had suffered the ugly indignity of having been anally raped by her captors.[35] Indeed, some obdurate commentators clung with remarkable tenacity to the initial Lynch-as-hero story even after the brutal realities of Lynch's very sad experience had been exposed. Thus, although an ideologically resolute reporter for Gannett News Service grudgingly acknowledged that the early reports of Lynch's battlefield exploits "were later questioned," he persisted in viewing Lynch as a hero who had "challenge[d] old conventions." In the view of this dogged ideologue, "the very fact that [Lynch] . . . survived capture with a back injury" entitled her to join the ranks of the war's greatest "heroes."[36]

The glaring discrepancy between the media image of Jessica Lynch and the unfortunate reality she experienced never in any way reflected a lack of truthfulness and candor on the part of the nineteen-year-old female supply clerk, who never asked to face battlefield danger and who never sought the media celebrityhood thrust upon her. She indeed repeatedly rebutted the fantasies built up around her name. But feminist ideology had given many journalists such a tremendous appetite for female heroics that the media enthusiastically generated these remarkably long-lived fantasies before even trying to learn the facts of her case. It was not the merely random inaccuracies that inevitably mar wartime reportage but rather the deep ideology of feminism that created the Lynch fantasies. "The gender factor," Roeper admitted, "played a huge role in the initial burst of publicity that [surrounded] Lynch."[37]

Feminist skewing of war reportage was even more apparent in the way the media handled the grim news of battlefield deaths. The deaths of male soldiers in Iraq frequently occasioned sharp criticisms of the Bush Administration's handling of the war, frequently drawing unpleasant comparisons to Vietnam. The tragic deaths of over 1,000 male soldiers in Iraq was thus often cited by media commentators as strong evidence that Bush's wrongheaded war policy had landed the United States in "another Vietnam."[38] The deaths of thousands of Iraqis—especially Iraqi civilians—likewise received attention in media criticisms of "[Bush's] invasion over false claims of weapons of mass destruction."[39] But media ideologues shifted into a remarkably positive tone—almost ebullient—when they began reporting on female soldiers who had fallen beneath the Grim Reaper's scythe.

Thus, when male GIs killed enemy soldiers, the media reported that fact as a deeply unfortunate wartime necessity. But some feminist ideologues could scarcely restrain their excitement when reporting that "female American troops in Iraq have killed Iraqis with bombs and bullets."[40] A tone of feminist triumph, verging on blood thirst, even pervaded some reports of the deaths of America's female soldiers themselves. For feminist ideologues, the fact that more women had died in Iraq than in any American war in the last century occasioned far less grief and dismay than pleasure and satisfaction over the mortuary evidence that America had reached "a historic moment" in gender equality.[41] Feminist commentators seemed to take it as a kind of social accomplishment that an unprecedented number of "female American troops in Iraq . . . [had been] killed by enemy fire and buried as heroes in Arlington National Cemetery."[42] So determined were some feminist pundits to see progress in the female military role in Iraq, that they apparently saw "women gain[ing] ground" even when that ground was the soil shoveled over female soldiers' coffins.[43]

Ideological commentators particularly celebrated—even exulted in—the battlefield death of twenty-three-year-old supply clerk Lori Piestewa, the first Native-American woman ever to die in foreign combat. Killed in the same military action in which Jessica Lynch was taken captive, this economically struggling and divorced single mother of two young children was the focal point of numerous laudatory media reports about her as an exemplary "Hopi warrior." She had a mountain peak in Arizona re-named for her and now holds a place in the women's military memorial at Arlington.[44] But for the most aggressive media ideologues, "the best way to honor [Piestewa] would be to remove the prohibition on women in combat."[45] Never mind that the death of Piestewa itself resulted from the Clinton-era success of feminist zealots in removing previous restrictions on combat involvement of female soldiers. Ideologues apparently do not mind that Piestewa never herself asked for exposure to battlefield danger that would imperil her life. Nor does it bother ideologues that putting women into front-line combat roles cruelly contradicts the pacific Hopi traditions in which Piestewa was reared. And ideologues seem utterly blind to the plight of Piestewa's two young children, left with no parent to care for them.

But while media ideologues seized upon Piestewa's tragic death as an irresistible opportunity to press for policies drawing more young mothers deeply into deadly combat, most Americans lamented Piestewa's passing and worried anxiously about the difficult circumstances her children would face. Consequently, while ideologues urged adoption of policies that would cost yet more mothers their lives as gender revolutionaries, more traditionally minded Americans called for renewed protection of these women in their home-centered maternal roles. Historian Allan Carlson thus spoke for the deepest feelings of many Americans when he responded to Piestewa's death by decrying the policies that put her in harm's way: "Healthy, responsible nations do not send the mothers of small children to or near the front lines—that violates the most basic human instincts."[46] Another voice for mainstream Americans, columnist Linda Chavez marveled at the social blindness of Americans who could not see the special tragedy of a single mother such as Piestewa: "As tragic as the death of a father is in a young child's life, it simply can't compare to the loss of a mother."[47]

Where's the Enemy?

What Chavez—and other Americans like her—could not quite grasp was that when feminist ideologues celebrated rather than mourned the battlefield death of military mothers such as Piestewa, it was precisely because motherhood meant nothing to them, precisely because they despised the traditional family. It was motherhood and all the other traditional family roles assigned to women that feminist ideologues most wanted to die. So when single mothers died in battle, these ideologues hoped—above all—that traditional family roles were perishing with them. So while America as a whole fervently waged a war against terrorism in order to defend motherhood and family, feminist ideologues reserved their fervor for those aspects of the war that could be turned against both.

Of course, radical feminists have always understood that not all of the American women they want to coax, persuade, or push into non-family social roles will need to face battlefield danger. But advancing the radical feminist project for re-making American society does require putting ever more women into the unmarried social status shared by Lynch and Piestewa. For it is deep hostility to wedlock and the complementary social roles that have traditionally defined it that largely explained media ideologues' enthusiasm for female soldiers in Iraq or Afghanistan, very few of whom were married and none of whom were dependent upon husbands for economic support. As one of the more candid authorities in women's studies, Elizabeth Fox-Genovese well understands the anti-marital dynamics of radical feminist psychology. "If truth be told," Fox-Genovese has written, " . . . feminists do not much like marriage. Indeed, many feminists would credit marriage with a primary responsibility for women's centuries-long subordination to men. . . . Second-wave feminists . . . sought not marriage's reform but...its abolition."[48]

But the radical feminist project of undermining wedlock does not in itself make women economically independent. Particularly if they become mothers, unmarried women need income and support from some surrogate. As economist Jennifer Roback Morse has pointed out, the "single mother" is almost always a myth. "Some third party is always in the background, helping the mother who is unconnected to the father of her child. . . . The person who appears to be raising a child all by herself has substituted for the other parent some combination of market-provided child care, employment income, and government assistance."[49] It is, of course, the militarized State that looms large as a surrogate parent in the lives of the tens of thousands of single mothers now in the military, relying on the armed forces for a paycheck and on the growing number of feminist-lauded military day-care centers for child care.[50]

But the fatherless families of single military mothers are actually only one manifestation of "the mother-state-child family" that feminist ideologues would like to multiply in their social engineering of the country. True, sociologists typically have in view welfare-dependent mothers when they speak of "the mother-state-child family."[51] But the family of the single military mother answers well to the same label. And even single mothers who receive benefits neither from a welfare office nor a military paymaster are often noticeably dependent upon the State to subsidize the care of their young children, to supervise the after-school activities of their older children, to collect child support from former lovers or husbands, and to advance their careers through Affirmative Action and Equal Opportunity programs. Is it any wonder that feminists are distinctively supportive of Big Government?[52]

Radical feminists' and hard leftists' partisan support for Big Government lent piquant irony to their criticisms of the Bush Administration for advancing a costly "neo-imperialism" that benefited profiteering corporations and jeopardized human rights by sending the military abroad. For with every year, it becomes clearer that feminist and leftist ideologues are building their own fiefdoms here at home, fiefdoms that grow rich and powerful by first attacking the "little platoons" of the family and then supplying palliative services to the rootless and legally disenfranchised remnants of those platoons. Of course, most of the government officials employed in these fiefdoms subscribe to the ideology of neither feminist ideologues nor hard leftists. Most are genuinely concerned about those they serve and deeply committed to helping improve their lives. But few of these officials ever pose the hard questions about how the erosion of family life multiplies the number of Americans needing their services, or about how the multiplication of that number serves the political interests of ideological opportunists.

Except when focusing on the female soldiers involved in its prosecution, ideological commentators have voiced numerous fears about the negative domestic and international consequences of the war against terrorism. Very early on, these commentators started worrying about "the soaring costs of the war in Iraq" and how those costs would affect the American economy.[53] Some of these ideologues expressed suspicions that as a result of the war in Iraq, "American corporations will colonize Iraq, and they'll make billions of dollars in the process."[54] Some of the more radical commentators discerned dark ulterior motives behind the official justifications for foreign campaigns against terrorism. They saw the Bush Administration using the military to establish an Iraqi regime that would "guarantee unfettered American access and influence," a puppet regime under which "the United States w[ould] unilaterally assume responsibility for decisions that w[ould] determine the future course of Iraq's oil and gas industries."[55] Some extremists even darkly suggested that the real reason for the invasion of Afghanistan was that of installing a puppet regime that would permit U.S. interests to build an oil pipeline through the country.[56]

Liberal media commentators have, it is true, generally not endorsed the more sweeping and ideological accusations and allegations of the hard left. But especially during the presidential campaign, liberal media commentators zealously pressed charges of wartime profiteering leveled against the Halliburton Corporation (former employer of Vice President Dick Cheney), so fostering the impression that America was now "fighting Halliburton's War."[57] What is more, the liberal media frequently opened their forums to the more extreme radicals who did characterize the war against terrorism as merely a cover for neo-imperialism and who warned ominously that such imperialism would bring upon America "the sorrows of Empire," including "a state of perpetual war" and "a loss of democracy and constitutional rights."[58] Far from protecting America, the war in Iraq served—in the view of these leftist critics— "only [to] create more terrorists and a more dangerous world for our children."[59] These leftist critics further alleged that Bush Administration policies had actually encouraged abusive military guards abroad to violate the rights of foreign prisoners and overzealous national security agents fighting the war against terrorism at home to violate the rights of American citizens, especially Arab-Americans.[60]

The Real "Sorrows of Empire"

With ceaseless vigilance, media ideologues have pointed out the high costs and political liabilities of a Big Government that tries to *defend* American families by sending (male) soldiers to fight terrorism abroad or empowers security agents to guard against terrorist strikes at home. But these same ideologues usually turn blind and mute when Big Government tries to *weaken* American families by paying a huge army of bureaucrats, lawyers, judges, and therapists to undermine traditional family ties and to supplant them with new politically engineered replacements. Left-leaning ideologues recognize "the sorrows of empire" when the American military effects the hegemony of American interests over foreign interests. They somehow cannot see the sorrows of empire when an American court or bureaucracy establishes an ideological fiefdom in which a leftist partisan coterie takes unjust advantage of—and often dismembers—ordinary families.

Thus media ideologues who complained loudly about the high costs to the taxpayer of putting men in Iraq will never complain about the rapidly escalating public costs of putting children in day care, of putting state officers on staff to collect child support, of putting lawyers on retainer to speak on behalf of children involved in divorce proceedings, or of putting more corrections officers into youth correction centers. These biased commentators will indeed only rarely acknowledge the way in which casual divorce and out-of-wedlock childbearing has driven up the public costs of providing Americans with welfare benefits, medical and psychological care, remedial education, drug therapy, and protection from crime.[61]

Left-leaning commentators may allege that America's foreign wars serve to set up puppet foreign regimes serving the interests of profiteering corporations; they will rarely acknowledge that in the endless ideological war against the family, single mothers have become mere puppets for "those who ha[ve] made an industry of 'helping them'"[62] Just how much they had become puppets of government bureaucrats came as something of a shock to some single welfare mothers when welfare reform suddenly forced them into employment. They suddenly discovered that they were as subject to the orders of government masters as female soldiers were subject to orders of military commanders. Poor single mothers who felt their children were "too young" to leave in day care while they went to work found that they were in much the same situation as single military mothers on orders to leave for Iraq.[63] But ideologues who never cared much about the disappearance of fathers have not worried overmuch about taking welfare mothers away from their children: Liberal media pundits have pronounced welfare reform "largely successful," though they have complained about the low pay in the jobs welfare mothers typically must take and have called for more public funding for pre-employment training, for housing and medical care, and—above all—for day care.[64] Calls for renewed appreciation for wedlock and for maternal child care have never found their way into the liberal media's critique of welfare reform).

During the run-up to the November 2004 election, media commentators often complained that conservative Republicans were "playing politics" with the War on Terror as they engaged in "scaremongering" that won them votes.[65] Left-leaning media ideologues have never acknowledged that some political opportunists are finding electoral advantage in excusing the casual divorces, the non-marital childbirths, the full-time maternal employment that make women more feminist.[66] Nor have left-leaning media ideologues ever criticized politicians whose political fortunes rise when policies encourage young people to cut their ties to family and to "shift allegiance increasingly to themselves and to the State."[67] During the election year, the media frequently aired suspicions about contracts granted to corporations linked to conservative Republicans. The ideologically biased media have remained curiously mute about the cozy ties between feminist politicians and the public bureaucracies that have become "almost a woman's preserve."[68]

Left-liberal media editorialists inveighed against Bush Administration policies that helped foster the abuse of Afghan and Iraqi prisoners at Guantanamo Bay and Abu Ghraib.[69] But they have rarely acknowledged that policies that foster divorce and illegitimacy also foster the abuse of American children in Detroit, Philadelphia, and Atlanta.[70] Nor have media ideologues ever acknowledged that the programs they favor for preventing child abuse—namely, educational programs in the schools—have yielded no demonstrable benefits and yet "overload children with suspicion and fear" in ways that "adversely affect [them] in their comfort with nonsexual contact between themselves and their parents."[71] The left-leaning media were quick to blame Bush's invasion of Iraq for "chaos in the streets" of Baghdad. But they have been exceedingly slow to acknowledge that the root cause of "the wave of black inner-city male violence that began building during the 1960s and 1970s . . . was the decline of stable two-parent families."[72]

Leftist guardians of the First Amendment have repeatedly complained that the Bush Administration has tried to censor and manipulate media coverage of the war against terrorism, thus "prevent[ing] the American people from seeing the truth about what's happening."[73] But these legal watchdogs have worried not at all about the way a left-leaning academic establishment enforces a "family taboo" that keeps from students' view any normative definition of family. Nor have they worried about how this pedagogical taboo confuses students by giving them "no explicit, objective definition of family" while offering instead "vague and inaccurate" ideological pronouncements: "a family is a group of people"; "a family is . . . 'the people you live with.'"[74]

In the Bush Administration's handling of Afghan and Iraqi prisoners, ideological opportunists have seen policies "allowing the war on terrorism to trump basic rights" and court proceedings that "d[o]n't look anything like justice" and instead suggest "kangaroo courts." Some journalists have even descried "a legal black hole" in proceedings that pronounce prisoners " 'guilty' without any trial." Even in its legal proceedings involving American citizens, media ideologues have accused the Bush Administration of "open hostility to protecting civil liberties" and of committing "egregious governmental abuses of power, all in the name of combating terrorism."[75] But Americans may well wonder just where all these leftist defenders of legal rights have been the last three decades when anti-family politicians, judges, and bureaucrats have stripped wives and husbands, mothers and fathers of many fundamental legal protections.

True, on rare occasions, a feminist commentator here or there has protested against the way permissive no-fault divorce statutes have impoverished betrayed wives denied the economic settlement and alimony that traditional divorce law would have given them.[76]

But where are the leftist guardians of legal rights who have ever decried the way new divorce laws have scripted a scenario in which "a blameless father . . . emerges from divorce courts with all the financial responsibilities of marriage and none of its emotional or economic rewards," as he is "saddled with children whom he never sees and who may even have been turned against him"?[77] Where are the leftist defenders of civil rights ready to denounce the legally abusive bureaucracy collecting child support (almost exclusively from non-custodial fathers, many of whom did not want to lose wife or children and did nothing to violate their wedding vows)? Judging from their thundering silence on the issue, Americans can only assume that left-leaning ideologues see nothing wrong with a bureaucracy that treats divorced fathers as "quasi-criminals," monitors their employment through a computerized system allowing "the government [to] keep closer tabs on where *everyone* is working," and adopts a presumption of guilt under which thousands of innocent men are "erroneously ensnared by computer error," and then forced to prove their innocence.[78]

The outspoken leftist champions of the legal rights of Afghans and Iraqis imprisoned in the war against terrorism have likewise been quite silent about the judicial-bureaucratic apparatus that has forced tens of thousands of blameless parents into costly court proceedings to prove their innocence and regain custody of their children. For all of their solicitude for imprisoned Afghans and Iraqis and for all their outrage over the legal defects in the way they have been handled, media ideologues seem remarkably insouciant about a national child-abuse system that "seems determined to err on the side of assuming [parental] guilt" and that consequently devastates "increasing numbers of families falsely accused of abuse." The same left-leaning media who roundly denounced the erosion of civil rights in the war against terrorism have said almost nothing about the emergence of a child-protection system marred by "a bias toward over-reporting and over-labeling child abuse and neglect" and by legal proceedings conducted entirely without "the legal system's traditional truth-finding tools—witness confrontation, cross examination, restrictions on hearsay and 'expert' opinion."[79] Apparently, ideologically blinkered commentators care much more about Afghans captured in Kandahar or Iraqis taken in Mosul than about parents falsely accused of abuse in Denver or Indianapolis.

In Afghanistan and Iraq, along the nation's borders and in its courtrooms, the war against terrorism will go on. Unfortunately, it promises to last a long time and to make demands upon all Americans. But let no one suppose that in their objectives or their hopes, Americans seeking for ways to safeguard their families will be fighting the same war as the ideologues intent on re-engineering those same families.

Notes

1.   Jim Marshall, "Media's Dark Cloud a Danger: Falsely Bleak Reports Reduce our Chances of Success in Iraq," *Atlanta Journal-Constitution* 22 Sept. 2003: A11.
2.   Tiahart qtd. in Norma D. Dicks, "'I Think We Can Do This,'" *Wall Street Journal* 3 October 2003: A18.
3.   John Leo, "Not Much Room for Good News in Media's View of Iraq," *Grand Rapids Press*, 4 Oct. 2003: A18.
4.   Rod Blum, "Double Take: Is Bush Administration's Course in Iraq Correct? Much Good Being Done, but Media Ignores It," *Telegraph-Herald* 5 October 2003: A17.
5.   Cf. Howard Kurtz, "War in Iraq Opens a Rift on the Right," *Washington Post* 25 March 2003: C8; John Donnelly, "Bush Shifts on Nation-Building," *Boston Globe* 26 June 2002: A1.

6.   Joseph Perkins, "David Kay and Bush's Blind Critics," *San Diego Union-Tribune* 30 Jan. 2004: B7.

7.   Joseph Perkins, "Leveling the Media Playing Field," *San Diego Union-Tribune* 15 Oct. 2004: B7.

8.   Cf. Robert Z. Nemeth, "Media Bias Mars Campaign 2004," *Telegram & Gazette* 5 September 2004: C2.

9.   Bob Levin, "Red America, Blue America," *Maclean's* 17 May 2004: 40-41.

10.   Cf. Steven Malanga, "The Real Engine of Blue America," *City Journal* Winter 2005: 66-73.

11.   Robert J. Bresler, "Media Bias and the Culture Wars," *USA Today Magazine* July 2004: 13.

12 . UCLA-University of Chicago Study Reported in Robert J. Barro, "The Liberal Media: It's No Myth," *Business Week* 14 June 2004: 28.

13.   Cf. Edmund Burke, *Reflections on the Revolution in France* (1790), ed. J.G.A. Pocock (Indianapolis, IN: Hackett, 1987), 41.

14.   Richard Roeper, "The News Is Different When Women Are Involved," *Chicago Sun-Times* 12 May 2004: 11.

15.   Keith Epstein, "Combat Questions Arise As Women Gain Ground," *Tampa Tribune* 4 April 2003: 1.

16.   Charity Vogel, "Doing Their Duty: With More Females Than Ever Serving in Military Combat Zones, Local Women Have Found Themselves in Life-Threatening Near-Miss Situations," *Buffalo News* 14 May 2004: A1.

17.   Jim Auchmutey, "War in the Gulf: Special Coverage: Women at War: G.I. Jane Fights Her Way Into the Service—and Danger," *Atlanta Journal-Constitution* 30 March 2003: D1.

18.   Matt Kelley, "Major Role of Female Soldiers Draws Little Comment at Capitol," *St. Louis Post-Dispatch* 4 Jan. 2004: A11.

19.   Gina Kim and Imran Vittachi, "In War Without Front Lines, Women GIs Caught In Chaos: The stories of Nichole Frye and Gussie Jones, 2 of 16 Female Soldiers Who Have Died in Iraq, Reveal Much About A Woman's Role in the Modern Military," *Chicago Tribune* 11 March 2004: 1.

20.   Epstein, op. cit.

21.   Qtd. in Kelley, op. cit.

22.   Scott Baldauf, "In Taliban Territory, GI Janes Give Afghans A Different View," *The Christian Science Monitor* 4 Nov. 2003: 1.

23.   Paisley Dodds, "Who's the Boss Now? Afghan Prisoners Taking Orders from Female Soldiers," *Grand Rapids Press* 27 Jan. 2002: A3.

24.   Cf. Maureen Dowd, "Driving While Female," *New York Times* 17 Nov. 2002: Sec. 4, page 11.

25.   Cf. Charles Krauthammer, "Abu Ghraib as Symbol," *Washington Post* 7 May 2004: A33.

26.   Cf. Kathleen Parker, "Dying of Political Correctness," *Orlando Sentinal* 30 May 2004: 63.

27.   Cf., for example, "Torture Policy." Editorial. *Washington Post* 16 June 2004: A26.

28.   Francine D'Amico, "The Women of Abu Ghraib," *Post-Standard* 23 May 2004: C1.

29.   Neva Chonin, "The Lynndie Hop," *San Francisco Chronicle* 29 August 2004: 20.

30.   Cf. Gavin McCormick, "Jessica Lynch Grapples With Fame—and Fate," *St. Louis Post-Dispatch* 4 April 2004: A7.

31.   Susan Schmidt and Vernon Loeb, " 'She Was Fighting to the Death': Details Emerging of W. Va. Soldier's Capture and Rescue," *Washington Post* 3 April 2003: A 01.

32. McCormick, op. cit.; David Lipsky, "*I Am A Soldier, Too*," rev. of *I Am A Soldier, Too* by Rick Bragg, *International Herald Tribune* 23 Dec. 2003: 18; "Jessica Lynch Arrives Home to a Hero's Welcome," *Irish Times* 23 July 2003: 9.

33. Lipsky, op.cit.

34. Cf. Joan McAlpine, "The Less Than Patriotic Truth About Private Jessica's Fable," *The Herald* 13 Nov. 2003: 16; Rowan Scarborough, "Crash Caused Lynch's 'Horrific Injuries,'" *Washington Times* 9 July 2003: A1; "Jessica Lynch Arrives Home to A Hero's Welcome," op. cit.

35. Cf. McAlpine, op. cit.

36. Chuck Raasch, "In Iraq, Some Heroes Challenge Old Conventions," *Gannett News Service* 7 April 2003:1.

37. Roeper, op. cit.

38. Cf. Susan Page, "Is Iraq Becoming Another Vietnam?" *USA Today* 14 April 2004; Associated Press, "Deadliest U.S. War Since Vietnam: Symbolic Figure Could Hurt Bush's Popularity," *Seattle Times* 18 Jan. 2004: A16.

39. Cf. Derrick Z. Jack, "The Victims We Don't Count," *Boston Globe* 7 Jan. 2005: A13.

40. Kelley, op. cit.

41. Vogel, op. cit.

42. Kelley, op. cit.

43. Epstein, op. cit.

44. Cf. T. R. Reid, "Hopi Soldier's Spiritual Return Home," *Washington Post* 7 April 2003: A19; Osha Gray Davidson, "A Wrong Turn in the Desert," *Rolling Stone* 27 May 2004: 66-70.

45. Cf. Ann McFeatters, "Let Our Women Fight," *Cincinnati Post* 21 April 2003: A8.

46. Carlson qtd. in David Crary, "Singe Moms' Role in Combat Gains Attention," *Telegraph-Herald* 11 May 2003: A4.

47. Linda Chavez, "Do We Really Want Women in Combat?" *Grand Rapids Press* 1 May 2003: A19.

48. Fox-Genovese qtd. in Lloyd Eby, "Difference of Attitude Biases Investigation of Effects of Divorce," *The World & I* Jan. 1998: 302-317.

49. Jennifer Roback Morse, *Love & Economics: Why the Laissez-Faire Family Doesn't Work* (Dallas, TX: Spence, 2001), 89.

50. Cf. Jacquelyn Swearingen, "Military's Day Care A Model for Nation," *Times Union* 13 Feb. 2001: A1; Elizabeth Simpson, "Navy Expands Options for '24/7' Child Care," *Virginia-Pilot* 13 July 2003: B1; Allan Carlson, "The Military as Social Engineer: Building 'The Total Army Family,'" *The Family in America* October 2002: 1-4.

51. Cf. Randal D. Day and Wade C. Madkey, "Children as Resources: A Cultural Analysis," *Family Perspective* 20 (1958): 258-262.

52. Cf. "Traditional Feminists Are 'Dependency Divas,' Peddling A Victim Mentality and Dependency on Government," PR Newswire, 2 Feb. 2004: 1.

53. Cf. Albert B. Crenshaw, "The High Cost of Low Taxes," *Washington Post* 30 March 2003: H4; P-I News Services, "Congress Upset Over Iraq: Soaring Costs, Need for Troops to Stay for Years to Come Cause Concerns," *Seattle Post-Intelligencer* 11 July 2003: A1.

54. Cf. Dan Radmacher, "Corporate Imperialism: The Real Reason for Iraq Invasion," *New York Review of Books* 9 Oct. 2003: 4A.

55. Cf. Robert Steinback, "Just Bring the Troops Home," *Milwaukee Journal Sentinel* 12 Sept. 2003: 4J; Leon Fuerth, "An Air of Empire," *Washington Post* 20 March 2003: A29.

56.   Acheson Intelligence Group, "Did the Planned Oil Pipeline Through Afghanistan Influence America's Decision to Invade and Install a New Government There?" *The Debate* 7 Jan. 2005 <www.thedebate.org/thedebate/afghanistan.asp>.

57.   Cf. Peter Carlson, "The Profitable Connections of Halliburton," *Washington Post* 10 Feb. 2004: C4; "The Iraq Reconstruction Bonanza," Editorial, *New York Times* 1 Oct. 2003: A22; Roy Ellis, "Stop Fighting Halliburton's War," Letter, *Augusta Chronicle* 17 April 2004: A4.

58.   Cf. Chalmers Johnson, *The Sorrows of Empire: Militarism, Secrecy, and the End of the Republic* (New York: Henry Holt, 2004), 285; George Scialabba, "American Empire an Its Grim Wages," *Boston Globe* 25 April 2004: D8; Stanley Kutler, "Foreign Policy as Moral Imperative," Rev. of *The Sorrows of Empire: Militarism, Secrecy, and the End of the Republic* by Chalmers Johnson, *Los Angeles Times* 4 Jan. 2004: R3.

59.   Cf. Alan Cooperman, "Bishop in Bush's Church in New Antiwar Ad," *Washington Post* 31 Jan. 2003: A18; "Rights and the New Reality," Editorial, *Los Angeles Times* 21 Sept. B22.

60.   Cf. Laura Sullivan, "U.S. Abuse Undermines Treaties," *Baltimore Sun* 5 May 2004: 4A; "Rights and New Reality: Security Without Bigotry," Editorial, *Los Angeles Times* 21 Sept. 2002: B22.

61.   Cf. Bryce Christensen, *When Families Fail . . . The Social Costs* (Lanham, MD: University Press of America/The Rockford Institute, 1991), 5-80.

62.   "There's Money in Poverty," Editorial, *Washington Post* 30 May 1989: A18.

63.   Cf. Judith R. Smith, "Commitment to Mothering and Preference for Employment: The Voices of Women on Public Assistance with Young Children," *Journal of Children & Poverty* 8 (2002): 51-66.

64.   Cf. "Progress Report on Welfare," Editorial, *Washington Post* 18 Nov. 2002: A20; Tony Lee, "Welfare Reform Is Not Working for Everyone," *Seattle Post-Intelligencer* 24 Aug. 1999: A11; "Welfare Vision," Editorial, *Boston Globe* 6 April 2004: A18; "Child Care Hostage," Editorial, *Los Angeles Times* 26 April 2004: B12.

65.   Cf. Dave Ford, "War on Terrorism: The Fear Offensive; Playing Politics with Terror Warnings," *San Francisco Chronicle* 26 May 2002: D3.

66.   Cf. Eric Plutzer, "Work Life, Family Life, and Women's Support of Feminism," *American Sociological Review* 53 (1988): 640-649; S. Philip Morgan and Linda J. Waite, "Parenthood and the Attitudes of Young Adults," *American Sociological Review* 52 (1987): 541-547; Jennifer Glass, "Housewives and Employed Wives: Demographic and Attitudinal Change, 1972-1986," *Journal of Marriage and the Family* 54 (1992): 559-569.

67.   Cf. Paul C. Glick, "The Family Life Cycle and Social Change," *Family Relations* 38 (1989): 123-189.

68.   "Why Women Get the Jobs," *Economist* 23 Aug. 1986: 13-14.

69.   Cf. "War Crimes," Editorial, *Washington Post* 23 Dec. 2004: A22.

70.   Cf. Martin Daly and Margo Wilson, "Child Abuse and Other Risks of Not Living With Both Parents," *Ethology and Sociobiology* 6 (1985): 197-209; Richard J. Gelles, "Child Abuse and Violence in Single-Parent Families: Parent Absence and Economic Deprivation," *American Journal of Orthopsychiatry* 59 (1989): 492-501.

71.   Cf. N. Dickon Reppucci, "Prevention and Ecology: Teen-Age Pregnancy, Child Sexual Abuse, and Organized Youth Sports," *American Journal of Community Psychology* 15 (1987): 10-12.

72.   David T. Courtwright, *Violent Land: Single Men and Social Disorder from the Frontier to the Inner* (Cambridge, MA: Harvard University Press, 1996), 198-280.

73.   Cf. Joel Rawson, "War in Iraq: Embedded Press Works on Several Levels," *Providence Journal* 20 April 2003: A17; "Ban on Coverage of War Dead Upheld," *Los Angeles Times* 22 June 2004: A13.

74.   Cf. Monte Bobele and Joseph Strabo, "The 'Family Taboo' Revisited," *Family Therapy* 14 (1987): 195-200; George F. Will, "Academia Stuck to the Left," *Washington Post* 28 Nov. 2004: B7; Paul Vitz, *Censorship: Evidence of Bias in Our Children's Textbooks* (Ann Arbor, MI: Servant, 1986), 37-38.

75.   "Captain Yee's Ordeal," Editorial, *New York Times* 14 Dec. 2004: Sec. 4, p. 10; "Guantanamo Farce," Editorial, *Los Angeles Times* 2 Sept. 2004: B12; Ray Moseley, "Guantanam: Detainees 'Guilty' Without Any Trial," *Chicago Tribune* 11 April 2004: 1; Joan Vennochi, "Ashcroft's Anti-Rights Legacy," *Boston Globe* 11 Nov. 2004: A19; M. Cheriff Bassiouni, "Don't Tread on Me: Is the War on Terror Really a War on Rights?" *Chicago Tribune* 24 Aug. 2003: 1.

76.   Cf., for instance, Sharman Stein, "New Allies Call for Alimony," *Newsday* 4 Sept. 1986: 4.

77.   Cf. Richard Neely, *The Divorce Decision: Legal, Economic, and Social Dilemmas* (Berkeley: University of California Press, 1986), 36.

78.   Cf. Bryce Christensen, "The Strange Politics of Child Support," *Society* November/ December 2001: 63-70.

79.   Cf. San Diego Grand Jury, "Child Sexual Abuse, Assault, and Molest Issues," Report No. 8, 29 June 1992; Donna L. Wong, "False Allegations of Child Abuse: The Other Side of the Tragedy," *Pediatric Nursing* 13 (1987): 329-332; Martin Guggenheim, *What's Wrong With Children's Rights* (Cambridge, MA: Harvard University Press, 2005), 194.

3

Dead-Beat Dads or Fleeced Fathers?
The Strange Politics of Child Support

Long before the war on terror began exacerbating tensions between the left and the right, Americans had reached consensus on one family issue. During the eighties and nineties, whether the speaker was a liberal Democrat or a conservative Republican, one theme emerged as a sure formula for uniting audiences in loud applause, not dividing them in controversy. On the left and on the right, the new phrase to conjure with became "child support." As *Time* reported, "the deadbeat dad" was accorded a place of singular dishonor as a "selfish fugitive condemned by liberals and conservatives alike."[1] For this reason, California attorney Leora Gershenzon regarded "child support [as] the best rhetoric in the world," a rhetoric unifying political figures "from [President] Clinton to [California's former conservative Republican Governor Pete] Wilson to your local DA...all say[ing] child support is a good thing."[2] And despite the new left-right tensions engendered by disagreements over the war against terrorism, this strange consensus about the beneficence of child support remains robust in the 21st century.

This consensus of support for collecting child support reflects deep public anxiety about the poverty and deprivation of children in female-headed households. The plight of these children does indeed deserve the attention of public officials and of the electorate at large. But as the British journalist G.K. Chesterton once observed, when considering any social evil, we must also keep in view the social ideal. When considering the evils darkening the lives of children in female-headed households, what social ideal should Americans and their elected officials focus on? A raft of sociological studies has now ratified traditional wisdom in identifying the intact two-parent family as the social ideal for anyone wanting to foster children's

41

well-being. The acknowledgment that many single mothers do succeed—against long odds—in rearing highly successful, law-abid-
ing, and well-balanced children should blind no sober analyst to the
overwhelming evidence indicating that children in intact two-parent
families enjoy higher levels of affluence, do much better in school,
succumb less often to the temptations to commit crime and abuse
drugs, and maintain better physical and mental health.[3]

In adopting aggressive child-support laws, few policymakers have
deliberately tried to obscure the social ideal of permanent wedlock.
A few ideologues, of course, do prefer to keep that ideal out of view.
But most of the policymakers who have supported strong new child-
support measures see their actions simply as pragmatic and necessary responses to real social need. But wise policymakers will not
only act to mitigate pain, but they will also analyze carefully the
causes of that pain.

To be sure, policies focused simply on reducing the economic
harm that parental divorce inflicts on children may deliver some of
these children from poverty. Yet because the politicians who have
framed such policies have done nothing to reinforce the social ideal
of keeping children in intact families, they have—however unintentionally—actually reduced the likelihood that children will enjoy the
tremendous economic, social, and psychological benefits which the
realization of that ideal could bring. Worse, by ignoring the need to
foster and protect intact marriages, the advocates of ever-more-ag-
gressive measures for collecting child support have trampled on the
prerogatives of local government, have moved us a dangerous step
closer to a police state, and have violated the rights of innocent and
often impoverished fathers.

Few Americans would dispute a father's obligation to provide for
his children. Throughout American history, any man who bore the
title *father* bore also the title of provider. In the days when most
Americans lived on farms, a man was more likely to discharge this
obligation by filling the family granaries and storage cellars than by
bringing home a paycheck—and, of course, his wife and children
helped him with the necessary agricultural labors. But in this century, as the number of family farms has dwindled, most Americans
have found themselves enmeshed in a cash economy in which few
fathers can work with their spouses and children in providing the
resources essential to the home. Until the 1960s, it was generally the
father alone who worked in the factory or office to support his home-

making wife and their offspring. Working away from home to earn a paycheck inevitably shrank a man's family role by making it much harder for him to teach or discipline his children in the way his great-grandfather did on the family farm. Still, despite deplorable exceptions, most American men continued to shoulder the responsibility of providing for their wives and children. Deprived of the larger family role possible on the family farm, many fathers even came to regard their responsibilities as an economic provider as the very key to their social identity. Fathers thus counted this obligation to provide for their wife and children as the most important and ennobling duty (next to that of conjugal fidelity) accepted through the vows pronounced at marriage.

Logic of the Shotgun Wedding

It was because of this perceived linkage between wedlock and a man's obligation to act as a provider that in the case of an out-of-wedlock pregnancy, the extended family and local community often pressured the responsible young man into a shotgun wedding. Marriage made the young man publicly take upon himself the duty to provide for the unborn child and its mother. This shared understanding of the social meaning of wedlock thus informed a 1923 ruling by the Supreme Court of the State of Kansas in which the Justices emphasize parents' "legal obligation...to support their *legitimate* child while it is too young to care for itself" (emphasis added).[4] The traditional horror of illegitimacy sprang in large part from a deep anxiety about the fate of an infant who was, in social identity, no man's child. Since no man had ever pledged to provide for that child by entering into wedding vows, the future of the child and its mother teetered in uncertainty.

True, traditional bastardy laws allowed the government to compel unmarried fathers to provide support for their children. But enforcing such laws was difficult since the disgraced mother and her family usually tried to keep the whole matter out of the public eye, often quietly putting the baby up for adoption so that a married father could assume the paternal responsibility of providing for the child. Even when bastardy laws were enforced, the modest aim was merely "to relieve taxpayer burdens, not to alter the economic or social standing of the mother of the child."[5] Certainly, it is not government coercion of an unmarried father which the renowned seventeenth-century jurist Samuel Pufendorf had in view when he observed that with regard to their obligation to provide for their children, "parents [chiefly fathers in his patriarchal age]…joyfully undertake and discharge their duty without the compulsion of the Civil Government."[6] In Pufendorf's era, it was widespread acceptance of the responsibilities implicit in the wedding vow which made compulsion by the Civil Government unnecessary.

So long as illegitimacy and divorce remained rare, fathers—with few exceptions—continued to support their children without any involvement by the Civil Government, except the licensing of their voluntary wedding vows. Divorce did begin to occur more frequently in a world in which fathers performed the task of breadwinning not on the family farm but far from home, often in daily association with women other than their wives. Yet even in the breach, the marriage vow defined a man's obligations to provide for his children and their mother. For under traditional fault-based divorce, it was the violation of the wedding vows which gave the court justification for denying the father custody of the children and for requiring him to pay alimony and child support.

But consider how much weaker the government's warrant for forcing a divorced father to make child-support payments to his former wife becomes once the question of fault has been eliminated from divorce proceedings, as it has under current law. For unlike traditional divorce statutes, no-fault divorce undermines rather than reinforces marriage as a social ideal. By allowing a faithless spouse to sunder the wedding vow with relative ease and without any legal condemnation, no-fault divorce trivializes marriage, making it weaker than the weakest of contracts-at-will. It is now easier to dispose of an unwanted spouse of twenty years than to fire an unwanted employee of one year. Nor do vigorous efforts to collect child support reinforce wedlock so long as violation of the wedding covenant does not materially affect how the court awards child custody or assesses child support. In fact, by allowing a faithless wife to keep her children and a sizable portion of her former spouse's income, current child-support laws have combined with no-fault jurisprudence to convert wedlock into a snare for many guileless men.

Some defenders of no-fault divorce have argued that its enactment had little or no influence on actual divorce rates, which were surging upwards before its passage. But statistician Thomas B. Marvell calculated in 1989 that the adoption of no-fault statutes had driven up state divorce rates "by some 20 to 25 percent."[7] And in a 1999 analysis, a team of statisticians determined that in the thirty-two states which had enacted no-fault laws by 1974, these laws "resulted in a substantial number of divorces that would not have occurred otherwise."[8] It particularly distresses attorney Steven L. Varnis that while no-fault divorce statutes have leached much of the legal meaning out of wedlock, "the content of marital vows" has remained the same as it was when traditional divorce laws were in force.[9]

Undermining marriage as a social ideal was not one of the objectives identified by the activists who pushed no-fault statutes through in the 1960s and 1970s. Indeed, many of these activists claimed that their legal innovation would actually strengthen wedlock by helping men and women trapped in bad marriages to move into good marriages. This argument looks very dubious to sociologist Norval Glenn, who cites national survey data indicating that since the enactment of no-fault laws, the probability of being in a bad marriage has "increased slightly." Glenn plausibly suggests that the shadow of casual divorce has actually made men and women less likely to "commit fully" to a marital union, thus reducing the likelihood of marital success.[10] Another reason for the ineffectiveness of no-fault divorce as a device for moving spouses out of unhappy marriages into happy ones is that aggressive collection of child support—initiated to limit the harm wrought upon children by parental divorce—"reduces remarriage probabilities among low-income fathers."[11]

The Wages of "No Fault"

Low income or high income, a good many innocent fathers have found that no-fault divorce delivers no happy new marriage and no chance of justice in resolving the custody and child-support disputes occasioned by the dissolution of what was for them a perfectly satisfactory union. Although it is frequently the case in divorce proceedings that the husband has violated the wedding vows and wants the divorce, no-fault statutes do not require any such finding in order to separate a man from his children and a portion of his income. In many cases, it is the wife who has broken her wedding vows. Yet no matter how faithless, when a wife files for divorce (and in two-thirds of all divorce cases, it is the wife who files the petition), she can count on the state as an ally. For as legal scholar Lenore Weitzman points out, no-fault divorce implicitly puts the state in alliance with the spouse who wants out of the marriage. "The new law," she writes, "elevates one's 'right' to divorce over a spouse's 'right' to remain married," so "shift[ing] the power from the spouse who wants to remain married to the spouse who wants to get divorced."[12] In the same vein, Varnis observes that "the law [under no-fault] generally supports the spouse seeking divorce, even if that spouse was a wrong-doer, by granting divorces with little regard for a spouse who may not desire it."[13]

Because of the continuing power of the "tender years" doctrine favoring the parent who has cared for the child during the early years, divorcing mothers still usually get custody of their children. And under no-fault, a mother's infidelities usually do not jeopardize her chances of winning a custody fight with a guiltless father.[14] Nor do a wife's infidelities reduce the amount of child support she is entitled to receive from her former spouse. "A blameless father," remarks Justice Richard Neely of the West Virginia Supreme Court, "often emerges from divorce courts with all the financial responsi-bility of marriage and none of its emotional or economic rewards." In many cases, Neely explains, the victimized man is "saddled with children whom he never sees and who may even have been turned against him."[15]

Under current jurisprudence, a betrayed father can expect to hear from the court whenever he falls behind in paying child support to a faithless former spouse, but he cannot ask the court to require his former spouse to give any account of how she spends that child support. In many cases, money paid for child support benefits a father's former spouse at least as much as his children. As Harvard scholar Martha Minow concedes, even though "child support is in-tended to benefit the child, not the custodial parent [generally the mother]," in fact, it is "difficult if not impossible to disentangle [the child's well-being] from the custodial parent's standard of living." Since it is impossible, for instance, to provide good housing to the child without also providing it to the custodial mother, a father's payment of child support often means "windfalls to the custodial parent."[16]

Nor can a divorced father expect much help from the court in guaranteeing his visitation rights. The state reserves all its legal rigor for the collecting of child support. Indeed, so far as custody and child support are concerned, the current rules for divorce appear to be premised not on no-fault but rather upon an unacknowledged presumption of paternal fault. For however guiltless he may have been in causing the divorce, the divorced father will probably lose his children and will thereafter live under court scrutiny—like a criminal on probation—to ensure that he pays the mandated child support until his children turn age eighteen.

Without question, many divorced fathers are guilty of having destroyed their marriages through perfidious or violent behavior and ought to have been denied custody of their children and ought to be under court order to pay not only child support but alimony as well. It is largely because no-fault has weakened the economic status of victimized former wives that feminist Betty Friedan, formerly a supporter, now admits, "I think we made a mistake with no-fault divorce."[17] But the plight of wives impoverished through no-fault in no way mitigates the injustice worked upon a father who never wanted a divorce or in any way neglected his marital duties—and then unexpectedly finds himself separated from his children and under court order to make child-support payments to a faithless former spouse who wastes the money he is forced to give her, while rearing their offspring in ways totally out of harmony with his beliefs.

Such injustices seldom receive attention from the politicians pushing for ever-more-stringent enforcement of child-support laws. In their view, it is in the best interests of the child to ensure full collection of child support, regardless of the reason for the divorce and regardless of the father's circumstances. "Concern about the effects of child support enforcement on the fathers themselves has been minimal," acknowledges a team of prominent researchers headed by Irwin Garfinkel.[18] But these effects have often been severe. Set by rigid formulae and often collected by garnisheeing wages, child-support payments often work great hardship on lower-income fathers. Urban Institute researcher Elaine Sorensen observes that bureaucratically established child-support orders often exceed poor fathers' ability to pay. Worse, she complains, when divorced fathers lose their jobs, have their wages or hours cut, or become sick or disabled, they find it very hard to get their child-support obligation adjusted accordingly. "The process for adjusting [child-support] orders is quite bureaucratic.... According to U.S. Census data, only 4 percent of non-custodial fathers who were paying child support under an order received a downward adjustment when their earnings fell by more than 15 percent between one year and the next."[19] Such numbers give substance to analyst John Smith's criticism that "get tough" child-support measures are "running [poor fathers] into poverty and homelessness."[20]

Should a divorced father fall into arrears in paying child support, he may lose his driver's license, his business license, or his professional license, even if the loss of his license deprives him of the ability to pay off the amount in arrears. One divorced father whose legal fight over visitation and support payments left him so penniless that he had to live in a tent in the Santa Cruz Mountains vehemently protested, "I have less rights than a damn criminal in jail."[21]

Punishing the Innocent

Harsh policies may be in order for fathers who have caused their divorce through culpable behavior. But under a legal regime which combines lax no-fault divorce laws with draconian child-support collection, fathers innocent of any pre-divorce offense against their spouse are treated much the same as fathers guilty of dark infidelities. For that matter, in the government's crusade to collect child-support payments, divorced fathers—guilty or innocent—receive much the same treatment as never-married fathers, now often identified by blood or DNA tests. Not surprisingly, never-married fathers typically resist the state's efforts to collect child support—much more so than most divorced fathers. After all, the unions which create illegitimate children have never been dignified by any voluntary public vows between the partners. And in an age of readily available contraceptives and abortion on demand, many unwed fathers regard childbearing as entirely a woman's decision, one for which he bears no responsibility. After all, he has no legal right to prevent the abortion of his child. The inconsistency in current child-support laws as they apply to unwed fathers is readily apparent to feminist lawyer Karen DeCrow, a leader of the National Organization for Women, who observes, "You can't have a unilateral decision in the hands of women and then say he [the father] has got to pay [child support]. Right now, the law is definitely unequal; men have no stake in the say of what's going to happen. It comes down to the whole right to choose parenthood or to choose non-parenthood.... [I]f abortion is legal, then men shouldn't have to pay child support for a child they did not choose to have."[22]

Unlike divorced fathers, who usually are quite willing to acknowledge their children and to help provide for them, never-married fathers often try to hide their relationship to children viewed as a former lover's accident. Biology alone cannot forge the kind of father-child relationship that marital child-bearing creates, even if the marriage later dissolves. Yet the same state which has devalued marriage through no-fault divorce also devalues marriage through child-support policies which put divorced fathers and never-married fathers under almost identical scrutiny, viewed alike as comparable classes of quasi-criminals, perpetually under corrective supervision. When Princeton researcher Anne Case analyzed the social effect of laws requiring identification of the fathers of illegitimate children (for the purpose of collecting child-support), she was stunned by the "perverse result" that legal measures requiring "paternity establishment to age eighteen" are "positively and significantly correlated with out-of wedlock childbearing." And she was greatly relieved that in more sophisticated multi-variable statistical models, "the passage of paternity establishment to age eighteen [for the purposes of collecting child support] is associated with a two-percentage-point reduction in the rate of out-of-wedlock childbearing."[23]

But the "perverse" correlation between paternity establishment and out-of-wedlock childbearing in the simpler statistical model may plausibly be interpreted as evidence that such measures for collecting child-support from never-married fathers are a corrective only belatedly adopted in areas in which marriage has already been sapped of its cultural and legal strength. Further evidence of the linkage between aggressive child-support policies and the erosion of wedlock as a social ideal may be gleaned from Sweden, a country with remarkably high rates of divorce, cohabitation, and illegitimacy, but with an international reputation as a country in which "child support enforcement is ferocious."[24] As they consider the Swedish example, Americans may well wonder how government child-support officials can ever reinforce wedlock as a social ideal while following essentially the same policies whether dealing with a promiscuous unwed father or a divorced father never untrue to his wedding vows. Such policies tend to reduce the never-married father and the divorced father alike to "sperm donors with checkbooks."[25]

No Substitute for Marriage

For advocates of vigorous child-support collection, a father's circumstances matter very little. All that matters is transferring resources from him to his child and the child's mother. Recent research validates their single-minded focus insofar as it does show that a father's payment of child support does enhance his child's well-being.[26] But will those who truly care about children settle for the relatively meager enhancement in their well-being to be secured through collection of child support? Should it be ignored that many of the adverse effects of parental divorce persist even when household income rises? No. Truly advancing the interests of children must mean reinforcing marriage as a social ideal. For living in an intact family confers tremendous advantages in physical and mental health, academic performance, and in resistance to delinquency and drug use. No matter how successfully they carry out their mandates, state officials collecting child support from divorced or never-married fathers can never bestow such advantages.

Defenders of the current regime of liberal laws for divorce and tough laws for child support may argue that the children's lives will not be improved by forcing incompatible parents to live together. But researchers report that children enjoy significant psychological and social advantages even when their parents characterize their marriage as "unsatisfactory"[27] and when they report moderate amounts of spousal conflict.[28] Varnis thus dismisses the argument that "it is better to have divorced parents without conflict than married parents with conflict" as "highly speculative and unsubstantiated."[29]

By endorsing a regime of casual no-fault divorce, America's policymakers gave the nation what Varnis calls "the idea of marriage as a serialized form of monogamous notarized dating with police approval, and divorce as part of a rational planned process."[30] When evidence began to accumulate that this rational, planned process was hurting children, these same policymakers responded not by reversing themselves and reinforcing matrimony. Instead, they began devising aggressive new strategies for collecting child support. But in hacking at the leaves of the problem rather than going to the root, policymakers have driven down the probability that children will enjoy the benefits of living in an intact family with both parents. Further, they have led a confused nation into a bureaucratic, legal, and political quagmire.

In 1988, Congress mandated that each state had to establish a computerized child-support registry. Nine years later, after the expenditure of $2.6 billion, only 15 states had complied, while most found themselves "plagued with technical glitches, cost overruns, and friction with counties and court systems, some of which maintain their own child-support records.[31] In its 1997 analysis of the situation, the General Accounting Office concluded that states had "underestimated the magnitude, complexity, and costs of their [computer] projects and operations" and had been given insufficient guidance from the federal government in trying to complete their computerized systems.[32] California alone spent $171 million in a failed attempt to meet Congress's 1997 deadline for creating their child-support registry. The state's second attempt likewise ended in fiasco in April 1999, with state officials in a fog even as to how much they had spent on the second failure. "It's an amazing mess," declared one exasperated state legislator.[33]

Not that things necessarily improve once child-support computers come on line. In one California jurisdiction (San Diego County) which succeeded in putting together a computerized system for identifying deadbeat dads, "a great number of people [have been] erroneously ensnared by computer error," with a good many men finding themselves in legal difficulty for "hav[ing] suffered from the coincidence of having the same or similar name as a father who hasn't paid up." "The computer," explained one San Diego official, " brings the benefit of serving a lot of cases, but it also is not real forgiving.... [H]ow do you keep the number of injustices down? It never goes to zero." Some measure of computerized injustice did not trouble Lucia Edmundson of the San Diego District Attorney's office, who stoutly defended "a child-support net so wide that a few bystanders get caught." Of the innocent but falsely accused, she said, "I can understand their feelings, but they still have to prove [their innocence]. If the only alternative is to come to court, then that's what they have to do."[34] In their push to collect child support, some public officials appear willing to push aside the traditional presumption of innocence.

Bureaucratic Nightmares

No improvement on San Diego's system, Wisconsin's statewide computerized network for collecting child support (dubbed the Kids Information Data System, or KIDS) has spewed out hundreds of erroneous child-support bills, forcing many innocent fathers to waste time and money clearing themselves. "Parents who owe nothing have been billed thousands of dollars," reports the Milwaukee Journal Sentinel, citing as an illustrative example the case of a sixty-five-year-old man whose children were all in their forties but who nonetheless received a bill for $60,000 in child support. Though the bill resulted from computer error, the man was compelled to clear his name.

Scores of other non-custodial parents (almost all fathers) have likewise had to pay attorneys to challenge erroneous computerized billings. Nine out of ten such challenges are eventually resolved in favor of the accused, but the state does not reimburse those incorrectly billed for child support for their legal expenses.[35]

When its computerized system malfunctioned in 6 percent of all 1998 child-support cases, the state of Virginia at least had the grace to apologize to the 2,300 non-custodial parents (again, almost all fathers) erroneously accused of delinquency in paying child support. But before receiving the official apology, many of those falsely accused of being child-support scofflaws had to gather the documents necessary to set the record straight.[36]

A different kind of computer snafu developed in Missouri, where the state's computerized child-support system sent out hundreds of checks to incorrect addresses and—incredibly—delayed the mailing of numerous checks in cases in which fathers bewildered the computer by paying more than they were legally obligated to do.[37]

But in their zeal to collect child-support payments, government officials are doing more than building costly and error-prone computer systems. They are also experimenting with new forms of coercion. In 1995, Florida led the way by employing dogs and a police helicopter to conduct a statewide arrest sweep for deadbeat dads.[38] On the federal level, government agencies such as the FBI, the IRS, and the Justice Department are taking on responsibilities previously outside their purview in order to identify deadbeat dads and jail the recalcitrant. Such measures do not impress Gershenzon, who believes that "the whole point is to collect money, and this approach is very expensive...The idea is to get cash for kids, not necessarily to put bad guys in jail. [Putting people in jail] may make you feel better, but it won't necessarily help children."[39]

The case of Timothy Lee Dean perfectly illustrates Gershenzon's point. Jailed for failure to pay $50,000 in back child support, Dean incurred more than $100,000 in legal fees contesting his debt. He finally ended up penniless, homeless, and almost blind in one eye because of a jail fight, yet his children received only a few dollars in child support—far, far less than the state spent prosecuting his case.[40]

Stubborn fathers are not alone in fighting against the newly aggressive efforts to collect child support. Some state legislators think that fundamental legal doctrines are being skewed in "the frenzy to boost [child] support payments."[41] Nebraska lawmakers, for instance, have railed against the new federal child-support directives—which states must adopt or lose federal funds—as "a form of blackmail, a usurpation of states' rights [which is] downright offensive." "This is a blatant attack on the state's ability to run the state," protested the Speaker of Nebraska's House of Representatives.[42] In Kansas, some lawmakers have complained that in its child-support directives, the federal government has gone "too far in imposing its will on state governments," with one legislator calling the federal plan a type of "extortion."[43]

The federal plan for collecting child support has also alarmed civil libertarians. To facilitate the collection of child support, federal officials have established a national employment registry allowing them to track the job changes of those who owe child support. Such a registry worries some observers, who see it opening "unexplored portals to surveillance" by enabling "the government [to] keep closer tabs on where everyone is working." Legal experts fear that the creation of this registry sets a dangerous precedent, increasing the likelihood that government will capture other databases originally collected for business purposes. In the opinion of one privacy expert, "It's the proverbial camel's nose under the tent door."[44]

Even if all of their computers work properly, even if federal and local officials can cooperate, and even if privacy concerns can be temporarily set aside, the child-support network makes a poor substitute for the intact family—even by strictly monetary measures. For in the first place, once a divorce takes place, creating two households instead of one, there are fewer resources available for parents or children, regardless of how those resources are divided up. "Two households," Minow remarks, "in most circumstances, will be unable to achieve the standard of living available to the one."[45] No child-support network will ever change this reality. Furthermore, while married fathers give their financial support directly to their children, government officials must expend one dollar for every four collected through their complex and coercive mechanisms.[46]

"Children Worse Off Overall"

Policymakers have trumpeted the increases in child support collected by the government in recent years: the $14.4 billion collected by federal and state officials in 1998 represents an increase of 80 percent over the $8 billion collected in 1992.[47] But by another measure, government officials are merely running faster on the social treadmill created by high divorce rates and ever-higher illegitimacy rates: of children living with single mothers, 31 percent received child support twenty years ago; the percentage is roughly the same today, despite the dramatic increase in government efforts to enlarge its child-support system.[48] Nor has the increase in government zeal in collecting child support come without emotional costs for the children and mothers who are supposed to be the primary beneficiaries, since recent research shows that "paying any child support increases the incidence of conflict between parents."[49] Because of such research findings, Garfinkel and his colleagues soberly concede—despite their own advocacy of more vigorous child-support measures— "stronger enforcement may make children worse off overall."[50]

Policymakers have had real social needs in view when devising ever-more aggressive measures for collecting child support. Those social needs were the unavoidable consequences of decades of family conflict and dissolution. But each year brings more evidence that responding to these needs with aggressive policies for collecting child-support hurts not only innocent fathers but quite possibly women and children as well, which should give them pause. Perhaps it is time for frenetic pragmatists to give place to insightful analysts. Perhaps it is time for policymakers to start thinking deeply about affirming the social ideal of marriage so effectively that such measures are not necessary. In truth, only such an affirmation really promises to help children in the long run. "Without increasing the number of children in two-parent families," columnist Ronald Brownstein has recently asserted, "the United States is unlikely to make the progress it wants at reducing the number of children in poverty."[51] Morley Glicken, a professor of social work at Cal State San Bernardino, goes further, suggesting that government leaders ought to "put some of [the money] spent on the collection of child support into family therapy and mandated mediation" so that "couples can work their problems out and stay together."[52]

Such a reallocation of funds will require government to once again endorse enduring marriage as a social ideal worthy of support as the best means of fostering children's well being. This reallocation will also require a repudiation of the anti-marital sophistry of ideologues, so forcing an overdue re-evaluation of the no-fault statutes that have so cheapened the wedding vow. It may also force a realignment of other government policies—such as the dubious experiments with gender-role engineering in the schools and in the military and the systematic dismantling of the family wage in the workplace. Most of all, recognizing wedlock as a social ideal will compel the surrender of the dangerous illusion that the bureaucratic machinery of child-support-collection can somehow obviate the need for the personal virtues that sustain marriage and family life. Once we have all surrendered this illusion, then we can—with T.S. Eliot—finally break out of the spells woven by political theorists "dreaming of systems so perfect no one will need to be good."[53]

Notes

1. David Van Biema, "Dunning Deadbeats," *Time* 3 April 1995: 49.
2. Gershenzon quoted in Teresa Moore, "Study Slams State Crackdown on Deadbeat Parents," *San Francisco Chronicle*, 23 March 1995: A15.
3. See Bryce Christensen, ed., *When Families Fail...The Social Costs* (Lanham, MD: University Press of America/The Rockford Institute, 1991), 5-82.
4. Doughty v. Engler, 122 Kan. 583, 585, 211 p. 619, 620 (1923); see Bryce Christensen and George Swan, "Double Bind: The Redefinition of American Fatherhood," *The Family in America* October 1988: 5.
5. Martha Minow, "How Should We Think About Child Support Obligations?" in Irwin Garfinkel et al., *Fathers Under Fire: The Revolution in Child Support Enforcement* (New York: Russell Sage, 1998), 304-305.
6. Samuel Pufendorf, *Of the Law of Nature and Nations* (Oxford: L. Lichfield, 1703), Bk. 4, ch. 11, IV, p. 374; see Christensen and Swan, op. cit.
7. Thomas B. Marvell, "Divorce Rates and the Fault Requirement," *Law and Society Review* 23(1989): 544.
8. Joseph Lee Rodgers, Paul A. Nakonezny, and Robert D. Shull, "Did No-Fault Divorce Legislation Matter? Definitely Yes and Sometimes No," *Journal of Marriage and the Family* 61(1999): 803-809.
9. Steven L. Varnis, "Broken Vows, Therapeutic Sentiments, Legal Sanctions," *Society* Nov.-Dec. 1997: 32f.
10. Norval D. Glenn, "The Recent Trend in Marital Success in the United States," *Journal of Marriage and the Family* 53(1991): 261-270.
11. David E. Bloom, Cecilia Conrad, and Cynthia Miller, "Child Support and Fathers' Remarriage and Fertility," in Garfinkel et al., op. cit.146.
12. Lenore J. Weitzman, *The Divorce Revolution: The Unexpected Social and Economic Consequences for Women and Children in America* (New York: Free Press, 1985), 27.
13. Varnis, op. cit.
14. See Matthew S. Cornick, *A Practical Guide to Family Law* (Minneapolis, MN: West, 1995): 220.
15. Richard Neely, *The Divorce Decision: The Legal and Human Consequences* (New York: McGraw-Hill, 1984), 17.
16. Minow, op. cit., 307.
17. Friedan quoted in Evan Gahr, "All the Fault of No-Fault," *Insight on the News* 28 October 1996: 41.
18. Irwin Garfinkel et al., Intro., op. cit., 2.
19. Elaine Sorensen, "A Little Help for Some 'Deadbeat' Dads," *Washington Post* 15 November 1995: A25.
20. "Child Support Collections" [Letters], *Los Angeles Times* 18 Oct. 1998: M4.

21.   See Steve Johnson, "Men Rebel Against Family Justice System," *Knight-Ridder Tribune News Service* 4 March 1996: 304K0269.

22   DeCrow quoted in Fred M. Frohock, *Abortion: A Case Study in Law and Morals* (Westport, CT: Greenwood, 1983), 78-79.

23.   Anne Case, "The Effects of Stronger Child Support Enforcement on Nonmarital Fertility," in Garfinkel et al., op. cit., 212.

24.   "Home sweet Home," *The Economist* 9 September 1995: 25f.

25.   "Letters from the People," *St. Louis Post-Dispatch* 23 March 1997: 2B.

26.   See Paul R. Amato and Joan G. Gilbreth, "Nonresident Fathers and Children's Well-Being: A Meta-Analysis," *Journal of Marriage and the Family* 61(1999): 557-573.

27.   See Carolyn Webster-Stratton, "The Relationship of Marital Support, Conflict, and Divorce to Parent Perceptions, Behaviors, and Childhood Conduct Problems," *Journal of Marriage and the Family* 51(1989): 417-430.

28.   See Thomas L. Hanson, "Does Parental Conflict Explain Why Divorce Is Negatively Associated with Child Welfare?" *Social Forces* 77(1999): 1283-1315.

29.   Varnis, op. cit.

30.   Ibid.

31.   Barbara Vobejda, "Nation's Child Support System Criticized," *Washington Post* 17 July 1997: A17.

32.   Adam Clymer, "Child-Support Collection Net Usually Fails," *New York Times* 17 July 1997: A16.

33.   Nicholas Riccardi and Greg Krikorian, "State's Child Support Computer Plan Rejected," *Los Angeles Times* 10 April 1999: A1.

34.   Leslie Wolf, "Collecting Support," *San Diego Union-Tribune* 20 Oct. 1997: A1.

35.   Mary Beth Murphy, "Audit Sought on Support System," *Milwaukee Journal Sentinel* 4 February 1997: 1.

36.   R.H. Melton, "Virginia Falsely Threatens 2,300 In Mistake on Child Support," *Washington Post* 29 January 1998: D7.

37.   Benita Y. Williams, "Problems Plague Child Support System," *Kansas City Star* 3 September 1998: 8.

38.   See Patricia Orwen, "Deadbeat Dads," *Toronto Star* 9 April 1995: A1.

39.   Gershenzon quoted in Marlene Cimons, "New Steps Seek to Boost Child Support Collection Efforts," *Los Angeles Times* 1 January 1999: A13.

40.   See Bill Callahan, "Deadbeaten," *San Diego Union-Tribune* 20 Oct. 1997: A17.

41.   See Katie Kerwin, "Child Support Collections Soar," *Denver Rocky Mountain News* 2 December 1996: A5.

42.   See Robyn Tysver, "Federal Mandate Criticized," *Omaha World-Herald* 20 April 1999: 1.

43.   Laura Scott, "A Fight Over Deadbeats," *Kansas City Star* 8 January 1998: C6.

44.   Penelope Purdey, "Eye on Privacy," *Denver Post* 2 March 1997: E1.

45.   Minow, op. cit., 305.

46.   See Varnis, op. cit.

47.   See Cimons, op. cit.

48.   See Elaine Sorensen, "Dead-Broke Dads," *Washington Post* 9 June 1999: A25.

49.   See Judith A. Seltzer, Sara S. McLanahan, and Thomas L. Hanson, "Will Child Support Enforcement Increase Father-Child Contact and Parental Conflict After Separation?" in Garfinkel et al., op. cit., 181.

50.   Garfinkel et al., Conclusion, op. cit., 333-334.

51.   Ronald Brownstein, "National Perspective," *Los Angeles Times* 28 June 1999: A5.

52.   Letter in "Child Support Collections," *Los Angeles Times* 18 Oct. 1998: M4.

53.   T.S. Eliot, Choruses from *The Rock*, VI, in *T. S. Eliot: The Complete Poems and Plays, 1909-1950* (New York: Harcourt, Brace, and World, 1971), 106.

4

Fostering Confusion: The Real Foster-Care Crisis

When policymakers went to work designing aggressive measures for collecting child support, they were responding—however myopically—to real human needs. In the same way, policymakers and activists who have in recent years called for more public money to expand and improve the foster-care system are likewise responding to real social needs. The inadequacy of the current foster care system is indeed obvious to almost all who have examined it—Democrats and Republicans, liberals and conservatives. The human significance of that inadequacy is all too clear in the life of one all-too-typical foster child, William Hagen.

Growing up was an ordeal for William Hagen. He was only six when his mother and her live-in boyfriend began to abuse him. Although the abuse ended with the intervention of state child-protection officials, the misery did not, as Hagen found himself being bounced around from one home to another in a foster-care system which deprived him of any sense of permanence or belonging. He never counted how many foster homes he passed through between the ages of six (when he was first taken from his mother) and nineteen when he finally left the foster-care system, but he estimates that it was between fifteen and seventeen homes. With periodic, but unsuccessful, attempts to return him to his mother, Hagen had to move at least thirty times during those years. Nor did his understanding of the reasons for the state's intervention ever fully enable him to accept it: "I was glad to not have the abuse happen," he now acknowledges, "but I had a strange sense of loyalty to my mother...I always wanted to go back."[1]

Lamentably, the number of children with similarly problematic experiences in foster care has skyrocketed in recent years, prompting many public officials and many prominent commentators to speak of a crisis in foster care. The well-being of hundreds of thousands of children, pundits have warned, depends upon the infusion of much more money into the foster-care system for the employment of more foster-care social workers and the recruitment and training of many more foster-care families.

Before lawmakers appropriate more money for enlarging the fos-ter-care system, however, perhaps they should take a sober look at the reasons for its troubles. For a thorough analysis of these troubles will reveal that the causes of these troubles extend far beyond the foster-care system itself. Under careful scrutiny, the problems that public officials now face in foster care turn out to be but the symp-toms of a much wider and deeper crisis: a crisis in American family life. Some commentators see nothing wrong with the foster care sys-tem that more tax money cannot fix. However, trying to resolve the problems in foster care without addressing the overall retreat from family life makes about as much sense as buying ever larger pumps to pump the sea water out of the Zuider Zee–without ever bothering to find out where the dikes are leaking and why the leaks are grow-ing. As the breaches in America's social dams grow, policies fo-cused narrowly on foster-care reform must prove both foolish and futile, sure to doom thousands of children to drowning in a wild and turbid flood. It is past time for merely bailing water; it is time to fix some dikes.

Numbers Crunched

Local and national officials now raising the cry of a "crisis in foster care" do not lack for statistics. In 1985, there were about 275,000 children in foster care in the United States (a figure already very high by historical standards), but by 2000, more than 540,000 children were in such care, despite the relatively depressed fertility throughout the period.[2] The number of children entering foster care is still growing "at a dizzying rate," and–what is worse–children now entering the system "tend to be younger and more distressed," with foster-care workers now seeing more "children who set fires, sexually abuse others, torture animals, and attempt suicide."[3]

Even as the number of deeply traumatized children entering the system has skyrocketed, the number of foster homes available to place them in has plummeted, dropping from 147,000 in 1991 to just 100,000 in 1995. In 2000, officials in Massachusetts reported that the state was short 2,000 foster parents, so creating "an emergency" in foster care.[4] In the same year, a single Florida city reported with alarm that it had "400 more foster kids than foster beds."[5] One consequence of this shortage of foster-care homes is that children are often "crammed into over-capacity homes," so exposing them to "greater risk of abuse by overstressed foster parents or other kids."[6] Moreover, foster children are consigned to "a longer stay in limbo" because overburdened caseworkers are forced to spend more time figuring out how to get new children into foster care and less time arranging for their release from foster care either through permanent reunification with their parents or through adoption. Inevitably, an extended stay in foster care means more bouncing around, especially at a time when so many foster families are now withdrawing from the foster-care system. In Nebraska (which is far from suffering from the worst foster-care problems), social workers report that the number of children who moved more than four times during their stay in foster care rose from 33 percent in 1992 to 47 percent in 1998. Similar trends have been reported in other jurisdictions. One New York boy was placed in a depressing thirty-seven different homes within two months; another lived with seventeen different families in just twenty-five days.[7]

These are the numbers, then, that officials have cited to buttress their claim that we now face "a foster-care emergency," a "system in crisis," a foster-care system "on the verge of collapse," a "system out of control," and "a foster-care crisis worse than ever before."[8] No set of statistics, no rhetoric of bureaucratic urgency can adequately represent what is really at stake here: the emotional and psychological well-being of tens of thousands of children. Public officials realize all too keenly that by forcing children to deal repeatedly with the pain of rejection, "it 're-traumatizes' children every time they are moved."[9] Yet the current upsurge in the number of children entering the foster-care system, at a time when foster families are dropping out far faster than they can be recruited, is forcing more and more children to deal with that pain. The current pressures on the system have also made inevitable the frequent separation of siblings–another cause of emotional trauma–and the increasingly common placement of foster children in distant jurisdictions, so rendering it difficult for extended family to visit.

In what probably constitutes the most galling irony of the foster-care quagmire, officials acknowledge that foster-care placement does not even do a very good job of shielding children from the evil which is typically the reason for their entering the system in the first place: child abuse. Although most foster parents demonstrate remarkable patience and love in caring for the troubled children in their care, a distressingly large minority not only fail to manifest such virtues, but actually abuse and victimize the children placed with them. One metropolitan jurisdiction found that "nearly a third of children taken from their families suffered some abuse by their foster parents."[10] The horror stories associated with foster care include verified cases of foster parents who beat their charges with belts, force them to bathe with Clorox, and even kill them with wanton cruelty.[11] In 1996 alone, fourteen children were killed while in foster care.[12] In the overcrowded foster homes increasingly relied upon by desperate social workers, it is often other foster children who are the abusers. A critic of the foster-care system points out that even "liberal definitions of abuse and neglect" yield a national incidence rate of between 2.3 percent and 4.9 percent in the general population, which is "far less maltreatment" than has been documented for the Seattle-based Casey Family foster-care program, regarded as "one of the very best in the nation" because of the low caseloads given its social workers and because of the special training given its foster parents. In this model program, 24 percent of female foster children who "aged-out" of foster care said that they had been "victims of actual or attempted sexual abuse" in the foster home in which they had stayed the longest.[13]

Subjected to the repeated traumas of relocation and abuse, denied the emotional support of siblings or relatives, many foster children slip over the edge into neuroses and depression. A 2000 study found that "children in foster care had Medicaid expenditures for mental health services that were more than 11.5 times greater than those expenditures for AFDC-eligible children," a comparison group which itself is "not notable for stellar health status."[4] It should surprise no one that almost half of foster-care children drop out of high school and that a disturbingly high percentage of foster-care children end up homeless, imprisoned, or institutionalized as adults.[15] As the Little Hoover Commission observed in 2000, "Despite benevolent intentions and billions of dollars, the government has proved to be a poor surrogate parent...In the end, troubled children often end up as troubled adults. The personal anguish becomes a public calamity."[16]

Fostering Problems

While some children come out of foster care healed and helped, the long-term track record for children who have spent time in such care is all too prominently marked with academic failure, crime, and homelessness. The true measure of foster-care pathos comes neither from sociologists nor social statisticians, but rather from the children themselves.

"It took me three or four years before I got adopted," recalls one former foster child. "And it's the pits going from foster home to foster home.... It's a killer. I wish kids didn't have to go through that."[17]

The autobiographical reflections of another former foster child provide more of the details of the "killer" existence:

> I stayed in foster care all my life–eighteen years. I went in, I guess when I was about three weeks old, and as I got older, I went into two other foster homes...I just wanted to know who my real family was, anything about my family....I felt as if, you know, Where would I be if I were with my natural parents? I wanted to figure out why, why...Why was I in a foster home?...At sixteen or seventeen, I ran away from home, and from then on when I came back for foster care, I was placed in another foster home. And I stayed there for maybe six or seven months. When I was placed back with the natural family, I was out of place because I didn't know any of them or any other people...Being in court I never knew if I was gonna go home. I never knew what was gonna happen–if I was gonna go home to a foster home or if I was gonna be placed somewhere in a group home or–I just didn't know.[18]

That the foster-care system is inflicting too much suffering on too many children, few will dispute. As to the right way to change the system so as to reduce that suffering, however, there is considerable disagreement. Many commentators and activists see no flaws in the current system which cannot be remedied with higher levels of funding, better staffing of the state's social-service agencies, and more aggressive recruiting of foster families. In this vein, Ames Alexander of *Knight-Ridder* writes that "much of the problem boils down to money." "Foster parents," he explains, "generally aren't well-paid or well supported...And many counties aren't recruiting effectively." "The funding squeeze," Ames adds, "has made it harder to recruit, train, and retain [foster-care] workers."[19]

On the other hand, many observers see the woes of foster care as too severe, too systemic, to be resolved by merely infusing more tax monies into the current system. "The foster care system, noble in intent, is a bureaucratic nightmare," in the opinion of journalist R. Bruce Dold, who sees "the revival of the orphanage" as the "unhappy, but unavoidable, choice" for policymakers.[20] Likewise endorsing the orphanage as an option superior to that available through foster care, social worker Dick Thompson suggests that "perhaps we've been too hasty in trying to de-institutionalize everything. What we're doing now [with foster children] is not working. The idea of returning to residential homes for security and stability has so much merit...We can't go and confuse all these kids by trying to love them like their mothers and dads, but we can give them honest care, permanence, and stability."[21] In endorsing this perspective, Federal Circuit Judge Estella Moriarty argues that "the foster-care system not only fails to prevent maternal deprivation, but also fails to provide the stability of place, friends, school and discipline that can be provided by an appropriate orphanage."[22]

Still, some experts decline to join in this new enthusiasm for orphanages, seeing in it desperation, not prudence. A professor of social work at the University of Calgary, Bill Cunes accuses advocates of orphanages of listening to too many former orphanage residents who have succumbed to the "Patty Hearst syndrome where the captive prisoner begins to identify with the captor."[23] Some critics of the current foster-care system come down in favor not of orphanages, but rather of the children's own parents. Thus, Richard Wexler of the National Coalition for Child Protection Reform dismisses both the campaign to recruit more foster parents and the crusade to bring back the orphanage, insisting that "the only way to fix foster care is to have less of it." In his view, state officials often remove children from homes because "poverty is confused with neglect," or because housing is judged to be inadequate. The truth, he asserts, is that "the typical foster child is taken away from parents who are neither brutally abusive nor hopelessly addicted." Because they remove "too many children too quickly," state child-protection officials find themselves "overloaded with children who don't need to be in foster care." As a consequence, these officials lack the time to identify properly those children who really do need to be in care. The result, in Wexler's assessment, is that children's workers make needless mistakes. "But nothing will change," he adds, "until the state confronts the problem of taking away too many children."[24]

Wexler's argument for taking fewer children from their parents deserves serious consideration for several reasons. One very simple but legitimate reason for reducing foster-care placements is that foster care, like welfare, puts economic pressure on married-couple families by forcing married couples, who are supporting their own children directly through their earnings, to support other people's children through taxes.[25] A far more fundamental reason for reducing the number of foster-care placements is that children almost always suffer emotional distress upon being taken from their parents and being placed in the hands of strangers, no matter how conscientious and loving those strangers. In a fairly typical case, when the foster family was asked about their six-year-old foster daughter, they responded: "Oh, she cries often...I think she misses her mom and dad."[26] Alexander suggests that as "wrenching" as abuse and neglect at home may be, for some children, "being taken from their families can be even more so."[27]

Given the trauma typically suffered when children are taken from their families, it is particularly troubling that, in more than a few cases, state officials take this action on the basis of what the *Washington Monthly* criticizes as an "overly broad definition of abuse"; using such a definition, state officials in many jurisdictions may take children from their parents and put them in foster care because of such dubious symptoms of sexual abuse as clinginess and thumb-sucking.[28] Let no one minimize the trauma caused when state officials unnecessarily take children from their parents based on groundless accusations of child abuse. This trauma was well documented in 1992 by a grand jury in San Diego, which found that an alarming number of children were being separated from their parents and placed in foster care for "extended periods of time," because state officials were "determined to err on the side of assuming guilt" and were, therefore, "accept[ing] reports of molest[ation] as true, notwithstanding that they may [have been] inherently incredible, made for motives of harm or gain, or the product of months or years of 'therapy.'"[29]

The arguments of Richard Wexler and the findings of the San Diego Grand Jury grow in gravity when viewed in historical context. For the lineage of the child-protection system (responsible for putting children in foster care) runs directly back to the problematic nineteenth-century movement of Child Savers, who frequently removed children from impoverished immigrant families judged to be insufficiently American. Though no state official would cite today such a justification for removing a child from a home, the legal doctrine of Parens Patriae ("the parenthood of the state"), first invoked by the Child-Saving zealots, remains the legal basis for today's foster-care system. This doctrine, as historian Allan Carlson points out, is not rooted in the American Constitutional tradition, but in English chancery laws. Yet, under its influence, the autonomy of the American family has been seriously compromised as "parents [have seen] their rights of custody stripped away, without the niceties of due process, through an inquisitorial hearing into their character."[30]

Some activists may claim that respecting the rights of parents accused of abusing their children will mean exposing more children to harm. However, given the sorry record of foster-care workers in trying to protect children, it is difficult to fault the logic of the Florida judge who declared: "I'm not going to take a child from his home to be put in a foster home where he will be abused. If he is going to be abused, let him be abused by people who love him instead of being abused by strangers."[31] Nor is it easy to dismiss the fears of those who worry that aggressive campaigns to recruit more foster-care families will increase the risk of foster-care abuse by attracting foster parents with mercenary–or even predatory–motives.[32]

Nonetheless, only the purblind can suppose that leaving children with their natural parents is a universal formula for minimizing children's suffering or that Child-Saver style overreaching by state officials constitutes the primary reason for the upsurge in recent years in the placement of children in foster care. By any reckoning, far more children are in distressing circumstances than was the case twenty-five or thirty years ago. As a consequence of what historian William Manchester has termed the "general revolt against constraints which characterized the 1960s," a revolt which continues today, Americans have seen "the discipline that knits a society together...weaken[ed] and at some points giv[e] way altogether."[33] Tens of thousands of children have been put at risk because of this disintegration of social discipline, with their neglectful or abusive parents–still living by the mindless mantras of the Sixties–doing drugs and violating every traditional precept of parental responsibility. As the news accounts of children beaten and even killed by live-in lovers make horrifyingly clear, the post-Sixties repudiation of marriage as the basis for parenthood has been particularly perilous for children.

Illegitimacy

It is, therefore, the rising tide of illegitimacy which Heather McDonald deplores as she questions the costly efforts of state officials to keep at-risk children in their single-parent homes rather than removing them for adoption or foster care. Though this endeavor bears the name of "family preservation," McDonald sees in it merely an attempt to "legitimate illegitimacy" and subsidize "family fragments," all the while exposing children to terrible risk in "the mother-child groupings that are forever moving in and out of combination with boyfriends, aunts, cousins, and grandmothers."[34] Brenda Nordlinger of the National Association of Homes and Services for Children underscores McDonald's point when she notes that too often social workers confront situations in which "the mother is on crack, and so is the grandmother [and the father is nowhere to be seen]–that's not a viable family."[35] "There is no evidence that social services can compensate for the lack of personal responsibility that is fueling America's epidemic of illegitimacy," McDonald remarks, as she assails the intellectual dishonesty of the typical "family preservation" initiative, which "studiously avoids any suggestion that there might be a connection between illegitimacy and family pathologies."[36] Insofar as the welfare of children is concerned, the politically correct amoralism of today's social workers offers no improvement over the zealotry of the high-minded Child Savers of the nineteenth century.

In highlighting illegitimacy as the primary reason so many children are now at risk, McDonald helps us get past much of the misleading rhetoric surrounding the crisis in foster care. So, too, does policy analyst Penelope Lemov, who acknowledges that "the reasons [that the number of families available to provide foster care is dwindling] have almost as much to do with society at large as with the system itself."[37] For whether we are looking for the reason more children are suffering harm than in the past or for the reason that fewer families are available to provide foster care to palliate that harm, the answer is the same: society–more specifically, family life–has changed in troubling ways. Since children are least likely to suffer abuse in an intact family, the decline in recent decades in the marriage rate and the sharp rise in divorce and illegitimacy rates has translated into a sad toll of abused children needing foster care.[38] Of course, these same changes have reduced the pool of families available to provide such care. The foster-care crisis is, therefore, merely the symptom of a much broader crisis in social life. It is the worst sort of foolishness to suppose that the crisis in foster care should be viewed as a discrete problem, amenable to managerial finesse, and not as the inescapable result of a widespread cultural malaise engendered by a broad retreat from family life. For the problems which bedevil the foster-care system are merely a bureaucratic concentration of problems increasingly prevalent as a consequence of family decay. Hence, the crisis in foster care may be taken as a portent, a sign of things to come, for all of society, if we do not reverse the retreat from family life.

For example, if we do not check the rising tide of illegitimacy, then many of the afflictions associated with foster-care abuse–academic failure, mental illness, adult homelessness, and imprisonment– will be visited upon more and more children, regardless of what is done with the foster-care system. For illegitimate children are highly vulnerable to all these afflictions, regardless of whether they are ever placed in foster care.[39] Consequently, policymakers will have done nothing for the overall welfare of children if they devote all their labor to improving the foster-care network, but do nothing to curb the epidemic of illegitimacy.

Divorce and Remarriage

Likewise, no one who worries about how foster care bounces children from home to home, caregiver to caregiver, can ignore the way in which divorce and remarriage often do something very similar, even if to a less pronounced degree. While some stepfamilies do succeed in establishing an atmosphere of love and harmony, they are unfortunately all too exceptional. Recent research has provided troubling validation of the traditional folklore in which the stepfamily appears as the setting for tension, discouragement, depression, and even abuse for children. Sociologists from Wright State University and the University of Dayton, for example, report that "children who experience the divorce and/or remarriage of their parents are at greater risk for psychological, academic, and health problems than are children who live continuously with both parents."[40] This profile of pathologies thus disturbingly parallels that limned among foster-care children.

Moreover, the emotional scarring experienced by foster children forced to move again and again has also been experienced by tens of thousands of stepchildren. Two out of three remarriages have failed in recent years, with these second (or third) divorces occasioning "new waves of grief and loss to every member of the family."[41] That grief and loss often translates into behavioral and psychological problems, academic failure, and crime. Whether we have in view foster children or stepchildren, we see the same "teeter-totter relationship" (sociologist David G. Myers's term): "As the percentage of children living with both their natural parents has gone down, the rates of...neglect, abuse, criminality, emotional disorder, and academic failure have gone up."[42] So long as the divorce rate remains high, reform of the foster-care system will not fix that teeter-totter.

Indeed, reform of the foster-care system alone will do nothing to free American families from the legal entanglements which surround both foster care and divorce. For just as foster families find themselves enmeshed in the red tape and protocols of government bureaucracy, so too, divorced-parent families (including stepfamilies) find themselves subject to the constant intrusion of child-support officers, custody lawyers, and divorce-court judges. In both the divorced-parent family and the foster family, we view what attorney George S. Swan regards as the erosion of the family as "a freestanding institution mediating between the individual citizen and the central government.... Today's family, continually threatened by dissolution, is less and less able to serve as the context in which millions of Americans...organize their lives independent of central political authority."[43]

Likewise reminiscent of the sad plight of foster-care children is the tragically elevated vulnerability to abuse which is found among stepchildren (as it is among foster children). One study found that "preschoolers living with one natural and one stepparent were 40 times more likely to become child abuse cases than were like-aged children living with two natural parents."[44]

Day Carelessness

Concerns about dangers faced by children not in the care of their natural parents might reasonably extend not only to children in foster care, but also to children in day care. For, like foster care, day care undermines children's sense of stable relationships of trust. The repeated changes in caregivers which emotionally impair a foster child can have a similar effect on a child in day care. It is, therefore, entirely predictable that what one prominent critic has said about foster care (that it moves children around "so much that they don't trust anyone after a while") nearly matches what a prominent child psychologist has said about day care: that it may be the way "history is preparing us for its future," a future which leaves "everyone out for himself" more than ever before.[45] The problem is not simply that placement in day care weakens the mother-child bond–though there is evidence indicating that this is so (especially for infants)[46]–the problem is also that once in day care, the young child is passed from caregiver to caregiver in a high-turnover institution. Because the best-informed analysts believe that "child-care wages are likely to stay at their extremely low levels," they predict that "the turnover rates in this occupation will continue to be high," meaning that children who form attachments to day-care workers–like foster children who form attachments to foster parents–will frequently feel the pain of having those attachments broken.[47] Improving foster care will do nothing to spare children in day care this emotional distress.

Further, the rise in maternal employment, which has made day care so popular, is making foster care more difficult to arrange for those who need it, while also hurting children who don't. In explaining the drop in the number of foster-care families, Lemov remarks, "More women are working, which means fewer mothers are at home to care for foster children."[48] In Lemov's observation, however, the word *foster* is superfluous; maternal employment outside the home means fewer mothers are home to care for their own children. This reality was quantified by a University of Virginia study concluding that "among families with preschoolers, mothers without a job spend 525 minutes in some contact with their children, more than twice the time of those with a job. Full-time mothers without a preschooler spend 355 minutes with their children [per week day], about two hours more [per week day] than their employed counterparts." This gap in maternal involvement showed up across "a wide range of activities" with "at-home mothers spending more time with their children than employed mothers in play, education, child care, homemaking and 'fun.'"[49]

Despite feminist efforts to put a favorable interpretation on this maternal deficit, research is accumulating which links it to depressed academic performance (especially, but not exclusively, among sons), to compromised "early affectional relationships between parents and children," to "very high levels of noncompliance" among preschoolers, to adolescent anomie, to "parental withdrawal," and to "lower well-being for daughters."[50] Whatever else it is doing, maternal employment appears to be giving their children problems recognizably similar to those found among foster children. No likely reform of foster care will do anything to improve the lot of the children of employed mothers.

The Family as Solution

Officials currently grappling with the crisis in foster care can take a number of positive steps to alleviate that crisis. First, they can reduce foster-care placements by defining child abuse more narrowly and clearly and by restoring the presumption of innocence to parents accused of abusing their children. Second, when foster-care placement is necessary, they can rely more heavily on kinship-based care, a policy proven to reduce sharply the risk of foster-care abuse.[51] Third, they can support and accelerate adoptions, thereby delivering children from foster care into a permanent home (however, it must be acknowledged that the number of families willing to adopt older children is not high).

Yet, even if all three of these prudent steps are taken, the number of children being abused, neglected, or abandoned will remain troublingly high; nor will any of these steps increase the number of strong and loving families willing to take on foster-care responsibilities. Real progress in reducing children's suffering, like significant progress in increasing the number of good foster-care families available, will require far more. It will require far more than any reform focused primarily on the foster-care system. The current passion for reforming bureaucratic systems–the child-care system, the child-support-collection system, the child-custody system–instead of renewing the family life for which such systems can never be more than poor surrogates, is itself symptomatic of our cultural malaise. An appropriate gloss on modern America's overweening faith in all government systems comes from the poet T.S. Eliot, who despaired of those carried away in "dreaming of systems so perfect that no one will have to be good" ("Choruses from *The Rock*," VI). Genuine progress in resolving not only the foster-care crisis, but also the more fundamental family crisis of which the foster-care crisis is a mere symptom, will require nothing less than that goodness which inspires enduring marital ties and strong parental commitments.

Although such goodness ultimately depends upon moral and religious impulses not at the command of government policymakers, these policymakers can at least reverse policies subversive of the family–such as the gender-role engineering which has undercut a man's ability to earn a family wage sufficient to support his wife and their children, so fostering maternal employment. Such policies have intensified what one commentator has called "the continuous self-destructive war against the family."[52] Reducing the social havoc of this war will be difficult because of the political clout of zealous ideologues—homosexuals, radical feminists, Marxists—indifferent or hostile to the family. The only alternative, however, to effecting a renewal in family life is that of watching as more and more of American life metastasizes into one huge and failing foster-care system.

Notes

1.   Hagen quoted in Candis McLean, "Maybe Dickens Was Wrong," *Albert Report* 20 September 1999: 24-28.
2.   Cf. Penelope Lemov, "The Return of the Orphanage," *Governing* May 1991: 30-35; cf. also Karen Gullo, "U.S. Adopts Tough Rules Regulating Foster Care," *Detroit News* 26 January 2000.
3.   Cf. R. Bruce Dold, "A Place to Call My Own," *Notre Dame Magazine* Summer 1995: 23-28; cf. also Ames Alexander, "Kids' Troubles Multiply," *Charlotte Observer* 30 May 1999: 1A.
4.   Cf. Dold, op. cit.; see also Jack Williams, "Guv Ignores Foster-Care Crisis," *Boston Herald* 11 February 2000: 29.
5.   Cf. "Crisis in Foster Care" (Editorial), *St. Petersburg Times* 10 March 2001: 16A.
6.   Ibid.
7.   Cf. Nancy Hicks, "Foster Care System Ailing," *Omaha World* 9 December 1999: 15; see also David Stoesz and Howard Jacob Karger, "Suffer the Children," *Washington Monthly* June 1996: 20-25.
8.   Cf. Jennie Tunkieicz, "Foster Care Crisis," *Milwaukee Journal Sentinel* 17 September 2000: 1B; Stoesz and Karger, op. cit.; Lemov, op. cit.
9.   Cf. Hicks, op. cit.
10.   Cf. Alisa Ulferts, "Foster Care Is in Crisis," *St. Petersburg Times* 27 February 2001: 5B.
11..   Cf., for example, Alexander, op. cit.
12.   Cf. Gullo, op. cit.
13.   Cf. Richard Wexler, "Foster Care: Less Is Better," *Seattle Post-Intelligencer* 14 May 2000: G1.
14.   Cf. Jeffrey S. Harman, George E. Childs, and Kelly J. Kelleher, "Mental Health Care Utilization and Expenditures by Children in Foster Care," *Archives of Pediatric and Adolescent Medicine* 154(2000): 1114-117; Abraham B. Bergman, "The Shame of Foster Care Health Services," *Archives of Pediatric and Adolescent Medicine* 154(2000): 1080-1081.
15.   Cf. Dold, op. cit.; Ezra Susser et al., "Childhood Experiences of Homeless Men," *American Journal of Psychiatry*," *Archives of Pediatric and Adolescent Medicine* 144(1987): 1599-1601; Peter Marquis, "Family Dysfunction as a Risk Factor in the Development of Antisocial Behavior," *Psychological Reports* 71(1992): 468-470.
16.   Little Hoover Commission quoted in Lynda Gledhill, "Demos Want to Fix Foster Care," *The San Francisco Chronicle* 8 March 2001: A6.
17.   Quoted in Patricia J. White, "Courting Disaster: Permanency Planning for Children," *Juvenile Justice* Spring/Summer 1994: 15-20.
18.   Quoted in White, op. cit.
19.   Cf. Alexander, op.cit.
20.   Cf. Dold, op. cit.

21.   Thompson quoted in McLean, op. cit.
22.   Moriarty quoted in McLean, op. cit.
23.   Cunes quoted in McLean, op. cit.
24.   Wexler, op. cit.
25.   Cf. Randal D. Day and Wade C. Mackey, "Children as Resources: A Cultural Analysis," *Family Perspective* 20 (1986): 258-262.
26.   Cf. Williams, op. cit.
27.   Cf. Alexander, op. cit.
28.   Cf. Stoesz and Karger, op. cit.
29.   San Diego Grand Jury, "Child Sexual Abuse, Assault, and Molest Issues," Report No. 8, 29 June 1992.
30.   Allan C. Carlson, *Family Questions: Reflections on the American Social Crisis* (New Brunswick, NJ: Transaction Publishers, 1988), 244.
31.   Quoted in McLean, op. cit.
32.   Cf. Robert Napolilli, "Foster Care Program Questioned" [Letter], *Courier-Journal* [Louisville, KY] 6 January 2001: 6A.
33.   William Manchester, *The Glory and The Dream: A Narrative History of America, 1932-1972* (Boston: Little, Brown, 1974), 2: 1267, 1392.
34.   Heather MacDonald, "The Ideology of 'Family Preservation,'" *Public Interest*, No. 115 (Spring 1994): 45-60.
35.   Nordlinger quoted in Lemov, op. cit.
36.   MacDonald, op. cit.
37.   Lemov, op. cit.
38.   Cf. Bryce Christensen, "The Child Abuse 'Crisis': Forgotten Facts and Hidden Agendas," *The Family in America* February 1989: 3,4.
39.   Cf. Viktor Gecas, "Born in the USA in the 1980's: Growing Up in Difficult Times," *Journal of Family Issues* 8 (1987): 434-436.
40.   Lawrence A. Kurdek and Mark A. Fine, "The Relation Between Family Structure and Young Adolescents' Appraisals of Family Climate and Parenting Behavior," *Journal of Family Issues* 14 (1993): 279-290.
41.   Bobbie McKay, *What Ever Happened to the Family: A Psychologist Looks at Sixty Years of Change* (Cleveland, OH: United Church Press, 1991), 29, 30.
42.   David G. Myers, *The American Paradox: Spiritual Hunger in an Age of Plenty* (New Haven, CT: Yale University Press, 2000), 60-97.
43.   George S. Swan, "The Political Economy of American Family Policy, 1945-85," *Population and Development Review* 12 (1986): 752.
44.   Martin Daly and Margo Wilson, "Child Abuse and Other Risks of Not Living With Both Parents," *Ethology and Sociobiology* 6 (1985): 197-209.
45.   Bruce McLay quoted in McLean, op. cit.; Jay Belsky quoted in Bryce Christensen, "Beware the Search for Utopia," *USA Today* 12 October 1989, Op-Ed Page.
46.   Cf., for instance, Peter Barglow et al., "Effects of Maternal Absence Due to Employment on the Quality of Infant-Mother Attachment in a Low Risk Sample," *Child Development* 58 (1987): 950-952.
47.   Victor R. Fuchs and Mary Coleman, "Small Children, Small Pay: Why Child Care Pays So Little," *American Prospect* Winter 1991: 75-79.
48.   Lemov, op. cit.
49.   Steven L. Nock and Paul W. Kingston, "Time with Children: The Impact of Couples' Work-Time Commitments," *Social Forces* 67 (1988): 59-85.
50.   Cf. Wendy A. Goldberg, Ellen Greenberger, and Stacy K. Nagel, "Employment and Achievement: Mother's Work Involvement in Relation to Children's Achievement Behaviors and Mothers' Parenting Behaviors," *Child Development* 67 (1996): 1512-1527; Jay Belsky and David Eggebeen, "Early and Extensive Maternal Employ-

ment and Young Children's Socioemotional Development: Children of the National Longitudinal Survey of Youth," *Journal of Marriage and the Family* 53 (1991): 1083-1110; Francis A.J. Ianni, *The Search for Structure: A Report on American Youth Today* (New York: The Free Press, 1989), 206-207; Rena L. Repeti and Jenifer Wood, "Effects of Daily Stress at Work on Mothers' Interactions with Preschoolers," *Journal of Family Psychology* 11(1997): 90-108; Maureen Perry-Jenkins and Sally Gillman, "Parental Job Experiences and Children's Well-Being: The Case of Two-Parent and Single-Mother Working-Class Families," *Journal of Family and Economic Issues* 21(2000): 123-147.

51.   Cf. Susan J. Zuravin, Mary Benedict, and Mark Somerfield, "Child Maltreatment in Family Foster Care," *American Journal of Orthopsychiatry* 63 (1993): 589-596.

52.   Mohammadreza Hojat, "Developmental Pathways to Violence: A Psychodynamic Paradigm," *Peace Psychology Review* 1 (1994/1995): 176-195.

5

Homeless America: Why Has America Lost Its Homemakers?

As family life has unraveled in America, social crises have multiplied so rapidly that they must compete with one another for public attention. Those raising warnings about—for instance—the crisis in foster care discussed in the preceding chapter must sometimes shout over the voices of those exercised over the looming crises in child poverty or homelessness. In the holiday season of 2002, it was the crisis in homelessness that captured the headlines. Officials in New York City reported in late November that over 37,000 were spending their nights in the city's homeless shelters, an unprecedented number, sharply higher than the 21,000 seen just four years earlier. Moreover, these numbers did not include the hundreds sleeping on the streets, on subway platforms, or cathedral steps. Nor was the problem peculiar to New York City: according to Nan Roman, president of the National Alliance to End Homelessness (NAEH), "the struggling economy and rising rents have combined to produce higher homeless rates across the country." NAEH, which put the number of American homeless at 735,000 in 1984, put the number of homeless people nationwide in 2002 at one million.[1]

Recognizing the media value of "one million" as a threshold statistic, some skeptics may have smiled, suspicious of yet another of the media's inflated "advocacy numbers." In truth, this was one case in which the activists clamoring for media attention were using numbers that dramatically understated the scope of the problem. For the true number of homeless in America has exploded in recent decades into the tens of millions, though few commentators seem to have noticed.

To be sure, the number of Americans who lack some kind of house or apartment to live in—those who show up in city shelters or who sleep on the streets or subway platforms—probably does stand at something like the one million Ms. Roman and her fellow activists have brandished as their unsettling statistic. However, that number does not begin to reveal the scope of homelessness in America. For since when did the word home signify merely physical shelter, or homelessness merely the lack of such shelter? The desperate people who lack such shelter, the people sleeping beneath sheets of cardboard above heating grates and probing for food in dumpsters, do deserve sympathetic attention, and the rise in their numbers should stir public concern. But those who lack housing are not the only Americans who lack homes, nor the only ones whose plight should excite concern.

For so long as English-speakers have used the word, *home* has signified not only shelter, but also emotional commitment, security, and belonging. Home has connoted not just a necessary roof and warm radiator, but a place sanctified by the abiding ties of wedlock, parenthood, and family obligation, a place demanding sacrifice and devotion but promising loving care and warm acceptance. Their lives anchored in some place fortified by the ties of marriage and family, the great majority of Americans have—until fairly recently—been able to refer to some special place as *home* and to do so with the full and rich meaning of that word. In recent decades, though, the number of Americans living without a real home has skyrocketed, even among those who entirely escape the attention of homeless activists because they do have adequate shelter.

The national epidemic of emotional and social homelessness can be limned in a grim litany of social statistics: an alarmingly high divorce rate (down from the stratospheric highs of the late 1970s and early 1980s but still more than 30 percent higher than in 1970); a plummeting marriage rate (down over 40 percent since 1970 and apparently still falling); a rising tide of out-of-wedlock births (33 percent of all births in 1998, up 300 percent from 1970); an explosion in the number of single-person households (now accounting for 26 percent of all households, up 70 percent since 1970); and remarkably low rates for completed fertility (languishing now for more than twenty-five years below replacement level).[2] These numbers do indeed reflect a distressing upsurge in the number of Americans who cannot claim that secure base of family ties that constituted what previous generations have recognized as the essence of a home. This is a distressing upsurge that advocacy statistics for on-the-street homelessness do not even hint at.

Perhaps no number reveals the prevalence of homelessness in contemporary America as well as does the little-noted renaming of a once very popular secondary-school organization: in 1999, the national organization known for more than fifty years as Future Homemakers of America (FHA) jettisoned its old name, choosing to be called hereafter as "Family, Career, and Community Leaders of America" (FCCLA). The new name was judged "more consistent" than the old name with a modern world in which young women, just like young men, take on "multiple roles of family member, wage earner, and community leader."[3] This collective repudiation of the title of "homemaker" speaks volumes about the real size of the homeless population in America today. For homes do not simply make themselves, and, in a nation without homemakers, real homes—not merely houses and apartments—must quickly grow as scarce as carriages in a nation without carriage-makers. And, while modern America can do quite well without carriages, its need for homes has perhaps never been greater.

But the leaders and members of FHA were acting on no mere caprice of nomenclature when they changed their name and abandoned the title "homemaker." Rather, they were responding to powerful economic and cultural forces far beyond their control. As these forces have combined to devalue the home—economically, politically, socially, and culturally—they have simultaneously devalued the labor and art of homemaking. Once highly honored, the social title of "homemaker" now carries deeply unfortunate connotations of incompetence, backwardness, and parasitism. The truth is that America still desperately needs homemakers and that by making tens of millions truly homeless, their disappearance is exposing growing numbers to psychological and social problems surprisingly similar to—if usually less acute than—those experienced by the desperate souls on the street. Even more surprising to many Americans is the hidden but very real linkage between the disappearance of homemakers and the rise not only of the emotional homelessness of the adequately housed, but also of the on-the-street homelessness of the unhoused.

The Real Traditional Home

Any real understanding of homemaking and its currently imperiled status must begin with an acknowledgement that, in economic terms at least, the 1950s-style homemaking—the homemaking of

Leave It To Beaver and *Ozzie and Harriet*—was but a shadow of the traditional homemaking of earlier eras. When most Americans lived on family farms, homemaking required mastery of a score of productive skills—not only cooking food, but making, preserving, and storing it; not only sewing clothing, but spinning thread and weaving cloth; not only caring for healthy children, but attending to all but the most severe childhood illnesses without medical assistance; not only negotiating marketplace purchases, but actually making candles, soap, buttons, and other items so that such purchases were kept to a minimum.[4] In fact, until the economic sea change that historian Karl Polanyi has called "The Great Transformation"—a sea change that gave the world money markets for cash, credit, and labor—most homemakers knew almost nothing about satisfying household needs through purchase but rather worked arduously with their husbands and children to make (or occasionally barter for) everything needed to run their homes.[5] And though it was usually husbands and sons who did most of the field work, homemakers and their daughters (homemakers to be) helped out with field tasks when needed.

But then the capitalist and industrial revolutions drew millions away into the cities and away from family farms. These revolutions also took men away from their homes—and it should be remembered that the Luddite riots of the early nineteenth century were led by male home-weavers understandably resistant to the social and cultural changes catalyzed by the use of factory-based power looms. These changes separated homemakers from their husbands in a new and problematic way. The Industrial Revolution also rendered many of the homemaker's productive tasks unnecessary, as factories turned out clothing, soap, candles, prepackaged foods, and all kinds of other household wares at low cost and with mechanized efficiency. Though this made life easier for the homemaker, it also—over time—had the demoralizing effect of making her social position an unskilled—or rather de-skilled—one.

Still, the processes that robbed the homemaker first of her productive tasks and then of her cultural esteem were gradual. Though the Industrial Revolution was well launched by the mid-nineteenth century, historian Glenna Matthews argues that American homemakers of that period still well understood that their "domestic sphere...was central to the culture."[6] And although his focus is London rather than a large American city, Charles Dickens portrayed the role of a typical late nineteenth-centry urban homemaker as one demanding a great deal of productive labor, with her "household affairs of the day" requiring that she engage in "weighing and mixing and chopping and grating...dusting and washing and polishing...snipping and weeding and trowelling and other small gardening...making and mending and folding and airing."[7]

By the mid-twentieth century, though, the powers of the manufacturer were fully integrated with the seductive allurements of the advertiser in ways that rapidly stripped the home of most of its remaining functions, so robbing the homemaker of her remaining productive skills and making her merely a domestic purchasing agent and manager of consumption. Historian Roland Marchand aptly identifies twentieth-century advertisers as "veterans in assimilation to modernity," who educated consumers (the economic role assigned to de-skilled homemakers) in the "pace and scale of modern life." The effect of this modernizing can readily be inferred from a 1920s article in the advertising journal *Printers' Ink*, in which G.A. Nichols identified home baking as the "greatest impediment to progress" for commercial biscuit companies and urged his fellow advertisers to deprecate this retrograde domestic practice while finding strategies "to educate the people into using more [commercially prepared] biscuits." In the same vein and at about the same time, Christine Frederick called on manufacturers and advertisers to effect a "household revolution" in which salesmen of household conveniences would "train the woman [homemaker] out of the handcraft age into a machine operative." A typical ad from the same decade thus urged the homemaker to use her power as a consumer to escape those "heavy household tasks that take [her] time and sap [her] strength." Historian Stuart Ewen perceptively points out that in the "displacement of crafts" which advertisers and manufacturers jointly effected, homemakers were freed from "old drudgery" only by "being divested of much knowledge and control of their work place."[8] Sociologist Pitirim Sorokin saw only too clearly what was happening when he remarked in the mid-twentieth century that because it was losing its "main socio-cultural functions," the home was fast becoming "a mere incidental parking place."[9]

Homemaking's Rise and Fall

This transformation of the home into an incidental parking place did provoke a few protests. Home economist Ann Richardson complained in 1929 that "the psychology of clever advertising is frequently pitted against the common sense of the homemaker, with the result that she is worsted in the struggle."[10] Ironically, though, Richardson's own discipline of home economics also turned against the homemaker. As Matthews explains, in trying to establish their field as an academically respectable pursuit, home economists felt compelled to emphasize "science and efficiency" and to "denigrate the quality of housewifely competence." They thus ended up "ignor[ing] most of what had produced the esteem for domesticity in the early nineteenth century," as they "strove to make the home as much like the male workplace as possible." Because "the idea that the home can be a source of redemptive values for other institutions was completely disregarded" within academic home economics, the new discipline helped foster a mid-twentieth-century culture in which "women's traditional skills and women's time were both undervalued," so making the role of homemaker "more problematic" than it had ever been before.[11]

The founding of Future Homemakers of America in 1945 may plausibly be interpreted as a rear-guard ideological attempt to shore up an increasingly precarious social role. With a membership that peaked at over 600,000 in 1966, this organization may have helped to temporarily retard the national repudiation of homemaking—so delaying our national epidemic of homelessness. But because of its close ties to academic home economics and its quasi-scientific denigration of traditional domestic crafts, the FHA's school-based functions partially replaced and so weakened grandmother-mother-daughter transmission of homemaking skills. Thus, an ostensible defender of homemaking—however unintentionally—further contracted the homemaker's role and accelerated the home-into-parking-place transformation.

Quite understandably, not many women have ever aspired to be parking-lot attendants. Ewen sees "the festering contradiction of modern womanhood" created by homemakers' loss of their traditional crafts and of their control of their work place as a prime reason for the "reinvigorated feminism" that surfaced in the 1960s.[12] Regrettably, very few feminist leaders recognized the need to rehabilitate homemaking by restoring and enlarging the home's productive functions. Rather, most have decisively turned against the home, denounced as a "prison of domesticity," as "patriarchy's chief institution," and as an obstacle to "equality with men in the world of jobs and careers."[13] Even many slogans underscoring what feminists do want are edged with contempt for the home as what they do not want. Consider, for example, the bumper sticker "A Woman's Place Is in the House...and the Senate" or the college poster promoting women's basketball depicting a stereotypical 1950s homemaker above the line "A Woman's Place..." and then, in a much larger picture, an aggressive female center muscling her way into position below the basket with the text "...Is In the Paint!" Such defiantly anti-homemaking rhetoric gives reason to suspect that feminist rejection of homemaking is a major reason that social critic Benjamin DeMott sees the traditionally feminine virtues of "care and sensitivity to others" simply vanishing from the culture. DeMott fears that our culture is being debased by a "tough guy feminism" premised on a "women-becoming-men fantasy" that promulgates a "hard-nosed egocentricity" and a "taste for pugnacity."[14]

In recent decades, though, many feminists are so fixated on gender equality that they seem actually to prefer a brutally Hobbesian war of each-against-all—so long as it is a gender-neutral war—over a more humane home-centered social order dependent upon gender-role differentiations. Feminist antipathy for the parking-lot-attendant role that homemaking was fast becoming in the twentieth century is quite understandable. But feminists have succumbed to a dangerously narrow cultural analysis when they fasten on the real deficiencies of 1950s-style homemaking as a reason for repudiating homemaking itself as an outmoded and dispensable artifact of one anomalous period of one misguided culture.

Family scholars Barbara Dafoe Whitehead and David Blankenhorn challenge the "individualistic and androgynous" rhetoric of egalitarian feminism as "antithetical to child-rearing on both biological and cultural grounds," and as discrepant with what both sociobiologists and cultural anthropologists teach about the universality of "mothering and fathering...as sharply differentiated (and complementary) activities. Fathers protect the vulnerable infant from physical harm by defending the perimeters of the domestic realm. Mothers provide emotional nurture to the child and sustain the domestic realm as the center of nurturance. This role differentiation does not derive primarily from either social convention or individual choice." In rejecting a role differentiation that allows homemakers to "sustain the domestic realm as the center of nurturance," feminists are thus losing sight of the home as "an independent moral realm con-

taining relationships and values different from those of the commercial realm."[15]

In a similar vein, American family ecologist Kathleen Slaugh Bahr
stresses that "family-care tasks" performed in the home have the
power to engender "a spirit of love" that causes us to "put aside our
own self-centered aims...to see more clearly the needs of others, and
then to respond to those needs in ways that help foster their growth
and well-being." In contrast, in labor performed "in a monetary
economy," we are influenced by "no such power."[16] Even historian
Christopher Lasch, who was hardly a political conservative and who
acknowledged "the justice of the central feminist demands" for economic self-sufficiency, believed that in their rejection of homemaking, feminists were guilty of "heedless disregard of the family and
the needs of future generations." Because, Lasch suggested, they
were too much in thrall to "the capitalist vision of individual self-
aggrandizement," feminists had become blind to "the deterioration
of care for the young" caused by women's flight from the home and
homemaking.[17]

Home Truths

Though feminists have been quite right to deplore the cultural
inadequacy of Cold War gender roles, they have been quite wrong
to suggest that the feminine role in homemaking was—like the household bomb shelters built during the era—just a curious American
aberration. Across time and across cultures, from the native tribes of
North America to the ancient Greeks and Romans, to the diverse
cultures of Africa and India and China, homemaking has defined a
central feminine task. As one cross-cultural survey of available an-
thropological data stresses, in society after society, a woman's "primary duties" have traditionally been those associated with "bearing
and rearing children," duties that "did not take her far from home."[18]
Indeed, one ancient Confucian commentator—about as far removed
from the world of *Ozzie and Harriet* as can be imagined—sums up
the collective wisdom of a diverse range of peoples in his pronouncement that in the family "the correct place of the woman is within; the
correct place of the man is without. That man and woman have their
proper places is the greatest concept in nature."[19]

Nonetheless, far too many feminists—ignoring the multicultural
richness in homemaking—have viewed homemaking almost exclusively through the distorted lens of the Fifties. What they see is what

Laurie Graham has shown her readers in her recent novel *The Future Homemakers of America*, in which Cold War-era American homemakers "bake, clean, mind children and swap scarves or tangerine lipsticks." Of course, the title of Graham's novel is ironic: by the time the novel concludes in the early Eighties, her main characters have left behind their tangerine-lipstick homemaking, along with their failed tangerine-lipstick marriages, and have become "determinedly independent" characters that "couldn't have been more different" from the "shiny homemakers" they had once been.[20]

Unfortunately, the rejection of homemaking Graham depicts on a small scale with a handful of fictional characters has played out on a national scale affecting tens of millions of real women, including the FHA leaders who—like the characters in Graham's novel—have said good-bye to homemaking. Having seen their organization dwindle to less than 100,000 members by the late 1990s, perhaps the Future Homemakers of America felt that only a new name (Family, Career, and Community Leaders of America) could stave off complete extinction.

An inexorable chain of causation dictates that the disappearance of homemakers means the disappearance of homes, which in turn can only mean an ever-more-ubiquitous plague of homelessness. Though not part of the statistics NAEH and other activist groups have pushed into the national headlines, this plague may be glimpsed in the nation's tens of thousands of day-care centers, where young children with employed mothers need a surrogate home just as acutely as the desperate souls clustering in municipal homeless shelters. It is thus entirely apt that the distinguished scholar Jacques Barzun should recently have referred to the day-care child as a "semi-orphan."[21] The semi-orphan title would also seem to apply to the growing number of children whose employed mothers rely on after-school programs as surrogate homes for their offspring.[22] The same need for surrogate homes also explains the remarkable growth in summer programs of all sorts (sports camps, computer camps, theater camps, art camps) sought out by employed mothers who do not want their children to be alone all summer in an empty house.[23] Of course, many children do spend their school-day afternoons and their summers home alone—watching TV, overeating, and all too often getting in trouble.[24] Though he does not use Barzun's term "semi-orphan," social critic Francis Ianni evokes a similar idea in describing the aimless suburban adolescents who wander the malls or commit petty acts of vandalism simply because they have no place to go except to an empty house. These "sullen and often disruptive bands of youngsters involuntarily liberated from parental guidance and supervision for several hours a day" are, in Ianni's opinion, "the suburban equivalents of the urban street gangs."[25]

The term "semi-orphan" might not apply, but some other term suggestive of a lack of home ties would also seem appropriate to describe the numerous solitary men and women whose residence is an unshared apartment and whose nightly meal is a microwaved freezer selection, or perhaps just a burger and fries, rather than a home-cooked meal shared with a spouse and family. In a 1986 book that helps to explain the astounding upsurge in single-person households, author Susan Littwin stressed the "change in men's and women's roles and the subsequent change in family life and society.... Young women will not be homemakers like their mothers; young men will not be providers like their fathers. It makes finding an identity interesting but confusing. Sorting it out takes time."[26] Though that sorting out often does eventually lead to marriage and some kind of family life, in a growing number of cases it now does not: demographers now expect that at least one in eight young Americans will never marry.[27]

Homeless Children

NAEH will not soon be including day-care children, latchkey children, adolescent members of suburban gangs, or the young men and women who live alone in apartments or houses in their homeless statistics. Such activist groups will, perhaps understandably, continue to focus on Americans who lack shelter. But the on-the-street homelessness that worries NAEH and the growing emotional homelessness caused by the widespread repudiation of homemaking are much more deeply linked than is commonly acknowledged.

One of the links that deserves scrutiny is the prevalence of poor mental health among both groups. Psychosis has indeed become part of the stereotype of the homeless person on the street. Some analysts, in fact, identify mental illness—and national policies deinstitutionalizing those suffering from it—as a leading cause of on-the-street homelessness. But investigative journalist Jonathan Kozol—who insists that it is mostly high housing costs that put people on the street—turns this argument on its head by suggesting that in many cases, it is the trauma and stress of living on the street that

makes people mentally unbalanced ("The lack of sleep," one homeless man on the street tells Kozol, "leaves you debilitated, shaky.
You exaggerate your fears. If a psychiatrist came along he'd say
that I was crazy. But I was an ordinary man...I lost my home. Now
would you say that I was crazy if I told you that I was feeling sad?").[28]

Kozol's insight that homelessness causes psychological disorders
will resonate with many researchers working with people whose
homelessness is emotional, not physical. All too often, the emotional
homelessness that triggers psychological malaise reflects the absence
of a homemaker. "Women's employment," writes Rutgers sociologist Sarah Rosenfield, "is negative for husbands' mental health,"
with relatively high income for wives predicting "demoralization,
sadness, anxiety, and hopelessness-helplessness" for their husbands.[29]
Often out-of-the-home employment also impairs a wife's mental
health as well by overloading her with stress. Researchers Beth Rushing and Annette Schwabe report that women in full-time employment frequently suffer from "role overload" and consequent mental
"distress" not found among women who devote all or most of their
time to homemaking.[30]

Perhaps it is children whose mental health suffers most from the
loss of the home consequent to the absence of a homemaker. Researchers who have looked carefully at day-care centers see children in "interaction patterns in which adults are less sensitive and
responsive than would be experienced in the home with mother,"
and they warn that this lack of sensitivity and responsiveness may
be "developmentally detrimental for the child."[31] Even some day-
care center operators have acknowledged "how children in day-care
suffer from separation, anxiety, and depression despite competent
staff."[32] That non-maternal care in a day-care center fosters "anxious and withdrawn behavior" in a significant number of children
has recently been documented by psychologists at the University of
Minnesota, who also measured abnormally elevated levels of blood
cortisol (a tell-tale symptom of psychological stress) in many day-
care children.[33]

Nor does a mother's devoting herself to out-of-home employment instead of homemaking threaten her children's psychological
well-being just because of the effects of day care. UCLA psychologists have found that "job stressors" for employed mothers often
translate into "parental withdrawal" and "negative emotional spillover
effects" for their children. The UCLA scholars fear that when em-

ployment stress degrades the quality of mother-child relationships day after day, "the cumulative effects of repeated failure to contain negative affect may be quite detrimental" to children's psychological development.[34] The adverse psychological effects of maternal employment help account for studies comparing children and adolescents growing up in the Fifties with those growing up in the Eighties and Nineties, in which psychologists see a shift "toward substantially higher levels of anxiety and neuroticism." So pronounced was this shift that "by the 1980s, normal child samples were scoring higher [in anxiety] than child psychiatric patients from the 1950s."[35] Perhaps, for all of its inadequacies, the homemaking of the Fifties was about more than just swapping tangerine lipsticks after all.

Given the way that the rejection of homemaking has jeopardized the mental health of the young, it should come as no surprise that researchers are now reporting results implicating out-of-home maternal employment in teen drug and alcohol abuse.[36] Nor should it astound anyone that researchers from the University of Colorado and Boston College have identified a rising female labor force participation rate as a strong statistical predictor of suicide and homicide among the young.[37]

Studies linking maternal employment to drug use and crime not only illuminate the great cost of America's national repudiation of homemaking, but also highlight yet another linkage between emotional homelessness and physical homelessness. For the drug use, suicide, and violence that become more prevalent when mothers abandon homemaking for outside employment give suburban America some of the grim characteristics of life on the city street for the physically homeless.[38] This linkage looks even stronger when it is acknowledged that wives' out-of-home employment increases the likelihood of divorce and that the divorce is the ugly precursor of a wide range of social pathologies—poverty, drug abuse, suicide, abuse (by a stepparent or a parent's live-in lover), and violent crime—all suggestive of the hellishness of life on the street.[39]

The Devalued Home

By increasingly devoting themselves to out-of-home employment rather than homemaking, American women have increased the likelihood of divorce in a number of ways. First, by devaluing the kind of home that only a homemaker can make, they have greatly diminished the horror of breaking such a home through divorce. This devaluing of the home and of the family solidarity it embodies may be glimpsed in a 1985 study finding that when women accept out-of-the-home employment, they "adopt a different perspective, see the world in a fundamentally different way," so that "basic definitions of equity have changed (from a family or community-based conception to an individualistic one)."[40] Identifying further reasons that wives' employment foster divorce, the authors of a 1988 study remark that "a working wife encounters a wider variety of men than a housewife and may increase her chances of finding an alternate mate. Entering the labor market also gives a wife another source of gratification, making her less dependent upon her marriage for happiness."[41] Wives' employment also increases the likelihood of divorce indirectly by sharply reducing fertility, since couples with few or no children are much more likely to divorce than those with large families.[42]

Lamentably, in the divorce-prone culture that some wives' deliberate rejection of homemaking helped to incubate, many women who had gladly chosen the role of homemaker found it cruelly stripped away from them in the divorce court. For the financial circumstances of a divorced woman almost always foreclose the option of homemaking and dictate out-of-the-home employment.

The divorces of a homemaker-unfriendly age have not only spawned the kind of psychological and social ills often associated with on-the-street homelessness, but have also greatly enlarged the actual on-the-street population. After extensive study, sociologist Peter H. Rossi has concluded that "homelessness is almost identical with 'spouselessness.'"[43] And a Boston Foundation study published in the 1980s predicted that "if the current rates of single-parent households continue to increase, it is probable that the number of families at risk of becoming homeless will also increase."[44]

The divorces of a homemaker-averse era have helped drive people into the street in another less direct way as well. Because an intact family needs but one house whereas a divorced family needs two, an upsurge in divorce inevitably puts new pressure on available housing stock, so driving up rent and housing costs. In a similar way, the multiplication of single-person households (also fostered by the national retreat from homemaking) increases the demand for housing, so inflating the cost of obtaining it. Quite understandably, advocates for the on-the-street homeless cry loudly for government-subsidized construction of more affordable housing. Perhaps they should instead be crying out for a rediscovery of wedlock and home-making. For if more Americans lived in intact marriages and fami-lies, if fewer lived in the isolation of divorce and singleness, fewer Americans would find themselves priced out of the housing market.

But it is not just by fostering divorce and singleness that the na-tional rejection of homemaking has made housing too costly for many Americans. When large numbers of wives turned away from homemaking and towards out-of-the-home employment, and when federal policymakers subsequently required banks to consider wives' second incomes in determining eligibility for mortgage loans, one-income households found themselves at a great disadvantage in com-petitive bidding for available housing. And not just in one area. By the1980s, real-estate analysts acknowledged that "the dual-career family...[was] having a broad impact on the housing market." [45] That impact led economist Kenneth J. Thygerson to assess a one-income family's difficulties in mortgaging a home with frank candor: "Let's face it, if you have no second income, you've got a problem."[46] That problem naturally affected rents as well as mortgages: in 1990, a social services official in an-all-too-typical Connecticut housing market acknowledged that "unless [families] have a second income, it's very tricky to pay rents here."[47]

In a housing market reshaped by the bidding of two-income fami-lies, many families face a painful dilemma. If the wife wishes to be a homemaker, the family then cannot afford a house for her to make into a home. As a consequence, many women who would have pre-ferred to be homemakers have settled for the far less satisfying and meaningful role of co-house-buyer. But, of course, in so doing, these families have thereby joined other two-income families in bidding up the cost of housing, making it still harder for other women to be homemakers. Many families have tried to make the best of this very bad situation by having the wife work just part-time, allowing her to be at least a part-time homemaker.

But in real-estate markets dominated by two-income families, it is single-parent families who face the truly insuperable problems. With no possibility of even a part-time second income, these families struggle to find any kind of housing at all. Failing in that struggle, too many end up on the street—and in NAEH's statistics.

NAEH and other activist groups deserve credit for drawing na-tional attention to the plight of the tens of thousands on the streets.

But the time has come for deeper thinking of the nature and causes of homelessness. Such thinking should awaken Americans to the inevitability of widespread homelessness so long as homemaking is despised and the home devalued. Such thinking should deepen skepticism about a type of feminism that, having recognized the deficiencies of Fifties-style homemaking, has turned against homemaking altogether. Such thinking should renew discussions about the long-neglected idea of "a family wage," a wage high enough for a father to support a homemaking wife and children.[48] Such thinking should kindle new interest in high-tech strategies—such as telecommuting and on-line data processing—for bringing back into the home productive activities for satisfying the needs of the outside world. Such thinking should restore interest in low-tech crafts—gardening, sewing, baking, cooking—for bringing back into the home productive activities for satisfying the needs of the family itself with products of higher quality than those hawked by the ad-men. Such thinking should excite widespread admiration for the homemaking pioneers who have made home-schooling a nationwide success[49] (If such pioneers were to receive the tax credits they so justly deserve for educating their own children without the help of tax-funded schools, more of the economic significance of this homemaking activity would be visible).

Such thinking needs to begin now. Economic subversion of and ideological hostility against homemaking has already pushed far too many Americans into the streets and into the homelessness of media and social-service statistics. Self-described conservatives often resist the ideological attack but ignore the economic subversion. Left-leaning social critics can see unrestrained consumer capitalism as socially destructive, yet they somehow never resist its subversion of the maternal homemaking role. Indeed, liberal-left activists press their own ideological attack—feminist and egalitarian—against homemaking. Thus, the two-pronged attack against homemaking continues, rarely checked by conservatives and positively applauded by feminists and leftists. This attack has already afflicted far too many adequately housed Americans with the psychological and social pathologies that mark them as sufferers of an emotional homelessness just as real, and far more widespread, than the on-the-street kind. It clearly is time for all of America—regardless of political affiliation—to rethink the social role of the homemaker. Perhaps if this thinking is deep enough, honest enough, thoroughgoing enough, the leaders of Family, Career, and Community Leaders of America will once again take up a very precious but now sadly discarded name: Future Homemakers of America.

Notes

1.   Erin McClam, "NY Sees Record Number of Homeless: Rate Is Rising All Over the Nation," *Chicago Tribune* 30 November 2002: 8.
2.   Cf. U.S. Bureau of the Census, *Statistical Abstract of the United States: 2000*, 18 Dec. 2002 http://www.census.gov/prod/www/ statistical-abstract-us.html.
3.   Cf. About FCCLA, Arizona FCCLA 18 Dec. 2002 http://ag.arizona.edu/fcs/fshd/ facs/fccla/htm and FCCLA History, North Dakota State Board of Vocational and Technical Education 18 Dec. 2002 www.state.nd.us/vtc/ programs/facs/history.html.
4.   Cf. Allan Carlson, *From Cottage to Work Station: The Family's Search for Social Harmony in the Industrial Age* (San Francisco, CA: Ignatius, 1993).
5.   Karl Polanyi, *The Great Transformation* (New York: Rinehart, 1943).
6.   Glenna Matthews, *'Just a Housewife': The Rise and Fall of Domesticity in America* (New York: Oxford University Press, 1987), xiii-xiv, 146-171.
7.   Charles Dickens, *Our Mutual Friend* (1864-65; rpt. New York: Penguin, 1976), 749.
8.   Cf. Roland Marchand, *Advertising the American Dream: Making Way for Modernity, 1920-1940* (Berkeley: University of California Press, 1985), chapter 6; see also Stuart Ewen, *Captains of Consciousness: Advertising and the Social Roots of the Consumer Culture* (New York: McGraw-Hill, 1976), 161-164.
9.   Pitirim Sorokin, *Social and Cultural Dynamics: A Study of Change in Major Systems of Art, Truth, Ethics, Law, and Social Relationships*, Rev. and abridged ed. (1957; rpt. New Brunswick, NJ: Transaction Publishers, 1985), 700.
10. Qtd. in Ewen, op. cit.,161-164.
11. Matthews, op. cit., xiii-xiv, 146-171.
12. Ewen, op. cit., 161-164.
13. Cf. Germaine Greer, *The Female Eunuch* (New York: McGraw-Hill, 1971), 216-220; Kate Millett, *Sexual Politics* (Garden City, NY: Doubleday, 1970), 33, 126-127; Christopher Lasch, *Haven in a Heartless World* (New York: Basic, 1977), xvi.
14. Benjamin DeMott, *Killer Woman Blues: Why Americans Can't Think Straight About Gender and Power* (Boston: Houghton, Mifflin, 2000).
15. Barbara Dafoe Whitehead and David Blankenhorn, "Man, Woman, and Public Policy: Difference and Dependency in the American Conversation," Institute for American Values Working Paper, Pub. #WP3, Feb. 1991.
16. Kathleen Slaugh Bahr, "The Power of the Home Economy," *The Family in America* February 2000: 3-4.
17. Lasch, op cit., xvi-xvii.
18. See Thomas Fleming, *The Politics of Human Nature* (New Brunswick, NJ: Transaction Publishers, 1988), 73-99.
19. *The I Ching or Book of Changes*, trans. Richard Wilhelm and Cary F. Baynes (Princeton, NJ: Princeton University Press, 1977), 3rd. ed., 570.
20. Katie Owen, Rev. of *The Future Homemakers of America* by Laurie Graham, *The Times* (London) 21 July 2001; Bernice Harrison, Rev. of *The Future Homemakers of America* by Laurie Graham, *Irish Times*, 27 July 2001.
21. Jacques Barzun, *From Dawn to Decadence: 500 Years of Western Cultural Life* (New York: HarperCollins, 2000), 780-790.
22. Cf. Debbie Kopyta, "After-School Programs Offering Alternatives to Home Alone," *Pittsburgh Post-Gazette* 11 Feb. 02: N8.

23.   Cf. Penny Carnathan, "Summer Camps Offer Variety of Activities," *Tampa Tribune* 6 April 2000: 1.
24.   Cf. Joan Treadway, "At Home and Alone Can Spell Trouble; Shortage of Programs for Teenagers Is Cited," *Times-Picayune* 17 December 2002: 1.
25.   Francis A.J. Ianni, *The Search for Structure: A Report on American Youth Today* (New York: Free Press, 1989), 84-85, 206-297.
26.   Susan Littwin, *The Postponed Generation: Why American Youth Are Growing Up Later* (New York: William Morrow, 1986), 17, 245-248.
27.   Cf. Robert Schoen, "The Continuing Retreat from Marriage," *Sociology and Social Research* 71(1987): 108-109.
28.   Jonathan Kozol, "Distancing the Homeless," *75 Readings: An Anthology*, eds. Santi Buscemi and Charlotte Smith, 8th ed. (New York: McGraw-Hill, 2001), 404-417.
29.   Sarah Rosenfield, "The Costs of Sharing: Wives' Employment and Husbands' Mental Health," *Journal of Health and Social Behavior* 339(1992): 213-225.
30.   Beth Rushing and Annette Schwabe, "The Health Effects of Work and Family Characteristics: Gender and Race Comparisons," *Sex Roles* 33(1995): 159-205.
31.   David A. Caruso, "Quality of Day Care and Home-Reared Infants' Interaction Patterns with Mothers and Day Care Providers," *Child and Youth Care Quarterly* 18(1989): 177-191.
32.   Cf. Edward M. Levine, "Day Care: Cons, Costs, Kids," *Chicago Tribune* 18 Sept. 1984: 15.
33.   Kathryn Tout et al., "Social Behavior Correlates of Cortisol Activity in Child Care: Gender Differences and Time-of-Day Effects," *Child Development* 69(1998): 1247-1262.
34.   Rena L. Repetti and Jennifer Wood, "Effects of Daily Stress at Work on Mothers' Interactions With Preschoolers," *Journal of Family Psychology* 11(1997): 90-108.
35.   Jean M. Twenge, "The Age of Anxiety? Birth Cohort Change in Anxiety and Neuroticism, 1952-1993," *Journal of Personality and Social Psychology* 79(2000): 1007-1021.
36.   Cf. Daniel J. Flannery, Laura L. Williams, and Alexander T. Vazsonyi, "Who Are They With And What Are They Doing? Delinquent Behavior, Substance Abuse, And Early Adolescents' After-School Time," *American Journal of Orthopsychiatry* 69(1999): 247-253.
37.   Fred C. Pampei and John B. Williamson, "Age Patterns of Suicide and Homicide Mortality Rates in High-Income Nations," *Social Forces* 80(2001): 251-282.
38.   Cf. Brian Bergman, "Hell on the Streets," *MacLean's* 19 Nov. 1990: 21; Kevin A. Yoder and Dan R. Hoyt, "Suicidal Behavior Among Homeless and Runaway Adolescents," *Journal of Youth and Adolescence* 27(1998): 753-771; Stephen W. Barun, "Street Youths and Substance Use: The Role of Background, Street Lifestyle, and Economic Factors," *Youth & Society* Sept. 1999: 3-26.
39.   Cf. Bryce Christensen, ed., *When Families Fail...The Social Costs* (Lanham, MD: University Press of America/The Rockford Institute, 1991).
40.   Kristi Anderson and Elizabeth A. Cook, "Women, Work, and Political Attitudes," *American Journal of Political Science* 29 (1985): 608-621.
41.   Bijou Yang and David Lester, "Wives Who Work Full-Time and Part-Time: Some Correlates Across the States of the USA," *Psychological Reports* 62(1988): 545-546.
42.   James De Fronzo, "Female Labor Force Participation and Fertility in 48 States: Cross-Sectional and Change Analyses for the 1969-70 Decade," *Sociology and Social Research* 64(1980): 272; Tim B. Heaton, "Marital Stability Throughout the Child-Rearing Years," *Demography* 27(1990): 55-63.

43.   Peter H. Rossi, *Down and Out in America: The Origins of Homelessness* (Chicago: University of Chicago Press, 1989), 43, 130.

44.   Qtd. in Nancy Rubin, "America's New Homeless," *McCall's* Nov. 1988: 118.

45.   Cf. Ellen Rand, "New Jersey Housing: 2-Career Families Are On the Rise," *New York Times* 14 Dec. 1980: Sec. 11, p. 26.

46.   Qtd. in Nancy Ross, "First-Time Home Buyers; Increasingly Families Need Two Incomes," *Washington Post*, 13 May 1978.

47.   Qtd. in Barbara Loecher, "In Affluent Towns, The Working Poor Are Filling Shelters," *New York Times*, Sec. 12CN, p. 1.

48.   See Allan C. Carlson, "Gender, Children, and Social Labor: Transcending the 'Family Wage' Dilemma," *Journal of Social Issues* 52.3(1996): 137-161.

49.   See Brian D. Ray, "Home Education Across the United States" (1997), Home School Legal Defense Association, 20 Dec. 2002, http://www.hslda.org/docs/ study/ ray1997/default.asp.

6

Queer Demand? Why Homosexuals Began Demanding What Marriage Had Become

In a nation so torn by family conflict and disintegration that millions find themselves psychologically—if not physically—homeless, men and women naturally find it increasingly difficult to think straight. Leisure for serious reflection and a stable context for reflection both disappear in the social tumult. Perhaps the lack of reflective thought and the absence of a stable context for such thought help explain the profusion of inapt and shallow responses to the unexpected twenty-first-century phenomenon of gay activism for marriage rights. Certainly, no prominent American commentator anticipated the rapid sequence of events that in early 2004 brought hundreds of homosexual couples—in Massachusetts, California, New York, Oregon, and elsewhere—before religious and public officials who were willing to pronounce them married.[1] Sympathetic observers marveled at the bravery of gay activists and compared their wedding ceremonies to the acts of black civil-rights demonstrators in the Sixties. Unsympathetic observers expressed dismay at how brazen homosexuals had become in violating moral tradition and in defying statutory law. Conservative groups subsequently set in motion a number of initiatives—voter referenda, legislative actions, and constitutional amendments—on both state and federal levels to prohibit further homosexual marriages and to invalidate those that had occurred. But amid all of the many pundits praising or damning homosexuals for breaking the marriage barrier, few reflected on just what kind of institution homosexuals—who had never previously laid hold of marriage—were starting to claim. Indeed, if Americans had scrutinized carefully the way the national culture had already redefined wedlock *for heterosexuals*, they may well have concluded that it was not homosexuals that had changed so much, but rather marriage itself.

Far from being some astonishing development reflecting unprecedented new attitudes among homosexuals, homosexual weddings constituted the predictable (not natural, but entirely predictable) culmination of cultural changes that had radically denatured marriage.

Once defined by religious doctrine, moral tradition, and home-centered commitments to child rearing and gender complementarities in productive labor, marriage had by the beginning of the twenty-first century become a deracinated and highly individualistic and egalitarian institution, no longer implying commitment to home, to Church, to childbearing, to traditional gender duties, or even (permanently) to spouse. Gone was the productive husband-wife bond defined by mutual sacrifice and cooperative labor, replaced by dual-careerist vistas of self-fulfillment and consumer satisfaction. That homosexuals now wanted the strange new thing marriage had become should have surprised no one: twenty-first-century marriage, after all, certified a certain legitimacy in the mainstream of American culture and delivered tax, insurance, life-style, and governmental benefits—all without imposing any of the obligations of traditional marriage (which homosexuals decidedly did not want). Thus, while the conservative attempt to deny homosexuals the right to marry was understandable and even morally and legally justified, such an attempt was foredoomed in the absence of a broader effort to restore moral and religious integrity to marriage as a *heterosexual* institution.

Generally favorable to homosexual causes, the mainstream media did little to identify the cultural metamorphosis of marriage as a primary reason that wedlock now attracts homosexuals. When, for instance, nationally syndicated columnist Ellen Goodman praised homosexuals in February 2004 for engaging in "the civil disobedience of wedding," she did not so much as hint that homosexuals now want marriage only because Americans have radically redefined the institution.[2] Numerous other commentators made much of "the parallel between the civil rights movement of forty years ago" and today's "gay marriage campaign," all the while maintaining a code of silence about how very different marriage itself has become in the intervening decades.[3] So when entertainer Rosie O'Donnell lauded public officials who accommodated homosexuals' desire to marry, hailing their "courage to stand up against injustice," she could hardly be expected to acknowledge that the courageous officials in question were actually beating up an institution already badly bloodied by decades of anti-marital public policy.[4] Unfortunately, even when the media did allow conservatives to voice their views of homosexual marriage, the focus typically remained fixed on the novelty of homosexual actions, as though marriage had not already been radically redefined in American culture before homosexuals rather belatedly joined in the assault. Conservative columnist Thomas Sowell, for example, understandably responded to homosexual marriages by decrying the "lawless" acts of a "headstrong minority" convinced that they were "above the law." But in his appeal for the "rule of law," Sowell failed to acknowledge that in many ways, American law had already subverted the institution to which homosexuals began laying siege.[5] When conservative commentator Mychal Massie denounced as "an outrage" the attempt to equate "something so offensive" as gay marriage with the Black Civil Rights Movement of the Sixties, he rightly sensed "something much deeper and more insidious" than a simple desire to marry. "They want to change the entire social order."[6] But Massie neglected to mention that long before advocates of homosexual marriage went to work, various other social activists had already decidedly turned "the entire social order" against marriage.

Only the ideologically blind would deny that homosexual marriage threatens harm to all the moral and legal traditions that have defined wedlock for millennia. Homosexual activists have themselves asserted that they aim at more than a "mere 'aping'" of heterosexual marriage: they want homosexual marriage to "destabilize marriage's gendered definition by disrupting the link between gender and marriage." They thus value the homosexual wedding ceremony in part because of the "transformation that it makes on the people around us."[7] But the disruptions in marriage and the accompanying transformations of the American people hardly began with homosexuals or homosexual marriage. To those who have been paying attention to what American culture, legislation, and jurisprudence have been doing to wedlock since at least the sixties, homosexual marriage looks all too much like the coup de grace administered only after numerous judges, educators, therapists, activists, and entertainers have already done their worst.

To understand the true significance of the new demands for homosexual marriage, it is thus necessary to recognize how profoundly heterosexual America had quietly acquiesced in or actively promoted radical changes in wedlock *before* homosexuals began laying claim to the institution. Any thorough scrutiny of the last fifty years of culture history will establish that homosexual marriage culminated a decades-long attack, rather than initiated a distinctively new assault.

Once strongly reinforced by both religious doctrine and legal statute, marriage stood for centuries as *the* socially obligatory institution that shaped the individual for an adulthood of self-sacrifice and cooperative home-centered labor focused especially on the tasks of childbearing and child rearing. For centuries, almost all Americans recognized marriage as a divinely ordained union of husband and wife entailing distinctive but complementary gender roles (cf. Gen. 2:24; 3:16-19) whose duty to God was to "multiply and replenish the earth" through childbearing (Gen. 1:28). Out of reverence for this sacred marital union, Americans generally decried pre-marital sexual relations as the sin of fornication (cf. I Cor. 6:18) and recoiled from divorce as an offense against God (cf. Mark 10:2-12).

Nor, until relatively recently, did the imperatives of marital theology lack for this-worldly reinforcement. As historian Allan Carlson has stressed, traditional patterns of "house-holding" assigned "reciprocal, complementary tasks [to] husbands and wives" engaged in various types of "household production, ranging from tool making and weaving to the keeping of livestock and the garden patch." Marriage thus defined the very foundation of "a basic economic unit," which "bound each family together" as a "community of work."[8] Sociologist Arland Thornton has in view the same kind of economically autonomous traditional marriages when he remarks that in the pre-industrial world, "there were few economic enterprises outside the home; and the family was the basic organizational unit for many important activities, including production and consumption." Within this "family economy," Thornton points out, "family roles—such as husband, wife, and child—implied and overlapped economic roles....The husband generally directed the economic activity of the family, which was often, but not always an agricultural enterprise. While the wife maintained a primary role in caring for the home and children, she often made an important contribution to the family economic enterprise."[9] Historian Steven Ozment sees married couples as the very heart of a traditional family enjoying cultural as well as economic autonomy. Such a family, he remarks "supported, educated, blessed, and entertained itself with minimal external instruction and coercion."[10]

Sustained by their religious beliefs and absorbed in the labors of maintaining an autonomous home, American couples made their wedding vows both fruitful and durable. The fruitfulness of the traditional American marriage accounts for the words of a nineteenth-century American congressman proudly inviting a foreign visitor to "visit one of our log cabins...There you will find a strong, stout youth of eighteen, with his Better Half, just commencing the first struggles of independent life. Thirty years from that time, visit them again; and instead of two, you will find in that same family twenty-two. That is what I call the American Multiplication Table."[11] Note that the nineteenth-century congressman assumed that after thirty years the typical husband and wife would still be together: a safe assumption given that in the second half of the nineteenth century only one American marriage in twenty ended in divorce.[12] Carlson has shown that even in the 20th century, religious conviction and inherited cultural traditions still melded lifelong marriages that produced "child-rich families" devoted to what Teddy Roosevelt identified as the nation's "great primal work of *home-making* and *home-keeping*." Thus, Carlson argues, Roosevelt spoke for a culturally united people when he praised the married couples producing the country's "best crop," its "crop of children" and when he denounced "easy divorce" as "a *menace* to the home."[13]

By the middle of the twentieth century, the American supports for marriage had weakened in a number of ways—none of them involving advocates of homosexual marriage. First, the transformation of America from a primarily agricultural country into a primarily industrial nation meant, as historian John Demos has pointed out, "Family life was wrenched apart from the world of work—a veritable sea-change in social history."[14] This sea change inevitably meant that most men left behind the traditional household economy which had reinforced wedlock for millennia, leaving their wives to work alone in a functionally diminished home. Immediately, advertisers, manufacturers, and educators conspired to take advantage of the social and economic isolation of the homemaking wife by making her into a "machine operative" and "general purchasing agent" for a home that had lost much of its productive function.[15] By the 1950s, the home's surrender of productive functions had become so complete (as was discussed in chapter 5) that Harvard sociologist Pitirim Sorokin saw it becoming a "mere incidental parking place" for consumption and relaxation.[16] Many wives consequently experienced what one social historian labeled the "festering contradiction of modern womanhood" as their traditional homecrafts lost economic value and cultural legitimacy,[17] so threatening to reduce their social status to that of menial parking-place attendants.

Still, for all of its monitory clarity about what could happen, Sorokin's parking-space metaphor need not have been anything more than hyperbole. The average American family of the fifties and sixties resisted in significant ways the economic pressures undermining the home economy that had traditionally reinforced marriage. Most mothers still cooked family meals rather than relying on restaurants or take-out; many still sewed some of their husbands' and children's clothing. Almost all mothers cared for their own young children rather than turning this task over to a paid surrogate. Fathers not only provided for their wives and children financially, but also performed many of the home repair and maintenance tasks. Though it had surrendered much, the American family still retained a significant core of its traditional autonomy and self-reliance.

Had America's policymakers and lawmakers in the fifties and sixties made preserving that core a high priority, they could have developed aggressively pro-natalist policies (tax credits and child subsidies) to support married parents producing America's "best crop." They could also have explored ways to bring technologically mediated work back into the home for both husbands and wives.[18] Policymakers and legislators might even have restored some of the domestic autonomy that Ozment finds so admirable in pre-modern families by encouraging families to home school their children. More fundamentally, had the nation's cultural elite cared deeply about wedlock, they could have deployed the persuasive powers of rhetoric, literature, and entertainment to (as Carlson puts it) summon "both men and women...to relearn and recommit to the deeper meanings of the ancient words *husbandry* and *housewifery*."[19]

Lamentably, during the sixties and seventies, America's cultural and political elite—none of whom were activists promoting homosexual marriage—chose to subvert rather than renew marriage, heterosexual marriage. In large part, the country's cultural elite chose to subvert marriage not by advocating new rights for gays and lesbians, but simply by acquiescing to the economic processes tearing apart the traditional home economy. After decades of such acquiescence, poet Wendell Berry could in 1990 fairly characterize the "typical modern household" created by a married heterosexual couple as something very like the "mere incidental parking place" which Sorokin had worriedly anticipated decades before fearing its malign consequences for marriage. "The modern household," Berry writes, "is the place where [a] consumptive couple do their consuming. Nothing productive is done there. Such work as is done there is done at the expense of the resident couple or family, and to the profit of suppliers of energy and household technology. For entertainment, the inmates consume television or purchase other consumable diversion elsewhere."[20] The marital and domestic world Berry describes could hardly be further removed from the marital and domestic world in which the family once "supported, educated, blessed, and entertained itself with minimal external instruction and coercion."

But the assault on wedlock during the Sixties and Seventies reflected cultural forces deeper than economics, cultural forces at work long before homosexuals began their strange parade to the wedding altar. Although its immediate effects remained confined to a relatively small elite, the intellectual atheism which historian James Turner sees emerging for the first time in the United States in the late nineteenth century had become by the mid-twentieth century a relatively potent force, one that "dis-integrated" our national culture by denying religious belief its traditional function as "a unifying and defining element of that culture."[21] Unbelief thus eroded the theological basis for wedlock by giving cultural license to well-placed and influential (though still not numerous) apostles of godless Nietzschean, Darwinian, Malthusian, and Freudian doctrines. Prayer disappeared from the nation's schools, and religious assumptions gradually faded from public discussions of morality and family life.

Without question, the fading of religious belief would eventually have emboldened homosexuals by weakening the cultural authority of theological prohibitions against homosexuality (cf. Lev. 18:22; Rom. 1:26-28). But most of the atheists who first warred against the country's Judeo-Christian marital and family traditions were freethinking *heterosexuals* advocating "sexual and familial experimentation" of the sort that finally helped incubate the New Left's Counterculture of communes, drugs, free love (overwhelmingly heterosexual), and rock music."[22] Although relatively few Americans directly participated in the Sixties counterculture, the prominence and cultural influence of those who did gave them remarkable power to reshape American institutions and behavior in the decades that followed.

That re-shaping dramatically reduced the power of traditional religious faith in America. As sociologist Timothy T. Clydesdale has remarked, religion held "an established cultural status" in America until "the cultural challenges of the 1960's disestablished this religious ethos."[23] Not surprisingly, then, Berkeley sociologists trace a "startlingly rapid" upsurge in the percentage of Americans claiming no religious affiliation to "more cohorts with a 1960's experience."[24] The impact of the Sixties may also be discerned in a remarkable "generation gap" in church attendance documented by University of Michigan sociologists in a 1989 study, with younger Americans evincing a significantly lower commitment than their parents to weekly worship.[25]

Even among Americans who continued to go to church, sociologists witnessed the emergence of dubious new religious attitudes in the post-sixties (but pre-homosexual-marriage) world. Pollster George Gallup reported in the eighties that many Americans who professed religious beliefs were beginning to "dodge the responsibilities and obligations" traditionally associated with such beliefs.[26] Post-sixties sociological inquiry indeed revealed that those still filling the pews were increasingly inclined to interpret "their religious commitments and beliefs in individualistic terms and less in terms of institutional loyalty and obligation. They [were] now looking to religion more for its personal meaning and less for its moral rules."[27] Even American Catholics—previously distinctive for their deference to hierarchy and tradition—became "more personally autonomous and less subject to traditional mechanisms of social control."[28]

Because so much of the traditional understanding of marriage rested upon religious doctrines, eroding popular commitments to those doctrines could only undermine marriage and family life. Writing in 1985, social commentator Barbara Hargrove thus saw "the authority of the Church over the family, and the family over the individual [fading into] the past."[29] And five years later, cultural critic Alvin Kernan acknowledged stark and clearly linked declines in religion and family life in the latter decades of the twentieth century.[30]

Sociologists predictably see a close linkage between declining church attendance among young Americans and a rising willingness to engage in premarital sex.[31] Young women eagerly availed themselves of the Pill in the sixties and seventies largely because they were simultaneously letting go of the New Testament: whereas only 29 percent of college age females reported having had premarital intercourse in 1965, that percentage had skyrocketed to sixty-three percent by 1985.[32] In the post-sixties world, young Americans were clearly taking their behavioral cues from someone other than St. Paul. By the 1980s—still long before homosexual couples challenged the religious doctrines denying them the right to marry—millions of heterosexual couples would flout the religious doctrines forbidding fornication: over two million unmarried heterosexual couples were living together in 1986, and 44 percent of all American heterosexual couples who married between 1980 and 1984 had cohabited before taking vows.[33] Thus many heterosexual couples had made a bad cultural joke of the traditional symbolism of the white wedding dress long before homosexuals tried to make optional a wedding dress of any sort.

Even when heterosexual couples did wed in the post-sixties world, an increasing number did so unencumbered by the scriptural prohibition against adultery (cf. Ex. 20:14; Matt. 19:18): in a 1983 survey of over 3,500 couples, fifteen to twenty-six percent allowed for "non-monogamy under some circumstances,"[34] while a parallel 1989 British study of married adults found that "of those surveyed under age thirty-five, over one fifth (twenty-two percent) entered their first marriage with no belief in sexual fidelity."[35] In 1991, British sociologist Paul Mullen warned that adultery was fast becoming "a participation sport indulged in by the masses," as "citizens increasingly assume the right to change and vary their erotic attachments."[36] A 1995 American study documented the very attitudes that so distressed Mullen, its authors reporting that "many married persons continue to search for an intimate partner, or at least remain open to the possibility of forming extramarital relationships, even while married."[37]

But the Sixties meltdown in religious orthodoxy harmed and denatured wedlock by destroying more than sexual restraint. As defined by religious tradition, marriage demanded—and taught—a deep capacity for self-sacrifice and selfless service (cf. Eph. 5:22-33). But self-sacrifice disappeared from the cultural catechism written by the Woodstock Generation of the sixties. In the same survey, sociologists who limned a decline in religious faith in the seventies and eighties also tracked a sharp rise in "hedonistic values," an increasing desire for "self-gratification," and an increasing absorption in the imperatives of "self-actualization."[38] This insistent emphasis on Self could only weaken and deracinate wedlock, regardless of whether homosexuals were ever permitted to take vows. For good reason, sociologists Howard Bahr and Kathleen Bahr express dismay that the kind of self-sacrifice that once served as "the essential glue of a moral society," particularly within marriage and family, came to be widely regarded as a "self-defeating behavior" or even a deplorable "personality defect" by modern commentators who were guided by "the assumption of self-interest and...the logic of utilitarian individualism."[39]   By the end of the twentieth century, many Americans no longer worshiped the God of Abraham, of Isaac, and of Jacob—the Deity who summoned husbands and wives to selfless devotion within the conjugal bonds of marriage—but rather adored only the Sovereign Self, unfettered by religious or moral restraints.

But even more astonishing than the widespread rejection of traditional Christian and Jewish doctrines governing marriage and family life was the headlong apostasy of many clergy, particularly in America's influential mainline Protestant denominations. As a disgruntled Episcopalian observer has remarked, many mainline Protestant leaders caved in to cultural pressures during the sixties and seventies, riding the turbulent currents of the sexual revolution as they catechized their parishioners in "being tolerant of non-marital liaisons" among heterosexuals and in accepting "new and non-traditional family forms," including single-parent and cohabiting-parent families.[40]   Catholic philosopher David Carlin marvels at how liberal Protestant clergy in the seventies and eighties "tried to hold on to their people by accommodating to the latest moral and intellectual fashions in the surrounding secular culture." "So far from struggling against secularist elements of culture," Carlin remarks, these progressive clerics "actually *embraced* them, attempting to incorporate them into a 'modernized' version of Christianity."[41] Predictably enough, such institutional apostasy drove attendance and membership in mainline Protestant denominations down during the latter decades of the 20th century. But tradition and inertia kept many perplexed parishioners in the pews, listening to clergy so permissive that they allowed couples (all heterosexual until very recently) to write their own bizarre wedding vows, so intensifying the spiritual and moral confusion about the true nature of wedlock and family life.[42]

The loss of the natural anchor of a healthy home economy and the supernatural sanctions of religious doctrine left marriage at the mercy of adverse economic, political, and cultural currents for decades before homosexuals ever sought state and church imprimatur for wedding vows. In curious ways, these currents have combined the wild anarchy of raw individualism with the focused fury of political ideology and corporate greed.

Once an essential element of the natural home economy, the gender complementarity of wedlock was exposed to particularly negative pressures in the sixties and seventies. As the distinguished economist Gary Becker demonstrated in a landmark study published in 1965—just when those negative pressures were gathering strength— marriage draws institutional strength from a complementary husband-wife division of labor.[43] Such a gendered marital division of labor had, of course, emerged spontaneously in pre-industrial agrarian cultures, but a somewhat artificial breadwinner/homemaker version of this marital division of labor had remained in place for decades in an industrialized United States, as labor unions demanded and employers and government officials acquiesced in a "family wage" system which paid a married father enough to support an at-home wife and their children, while deliberately keeping married women out of the labor market. Scriptural sanction for a gendered division of labor in marriage (cf. Gen. 3:16-19; Titus 2:4-5) fostered acquiescence so long as religion remained a powerful force in American public life. However, as religion lost cultural strength in the firestorm of the Sixties, employers and government officials turned decisively against the "family wage" system and the marital gender roles it protected. Indeed, during the sixties and seventies, lawmakers outlawed the deliberate gender discrimination essential to the "family wage" system.[44]

Corporate employers needed no encouragement for abandoning the family-wage system and attacking marital complementarities; these employers had long recognized that bringing wives into the labor market would drive down wages. Politicians turned against marital complementarities for a more complex mix of reasons. Some were simply responding to the lobbying of corporate employers. Others resonated—consciously or unconsciously—to the ideological imperatives of utopian thinkers (Plato, Campanella, Bellamy, Morris, Wells, Skinner) who dreamed of making all citizens completely devoted to the ideal state as they abolished (or at least weakened) the competing loyalties of marriage and family.[45] The feminist elements of such utopian ideology gained strength in the Seventies as doctrinaire gender-egalitarians rallied round the Equal Rights

Amendment, drawing intermittent support from confused wives frustrated and disheartened by the economic and cultural marginalization of their homemaking.

Quietly undermined by the continual erosion of the home economy, directly assaulted by feminist egalitarians, and rendered economically precarious by the disintegration of "the family wage," the economic gender complementarities of marriage disappeared for millions of couples as millions of wives moved out of the home and into paid employment. Hence, long before homosexuals challenged the male-female sexual complementarities of marriage, the economic complementarities of marriage had already disappeared. In these couples—as sociologist Steven Nock pointed out—"being a 'good' mother" had come to mean "the same thing...as being a 'good' father [had]...for years—the provision of adequate material/financial resources" for the family.[46] In economic terms at least, a growing number of American children had two "fathers" long before advocates of homosexual marriage ever attempted to give children two biologically male parents.

However, the transformation of wives into economic clones of their husbands had the entirely predictable effect of sweeping away most of the remnants of the home economy, as harried employed women increasingly relied on the restaurant for meal preparation and the day-care center for child care.[47] But the obliteration of the economic distinction between husband and wife also inevitably suppressed the biological event that most forcibly defined gender complementarities: childbirth. Marital fertility plummeted in the Seventies, pushing overall fertility in the United States below replacement level in what policy analyst Ben J. Wattenberg called "a birth dearth."[48] Although the U.S. population continued to grow in the Nineties because of immigration and increased longevity, the birth dearth continued as the number of DINK (Double Income, No Kids) marriages multiplied.[49]

Though it worried Wattenberg and others, certain activist groups rejoiced in the disruption of the cultural pattern that traditionally made marriage the foundation for a "child-rich" family. For policymakers and judges in thrall to the Malthusian scare propaganda of a population explosion, the child-poor family was the ideal. In order to discourage married couples from having children, Malthusian policymakers deliberately turned tax policy against large families. Meanwhile, an activist Supreme Court joined in the war against childbearing directly by creating a legal right to elective abortion (*Roe* v. *Wade* [1973]). Further, the Court undermined the marital integrity that had previously given a married father legal standing in life-death decisions about his unborn children (*Planned Parenthood of Missouri* v. *Danforth* [1976]).[50] By making childbearing entirely a female decision, the High Court's decisions helped make the shot-gun marriage a rarity, as the percentage of children born out of wed-lock rose from just 5 percent in 1960 to 33 percent in 1998.[51] The rise in the illegitimacy rate accelerated under welfare policies making Uncle Sam a reliable surrogate spouse. By the Eighties, "mother-state-child" families predominated in some inner-city areas.[52]

Judge-made policy not only helped sever the linkage between childbearing and marriage, but it also helped further weaken the already severely compromised link between marriage and sexual activity. Seven years before the High Court legalized abortion, it exacerbated the growing effects of the sexual revolution by giving pornographers a startling victory in its notorious *Fanny Hill* decision of 1966. With law officials powerless to stop them, pornographers carried out what one of their champions, writing in 1973, called "the obscening of America," inciting ever more licentious behavior until "nothing was reduced to less recognizable rubble than the revered...Institution of Marriage."[53] With the advent of the Internet, pornographers were able –without little or no help from homosexuals—to continue "the obscening of America" through cyberspace, pulverizing marriage even more.

Even if not subverted by pornography and licentiousness, sterile marriages of economic clones became contentious and unstable in post-sixties America. As Berry pointedly remarks, when marriage became merely "two careerists in the same bed," it degenerated into "a sort of private political system in which rights and interest must be constantly asserted and defended." Such a system actually turned marriage into a "form of divorce: a prolonged and impassioned ne-gotiation as to how things shall be divided."[54] The sixties and seven-ties did in fact see divorce rates skyrocket, rising by 145 percent between 1960 and 1980.[55] Rather than resist this trend, state legisla-tors—urged on by a well-organized coterie of activists—enacted "no-fault" divorce laws—laws that reduced marriage to less than the weakest contract-at-will and put the state for the first time in alliance with the spouse who wanted the divorce (often a calculating be-trayer) against the spouse who wanted to preserve the marriage.[56]

As marriage became more insubstantial and impermanent, the family that couples formed through marriage ceased to create the kind of autonomy Ozment finds so admirable in early modern families. As the legal scholar George Swan looked at the divorce-prone modern couple of the eighties, he could not see them creating "a freestanding institution" in their home: "Today's family, continually threatened by dissolution, is less and less able to serve as the context in which...Americans organize their lives independently of central political authority."[57] Rather than the foundation of a sphere of autonomy, the modern marriage—bereft of a healthy home economy, frequently devoid of children, and threatening to dissolve at any moment—metamorphosed into merely a convenient social arrangement for securing and regularizing the household's dependency on insurance, employment, and government benefits (such as Social Security).

The radical redefinition of marriage during the latter decades of the twentieth century—its legal, economic, and cultural decimation—largely accounted for the sharp drop in the marriage rate after the sixties. By the nineties, marriage had lost so much of its cultural substance that it hardly seemed worth the bother to many young Americans. Between 1970 and 2000, the marriage rate dropped an astonishing 40 percent.[58] Marriage became so culturally and socially marginal for Americans—*heterosexual* Americans—that in 1998 one social scientist declared that, in a development that was "novel, perhaps even unique, in human cultural history," marriage had ceased to be "the definitive criterion for the transition to adulthood" in American society.[59]

It was in truth the cultural devaluation of marriage that explained why some homosexual activists reacted to the push for homosexual marriage by asking, "Why should we scramble to get onto a sinking ship?"[60] But most homosexual couples who started seeking to be married were doing so precisely because so much of the traditional freight of marriage—complementary gender roles, work in a real home economy, childbearing, sexual fidelity, permanence—had been thrown overboard as the marital ship settled ever lower in the water. The strangely denatured and deracinated thing that marriage had become appealed to homosexuals because it now offered insurance, employment, lifestyle, and government benefits, while imposing almost none of the obligations it once had. Conservative opponents of homosexual marriage spoke the truth when they protested that

America was making a mockery of wedlock if it licensed vows for couples who could never have children (without resorting to surrogate mothers or sperm donors), would not resist the temptations to extramarital affairs, and would not preserve their union for a lifetime.[61] But the mockery of wedlock began decades ago when hundreds of thousands of *heterosexual* DINK couples started buying basset hounds rather than bassinettes, started indulging in extramarital affairs, and started fulfilling divorce attorneys' dreams of avarice. It was indeed by trivializing the marital traditions of fertility, fidelity, and permanence that heterosexuals so completely changed the character of marriage that homosexuals finally *wanted* to claim the very odd thing it had become.

Thus conservative commentators missed the point when they opposed homosexual marriage on the grounds that it "would undermine traditional understandings of marriage."[62] It was only because traditional understandings of marriage *had already been severely undermined* that homosexuals began laying claim to it. Carlin assessed the situation astutely when he asserted that "gay marriage is...worth opposing not as an end in itself...but [only] as the first step toward the rolling back of the progressive delegitimization of marriage that has occurred in the past few decades." If it became merely a separate and discrete initiative, unconnected to the broader task of restoring substance to marriage, then Carlin judged the effort to outlaw homosexual marriage to be a "game...not worth the candle." "If," Carlin wrote, "we are not interested in this rollback [of the delegitimization of marriage], we might as well permit gays and lesbians to marry."[63]

Though restoring substance to marriage will entail many legal, political, economic, and cultural tasks, it will require above all two things: (1) restoring substance to the marital home economy; (2) reinvigorating religion as a basis for marital and family life. Berry clarifies what is required to restore marriage to a healthy home economy when he writes about how "a household economy... [should involve] the work of both wife and husband [and]...[give] them a measure of economic independence and self-protection, a measure of self-employment, a measure of freedom, as well as a common ground and a common satisfaction. Such a household economy may employ the disciplines and skills of housewifery, of carpentry and other trades of building and maintenance, of gardening and other branches of subsistence agriculture, and even of woodlot management and woodcutting. It may also involve a 'cottage industry' of some kind."[64]

The renewing of religion, on the other hand, requires deeper and more challenging changes. However, the prophet Isaiah holds out the promise that "they that wait upon the Lord shall renew their strength; they shall mount up with wings as eagles..." (Isa. 40:31). Eagles, it should be recalled, mate—male and female—for life.

Notes

1. Pam Belluck, "Gay Marriage, State by State," *New York Times* 7 March 2004: Sec. 4, p. 2.

2. Ellen Goodman, "Center Has Shifted," *South Florida Sun-Sentinel* 21 February 2004: 19A.

3. Jennifer Peter, "Massachusetts' Gay Marriage Debate Taking on Form, Rhetoric of Civil Rights Movement," *Associated Press Worldstream* 15 January 2004.

4. O'Donnell qtd. in Paige Wiser, "Riveting Rosie," *Chicago Sun-Times* 27 February 2004: 60.

5. Thomas Sowell, "Democracy Needs the Rule of Law for its Survival," *Albany Times Union* 5 March 2004: A11.

6. Associated Press and Fox News, "Blacks Balk at Gay Marriage-Civil Rights Links," *Fox News* 28 November 2003, 10 March 2004 *http://www.foxnews.com*.

7. Barbara J. Cox, "A (Personal) Essay on Same-Sex Marriage," *National Journal of Sexual Orientation Law* 1.1 (1995): 88-89.

8. Allan C. Carlson, *From Cottage to Work Station: The Family's Search for Social Harmony in an Industrial Age* (San Francisco, CA: Ignatius, 1993), 1-2.

9. Arland Thornton, "Reciprocal Influences of Family and Religion in a Changing World," *Journal of Marriage and the Family* 47 (1985): 382.

10. Steven Ozment, *Flesh and Spirit: Private Life in Early Modern Germany* (New York: Village, 1999), 262-265.

11. Qtd. in Paul Johnson, *A History of the American People* (New York: HarperCollins, 1997), 284.

12. Cf. Thornton, *op. cit.*, 384.

13. Cf. Allan Carlson, *The 'American Way': Family and Community in the Shaping of the American Identity* (Wilmington, DE: ISI Books, 2003), 8-13, 16.

14. Qtd. in Carlson, *From Cottage*, 2.

15. Cf. Stuart Ewen, *Captains of Consciousness: Advertising and the Social Roots of the Consumer Culture* (New York: McGraw-Hill, 1976), 161-164; Roland Marchand, *Advertising the American Dream: Making Way for Modernity* (Berkeley: University of California Press, 1985), Chapter 6.

16. Pitirim A. Sorokin, *Social and Cultural Dynamics: A Study of Change in Major Systems of Art, Truth, Ethics, Law and Social Relationships*, rev. and abridged ed. (1957; rpt. New Brunswick, NJ: Transaction Publishers, 1985), 700.

17. Cf. Ewen, op. cit., 164-166.

18. Cf. Carlson, *American Way*, 166.

19. Carlson, *From Cottage*, 168.

20. Wendell Berry, *What Are People For?* (San Francisco, CA: North Point, 1990), 180-181.

21. James Turner, *Without God, Without Creed: The Origins of Unbelief in America* (Baltimore, MD: Johns Hopkins University Press, 1985), 263.

22.   Cf. Eli Zaretsky, *Secrets of the Soul: A Social and Cultural History of Psychoanalysis* (New York: Alfred A. Knopf, 2004), 208, 317.
23.   Timothy T. Clydesdale, "Family Behaviors Among Early U.S. Baby Boomers: Explaining the Effects of Religion and Income Change, 1965-1982," *Social Forces* 76 (1997): 607.
24.   Michael Hout and Claude S. Fischer, "Why More Americans Have No Religious Preference: Politics and Generations," *American Sociological Review* 67 (2002): 165-190.
25.   Arland Thornton and Donald Camburn, "Religious Participation and Adolescent Sexual Behavior and Attitudes," *Journal of Marriage and the Family* 51 (1989): 641-653.
26.   Qtd. in Howard M. Bahr and Bruce A. Chadwick, "Religion and Family in Middletown, USA," *Journal of Marriage and the Family* 47 (1985): 410.
27.   Thornton, op. cit., 385.
28.   William V. D'Antonio, "The American Catholic Family: Signs of Cohesion and Polarization," *Journal of Marriage and the Family* 47 (1985): 399.
29.   Qtd. in Patrick H. McNamara, "The New Christian Right's View of the Family and Its Social Science Critics: A Study in Differing Presuppositions," *Journal of Marriage and the Family* 47 (1985): 450.
30.   Alvin Kernan, *The Death of Literature* (New Haven, CT: Yale University Press, 1990), 8.
31.   Thornton and Camburn, op. cit.
32.   Ira Robinson *et al.,* "Twenty Years of the Sexual Revolution, 1965-1985: An Update," *Journal of Marriage and the Family* 53 (1991): 216-220.
33.   Cf. Arland Thornton, "Cohabitation and Marriage in the 1980's," *Demography* 25 (1988): 501-506; Patricia A. Gwartney-Gibbs, "The Institutionalization of Premarital Cohabitation: Estimates from Marriage License Applications, 1970 and 1980," *Journal of Marriage and the Family* 48 (1986): 423-434; Martha Farnsworth Riche, "The Postmarital Society," *American Demographics* November 1988: 26.
34.   Arline M. Rubin and James R. Adams, "Outcomes of Sexually Open Marriages," *Journal of Sex Research* 22 (1986): 311-319.
35.   Annette Lawson and Colin Samson, "Age, Gender, and Adultery," *The British Journal of Sociology* 39 (1988): 409-439.
36.   Paul E. Mullin, "Jealousy: The Pathology of Passion," *British Journal of Psychiatry* 158 (1991): 593-601.
37.   Scott J. South and Kim M. Lloyd, "Spousal Alternatives and Marital Dissolution," *American Sociological Review* 60 (1995): 21-35.
38.   Cf. Arthur G. N. Neal, Theodore Groat, and Jerry W. Wicks, "Attitudes About Having Children: A Study of 600 Couples in the Early Years of Marriage," *Journal of Marriage and the Family* 51 (1989): 313-328; Lawson and Samson, *op. cit.*
39.   Howard M. Bahr and Kathleen S. Bahr, "Families and Self-Sacrifice: Alternative Models and Meanings for Family Theory," *Social Forces* 79 (2001): 1231-1258.
40.   Dianne Knipps, "Exploding Myths About the Episcopal Church Crisis," *AAC News,* 10 January 2004, American Anglican Council 10 March 2004 *http://www.americananglican.org.*
41.   David Carlin, "Open or Closed Religion?" *Homiletic & Pastoral Review* November 2001 10 March 2004 *http://www.catholic.net.*
42.   Cf. Kerry A. White, "Words to Marry By: The Do's and Don'ts of Writing Your Own Wedding Vows," *Baltimore Sun* 2 June 1996: 21.
43.   Cf. Carlson, *From Cottage,* 154.
44.   Allan C. Carlson, "Gender, Children, and Social Labor: Transcending the 'Family Wage' Dilemma," *Journal of Social Issues* 52.3 (1996): 137-161.

45.   Cf. Bryce Christensen, "The Family in Utopia," *Renascence* 44 (1991): 31-44.
46.   Steven L. Nock, "The Symbolic Meaning of Childbearing," *Journal of Family Issues* 8 (1981): 373-393.
47.   Cf. W. Keith Bryant, "Durables and Wives' Employment Yet Again," *Journal of Consumer Research* 15 (1988): 37-45.
48.   Ben J. Wattenberg, *The Birth Dearth* (New York: Pharos, 1987), 127-130.
49.   Cf. "DINKs," *Investopedia* 10 March 2004 *http://www.investopedia.com.*
50.   Cf. Bryce Christensen, "Double Bind: The Redefinition of American Fatherhood," *The Family in America* October 1988: 3-4.
51.   Cf. George A. Akerlof, Janet L. Yeller, and Michael L. Katz, "An Analysis of Out-of-Wedlock Childbearing in the United States," *The Quarterly Journal of Economics* 111 (1996): 277-317; U.S. Bureau of the Census, *Statistical Abstract of the United States* 2 September 2003 *http://www.census.gov.*
52.   Cf. Randal D. Day and Wade C. Mackey, "Children as Resources: A Cultural Analysis," *Family Perspective* 20 (1958): 258-262.
53.   Allan Sherman, *The Rape of the A*P*E (American *Puritan *Ethic): The Official History of the Sex Revolution* (Chicago: Playboy Press, 1973), 11, 338-339.
54.   Berry, *op. cit.*
55.   U.S. Bureau of the Census, *Historical Statistics of the United States: Colonial Times to 1970* (Washington: U.S. Government Printing Office, 1975), 1: 20, 64; U.S. Bureau of the Census, *Statistical Abstract of the United States* 2 September 2003 *http://www.census.gov.*
56.   Cf. Lenore J. Weitzman, *The Divorce Revolution: The Unexpected Social and Economic Consequences for Women and Children in America* (New York: Free Press, 1985), 27; Herbert Jacob, *Silent Revolution: The Transformation of Divorce Law in the United States* (Chicago: University of Chicago Press, 1988), 65-59, 150-151.
57.   George S. Swan, "The Political Economy of American Family Policy, 1945-85," *Population and Developmental Review* 12 (1986): 752.
58.   Cf. Robert Schoen, "The Continuing Retreat From Marriage: Figures From 1983 U.S. Marital Status Life Tables," *Sociology and Social Research* 71 (1987): 108-109; U.S. Bureau of the Census, *Statistical Abstract of the United States* 2 September 2003 *http://www.census.gov.*
59.   Jeffrey Jensen Arnett, "Learning to Stand Alone: The Contemporary American Transition to Adulthood in Cultural and Historical Context," *Human Development* 41 (1998): 295-315.
60.   Cf. Johann Hari, "If It Looks Like A Marriage, Then Call It A Marriage," *The Independent* (London) 20 January 2003: 17.
61.   Cf. Timothy J. Dailey *et al.*, *Getting It Straight: What the Research Shows About Homosexuality* (Washington: Family Research Council, 2004), Chptrs. 4-5.
62.   Cf. Stanley Kurtz, "Seeing the Slip," *National Review online* 14 April 2003, 10 March 2004 *http://www.nationalreview.com.*
63.   Carlin, op. cit.
64.   Berry, op. cit.

7

The End of Patriotism: Family Tumult in "the Seedbed of the State"

When homosexuals began appearing before government officials to be married, the sight should have prompted the country's heterosexual majority to ponder just how much they themselves had done to de-nature wedlock. It also should have occasioned much-needed reflection on how reflexively many Americans—straight and gay—now routinely turn to government to satisfy their own needs, not to discharge their duties. American attitudes were once quite different.

"I only regret that I have but one life to lose for my country." For more than 200 years, the brave words of Nathan Hale stood for something more than the courage of one American spy. For millions of grateful Americans, these words typified the selfless patriotism of an entire generation, willing to pledge their lives and sacred honor to their new nation. Unfortunately, this kind of patriotism had dwindled remarkably by the 21st century. As is discussed in chapter 9, the nightmare of 9/11 did prompt a remarkable upsurge in patriotic fervor and sentiment. But as chapter 9 also notes, this upsurge proved troublingly short-lived, suggesting that the post-9/11 displays of patriotism lacked deep substance. Before long, many Americans seemed slightly embarrassed at ever having been caught up in all the flag-waving and anthem-singing. And unlike 1941-42 when Pearl Harbor prompted hundreds of thousands of American men to volunteer for military service, 2001-02 did not see a marked upsurge in voluntary military enlistments. Indeed, the attitude which again prevailed not long after 9/11 among large numbers of young Americans might be summed up as the antithesis of Hale's stirring declaration: "I only regret that I cannot get more out of my country during one lifetime."

That expressions of selfless patriotism had largely disappeared by the late twentieth century, few would deny. Writing in 1999, journalist David Brooks acknowledged that "patriotic eloquence went into long-term decline" during the twentieth century and that in the waning years of that century, "America ha[d] struggled to rediscover a compelling patriotic language." As a people, Brooks suggested, Americans had retreated into "the easy comforts of private life," so completely losing touch with "higher, more demanding principles and virtues" that we had begun to "look on everything that does not immediately touch on our own lives with an indifference that is laced with contempt."[1] Even when commentator Cynthia Crossen insisted that patriotism endured in late-twentieth-century America and indeed was "booming along with the economy," she wrote of a patriotism light years away from the self-sacrifice of Nathan Hale. "The newest breed of patriots," she conceded, "distances itself from the word [*patriotic*]" because of "its recent connotations of right-wing extremists and militias." But Crossen argued that Americans were still patriots nonetheless because "they love the opportunity, the personal freedom, and the beauty of America." After all, as Americans, "we've got Microsoft, we've got Disney, we've got FedEx."[2] Somehow, the national outlook that Crossen dubbed "patriotism" bore many of the marks of the "easy comforts of private life" that Brooks condemned as its opposite.

The need to regain an authentic patriotism of self-sacrifice indeed defined one of the major themes of Senator John McCain's failed 2000 campaign for the presidency. "The spirit of America is dissipating," he lamented. "People are not proud any more of their institutions. They are not eager for public service or willing to work for a cause greater than themselves.[3] Corroborating McCain's perception, a 1999 Roper Center study concluded that for almost two-thirds of Americans, patriotism no longer involved "making active sacrifices for the public good"; consequently, "someone does not actually have to do anything in order to be patriotic."[4]

Arguably, the decline in selfless patriotism could be traced in part to the debacle in Vietnam and the tawdry deceptions of Watergate, which made the country look less worthy of personal sacrifice by its citizens. However, the self-absorption of which Brooks wrote and McCain spoke reflects unwillingness on the part of American citizens to make sacrifices for any cause or institution larger than self, no matter how noble. Neither Vietnam nor Watergate can be blamed for that. What can be blamed to a great degree is the national retreat from family life. For it is only within the family that we are likely to acquire those moral attitudes which make possible selflessness of any sort–including that of patriotism. Because of the family's claim to a type of immortality, the family can invest sacrifices made for its sake with profound meaning–at once biological and religious—a meaning that can extend to sacrifices made for a government perceived to be the ally of the family. But when the family disintegrates, so too does the selflessness necessary for patriotism.

"Mothers give us life," remarks Jehan Sadat, widow of Egyptian Prime Minister Anwar Sadat. "They are our first teachers, giving us the lessons and values we will carry for the rest of our lives."[5] America, just as much as Egypt, needs young citizens who have acquired from their mothers the values of lawfulness, integrity, and selflessness. Even the framers of very modern nontraditional theories of morality require mothers and families just to get started with their theorizing. As ethicists Owen Flanigan and Kathryn Jackson critically observe, modern theories of justice "need to assume that there will be loving parents in order to ensure the stability of a just society and the development of a sense of justice in new members." "Theories of obligation," they point out, "...must take out a loan not only on the natural duty of parents to care for children...but on the natural virtue of parental love... The virtue of being a loving parent must supplement the natural duties and obligations if the just society is to last beyond the first generation." "For any human interaction to take place, there must be family and nurturance. Otherwise, the helpless infant will not survive its first night."[6]

Of course, a helpless infant at home will generally be found in her mother's arms. But a mother's ability to imbue her children with such values depends heavily upon her family circumstances. A raft of studies indicate that married mothers achieve far greater success than single mothers in instilling essential moral values in their children. In a 1999 study of preschoolers and their families, for example, researchers found that single mothers were more likely than married mothers to use "negative controlling behaviors" with their children, resulting in "increased children's aggressiveness" among the offspring of the unmarried mothers.[7] Likewise, in a 1998 study of inner-city grade-schoolers, researchers documented "harsher parenting" in single-parent households with "poorer behavioral adjustment" among the children as an apparent consequence.[8] Not surprisingly, then, rates for juvenile delinquency, drug use, and academic failure all run higher among the children of single mothers than among peers reared by married mothers.

Family and Human Values

Clearly, it is the intact family to which Americans must look for the instilling in children of the moral orientation which engenders selfless patriotism. For good reason, Cicero wrote of the family as "the seedbed of the state."[9] Without the family, the civic and patriotic impulses which inform a healthy country soon disappear. Consequently, America's greatest leaders have, with Cicero, recognized the nation's need for the morality which only the family can inculcate. It was George Washington himself who emphasized that "Virtue or morality is a necessary spring of popular government. The rule indeed extends with more or less force to every species of Free Government. Who that is a sincere friend to it can look with indifference upon attempts to shake the foundation of the fabric?"[10] And as one who praised his own "revered Mother; by whose Maternal hand...I was led from childhood,"[11] Washington knew who laid that foundation.

Family devotion also informed the patriotic vision of Abraham Lincoln, whose political integrity preserved what Washington had founded. Speaking of his own mother, Lincoln said, "God bless my mother; all that I am or ever hope to be I owe to her."[12] The theme of debts owed to family also ran through the words Lincoln spoke to troops summoned to make great sacrifices for their country. "There is involved in this struggle," he stressed, "the question whether your children and my children shall enjoy the privileges we have enjoyed." "We should," he urged, "perpetuate for our children's children this great and free government."[13] The same commitment to family which could motivate men to acts of self-sacrifice for their country could also impel them to selfless vigor against an institution which the Great Emancipator hated for the way it "separated [men] forever from...their fathers and mothers, and brothers and sisters, and many of them, from their wives and children."[14]

Even in the far less articulate and less acclaimed American patriot Dwight Eisenhower we may see the importance of the family in fostering selfless valor. Eisenhower's biographer Kenneth S. Davis traces the "selfless integrity" which carried Eisenhower to victory against the Nazis to the "moral tenets" which he acquired from the "happy stable family" of his boyhood. "Of a healthy society the family is not only a portrait in miniature," writes Davis, "it is also the vessel...through which the roots of the living culture can draw nour-

ishment from a warmly human past. Out of it grow the human values which are the substance of social justice, the very essence of
democracy: the values of tolerance, sympathetic understanding, self-
discipline, and self-sacrifice in the common good."[15] America's
dependence upon the family as the institution which can best culti-
vate such values is particularly acute because of our political tradition separating Church and State (a tradition taken to secularist ex-
tremes in recent decades). If the family does not instill this vital set
of values, no other American institution can serve as an adequate
substitute.

Since the transmission of internalized moral values–including selfless patriotism–depends heavily upon mothers and families, the nation risks a rupture in civic culture whenever society changes in
ways that deprive children of maternal care in an intact family. We
should therefore attend with particular concern to the findings of a
1988 study of day care which discovered that while mothers try to
teach their children obedience, paid day-care workers seek to make
children focus on their own desires while acting independently. The
authors of the study consequently warn that day care "may be alter-
ing a social pattern characterized by a willingness to sacrifice one's
needs to those of the family."[16] Perhaps it was with such findings in
view that the prominent child psychologist Jay Belsky conjectured
that day care may be preparing children for a future in which "everyone is out for himself."[17]

Strangely, despite the nation's need for citizens willing to make
selfless sacrifices, the federal government has in recent decades sub-
sidized non-family, non-maternal child care at the expense of higher
taxes for traditional one-earner families who care for their children
at home. Worse, tax subsidies for day care count as only one of the
ways government has subverted family life in recent decades.

The federal government indirectly weakened family life in a se-
ries of post-war decisions which made it very hard for families to
perpetuate the agricultural way of life which had for generations
reinforced generational and marital ties. As historian Allan Carlson
has written, the government turned against "farm families on farms
[considered] too small or too unproductive or both." "Federal policy
was reshaped, often in subtle ways," Carlson observes, "to encourage the consolidation of these farms into larger units and the movement of the 'surplus' agrarian population into other jobs."[18] With the
near disappearance of the family farm, parents–no longer working

with each other and alongside their children in home, barn, or field–
lost priceless opportunities to shape their children's moral attitudes. But the State also lost something vital to its health. It is the
"intimate connection between family feeling and preservation of
the land" which Tocqueville has in view when he asserts: "Where
family feeling is at an end, personal selfishness turns again to its real
inclinations. As the family is felt to be a vague, indeterminate, uncertain conception, each man concentrates on his immediate convenience."[19]

But federal policies not only drove families off the farm, but they
also made it harder for fathers to earn enough in urban employment
to support a home in which his wife could stay home to care for their
children. As Carlson has shown, a shift in federal policy away from
"women's home-centeredness" helped destroy the "complex sexual
division of labor" which had created "the Western family wage,"
which had previously sustained one-earner families with homemaking mothers.[20] Reflecting such policy shifts, the percentage of young
men ages twenty to twenty-four who earned enough to keep a family of three out of poverty–above 60 percent as late as the 1970s–
fell to 40 percent by the mid-1980s.[21]

Family life sustained a more direct blow from the government in
1973 when the Supreme Court, with only the flimsiest pretense to
constitutional logic, struck down the anti-abortion statutes of all fifty
states with subsequent rulings denying parents of unmarried daughters and husbands of wives any legal standing in an abortion decision. Similarly dubious jurisprudence gave unmarried women legal
access to the Pill. Government policy thus helped heat up the sexual
revolution and destroy the sexual self-restraint essential to family
life. It has also increased illegitimacy by fostering the perception
that women alone bear responsibility for pregnancy and childbearing decisions. Hence, researcher Janet L. Yeller and her colleagues
conclude that legalized abortion and contraception have helped drive
up the illegitimacy rate (surprising many who anticipated the opposite effect) because "the technological shock of abortion and female
contraception" effected "changes in sexual and marital customs."
Specifically, abortion and contraception made young women far more
willing to "participate in uncommitted premarital sex," while making young men far more loathe to accept responsibility for "women
who passed up available contraception and abortion options." So
emerged a new social world in which "men who wanted sexual ac-

tivity, but did not want to promise marriage in case of pregnancy, were [no longer]...expected or required to do so."[22]

But while government policy was undermining wedlock, it was also making it less economically necessary for women and children who increasingly relied for their support on a welfare state which grew dramatically under Lyndon Johnson's Great Society initiative.[23] Pushing down marriage rates and pushing up illegitimacy rates, welfare largesse created what sociologists Randal Day and Wade C. Mackey have called "the mother-state-child family." Because of the proliferation of this family form, Day and Mackey assert that married fathers must now "pay directly for their own children, and, in addition, must pay a heavy tax burden to support the state, as the state takes the role of the supportive 'traditional father'" to the children of unwed and divorced mothers.[24]

Even if defenders of the welfare state deny anti-family motives, sociologist David Popenoe argues that "the inherent character of the welfare state by its very existence help[s] to undermine family values or familism–the belief in a strong sense of family identification and loyalty, mutual assistance among family members and a concern for the perpetuation of the family unit."[25] And though much ballyhooed as an improvement, the reform of the 1990s may actually have made the welfare system more subversive of the family. For while the Great Society welfare system fostered fatherless families, the new post-reform welfare system has created parentless families by forcing unwed mothers into low-paying employment while putting their young children into tax-subsidized day care.[26] But then, tax subsidy of day care for welfare mothers constitutes part of a much larger government commitment to push mothers–married and unmarried–into paid employment, a commitment manifest in ever-more-ambitious programs for federalizing day-care costs.[27] Because of its commitment to a "fully mobilized workforce"–male and female–the federal government has focused (in the words of two critical analysts) "less on what is best for the parent-child relationship than it does on what is best for the labor force. To the degree, for example, that the mother-child relationship conflicts with the mother-job relationship, the mother-job relationship is almost always treated as primary."[28]

Government efforts to keep women linked to employers contrast sharply with government indifference to the dissolution of their unions to their husbands. In truth, since the enactment of no-fault divorce laws, the government has actually made itself the ally of the disloyal spouse who wants to break the marriage vow. As attorney Steven L. Varnis points out, "The law [under no-fault] generally supports the spouse seeking divorce, even if that spouse was a wrongdoer, by granting divorces with little regard for a spouse who may not want it."[29]

Nor is the State's moral obtuseness in family matters limited to the divorce court, an institution many Americans still manage to avoid. For although many teachers and administrators still believe in the family and the moral principles which sustain it, enemies of the family have made astonishing strides in gaining control over what is taught in the public school, a government institution much harder to avoid than the divorce court. In the opinion of education critic Edward Wynne, the public schools have stopped teaching moral principles supportive of the family and have even become "indifferent or hostile to such efforts."[30] This indifference to a family-nurturing morality may be glimpsed in social-science textbooks giving "no explicit, objective definition of family," but instead "vague and inaccurate" notions such as the idea that "a family is a group of people" or "a family is defined as 'the people you live with.'"[31] Stanford scholar Kingsley Davis goes so far as to speak critically of "the school system, one of the main functions of which appears to be to alienate offspring from their parents."[32] Certainly, since the enactment of Title IX in 1972, many public educators have been working overtime to separate young people from any traditional gender roles their parents may have tried to teach.

The 'No Sacrifice' Soldier and Sailor

Given that the public schools once helped the family to inculcate chastity, fidelity, and filial devotion, many Americans must regard their current indifference and hostility to the family as a stunning reversal. But an even more astonishing reversal has occurred in the American military, an institution which until recently honored the family as the wellspring of loyalties which inspired soldiers' highest martial and patriotic aspirations. American soldiers fought not only to protect their public institutions, but also—and often more importantly—their wives, their children, their sisters, and their parents. Thus, sacrifices made for the military were a natural extension of family responsibilities.

But by the late twentieth century, the military had largely given up on asking soldiers for sacrifice. No longer were soldiers being summoned to enlist because of national need ("Uncle Sam Needs You"), but instead were being promised excellent career training ("Be All You Can Be!"). But then, appeals to naked self-interest were not working very well in attracting recruits before 9/11 and the invasions of Afghanistan and Iraq and became even less effective thereafter. However the old-fashioned appeals to a family-instilled sense of sacrifice hardly made sense in looking for recruits for the new military feminist social engineers created during the final decades of the twentieth century. These social engineers so fully captured the military that a family-instilled willingness to sacrifice seemed as out of place in the ranks as a single-shot musket.

Any doubt as to the triumph of anti-family ideology in the military was dispelled in 1994 when a Navy commander was relieved of his duties and twice recommended for dismissal when he resisted policies putting women into his combat unit. The officer in question explained that his reading of the Bible taught him that it was a man's responsibility "to protect and provide for the family" and that "part of that is you don't subject women to violence." The Chief of Naval Operations did finally reject the repeated recommendations that this pilot be dismissed for "substandard performance of duty based upon failure to demonstrate acceptable qualities of leadership." After all, the officer's "record of service and performance was impeccable." But it was universally understood that this man could never again hope for career advancement within the military.[33] Once a critical inducement to military ardor, a desire to protect wives and daughters from violence now disqualifies a man from military leadership.

No wonder, then, that even before casualties in Iraq sent re-enlistment rates plummeting, the military found itself demoralized and paralyzed by sex scandals and gender tensions. Military leaders could scarcely worry about inspiring patriotism while trying to make male soldiers less sexually aggressive in the gender-integrated ranks. And it was not patriotism but confusion they sowed when these same leaders also tried (as they continue to do) to teach male soldiers not to attempt potentially dangerous measures to protect female comrades from rape or other sexual abuse at the hands of enemy soldiers. "It is impossible to believe," hazards jurist Robert Bork, "that both efforts can succeed simultaneously."[34]

But then, most young men are now avoiding both aspects of the military's schizophrenic gender-role training by simply opting out of the new feminized armed services. By the late Nineties, military officials were admitting that recruiting difficulties had become "the worst they'[d] seen since the mid-1970s when Americans were grappling with the aftermath of the Vietnam War." The perils of potential service in Afghanistan and Iraq have only exacerbated these recruiting challenges. Gone are the "young men low on money but high on a sense of adventure and patriotism"; young men are simply "spurning the military for other options." Conceded one top recruiter, "This is as serious as any recruiting shortfall we've since the end of the draft.[35] "The waning allure of a military career for young men," explained Wesley Pruden, could at least in part be traced to the ascendance of feminist ideology: "When young men are told that fighting wars–killing people and breaking things for their country's sake–is something that women can do as well as men, a lot of young men who would otherwise be drawn to a warrior career will say 'to hell with it.' Army recruiters have to make up the slack with more women, which further changes the culture, which further repels young men, which requires recruiting more women, which...."[36] Though military officers fear career-destroying discipline for speaking out on the issue, more and more evidence substantiates Bork's judgment that "feminist ideology is inflicting enormous damage on the readiness and fighting capability of the armed forces," auguring a day when "engagements are lost, or won at unacceptably high costs."[37]

But Americans need not wait for a future war against a foe wielding weapons more potent than car bombs to see many of the wounds that the national retreat from family life has inflicted on the body politic. Deprived of the moral impulses which only a strong family life can instill, many Americans now lack the minimal degree of selflessness to give community service, to work for a political or civic organization, or even to obey the law. What psychologist David Myers calls "the triumph of individualism" has meant a sharp decline in community participation, evident in lower rates of involvement in scouting, the Red Cross, the PTA, and the Jaycees. It has also meant falling attendance at public meetings on town or school issues, declining involvement with political parties, reduced willingness to hold or run for public office or even to vote. Opinion surveys find public trust at historic lows while political cynicism now runs very high.[38] To try to reverse this decline in public-spiritedness, the Clinton Administration launched the AmeriCorps national service program, seeking to enlist young volunteers to work in schools, parks, or auxiliary police at minimum wage (with $5,000 in student loans forgiven). But from the outset, critics were dubious that many young people would respond, and they warned that "a failed national service plan [would] be worse...than nothing."[39]

Meanwhile, although politicians tried to make much of the declines in violent crime in the 1990s, violent crime never dipped below levels four times higher than those seen in the early 1960s. Violent crime remained (in the words of one criminologist) "still off the charts and... at an unacceptable level."[40] "The crime statistics should have been falling," stressed historian David T. Courtwright in 1996, who pointed to the predictable demographic effects of the baby bust of the 1970s. Despite this birth dearth, juvenile violent-crime arrests more than tripled between 1965 and 1990, and the declines during the Nineties still left juvenile crime and violence at "unprecedented levels."[41] Even during the period of modest national declines in crime rates, youth violence and homicide continued to climb in some large cities, including Washington and Philadelphia.[42]

Other evidence of the unraveling of the civic culture has received less media attention, but should alarm us nonetheless: revenue authorities have reported that "tax cheating is on the rise," with tax evasion now costing the federal government at least $80 billion annually.[43] Nor can government officials hope to see greater honesty and compliance in paying taxes among the next generation of taxpayers since school officials are now seeing an "erosion of conscience at every level of education," manifest in an unprecedented epidemic of cheating and "deceits [which] devalue learning."[44]

The temptation to cheat in paying taxes has naturally grown stronger as anti-family policies have increased the tax burden. As Oxford philosopher Basil Mitchell has pointed out, government policies which ignore or attack the family must invariably "weaken the moral ties which bind society together." The result is then "an increasingly heavy burden upon the State apparatus. The process is cumulative—the greater the number of marriage breakdowns, the greater the number of one-parent families in need of support; the greater the number of sexual relationships in which no definite responsibilities are assumed; the greater the insecurity of any children born to them; while in turn, the official acceptance of such relationships, combined with an emphasis on the needs of children as the sole consideration tends inevitably to diminish the standing of marriage...So there are more casualties for the State to rescue, and the more single-mindedly it concentrates on this task, the more unmanageable the task becomes."[45] Citizens consequently witness the sorry spectacle, decried by Jacques Barzun, of "public agencies...disintegrating, working against their best interests, and unable to change."[46]

In view of the terrible social and civic chaos produced by family decay, Americans may well wonder just what judicial theorists and political leaders (Republican and Democratic alike) have been thinking in recent decades as they have turned against the family. Have they intended to plague the country with crime, dishonesty, bureaucratic overload, and civic apathy? Probably not. But for at least three decades, many of America's political elite have succumbed to a very old utopian illusion: the belief that the State's power to perfect society can be enhanced by weakening or destroying the family as a competing seat of authority and governance. From Plato to Bellamy, utopians have supposed that once loyalty to family has been vanquished, perfect loyalty to the State will be possible. The seventeenth-century utopian Thomas Campanella, for instance, confidently asserted that once the family is destroyed, "there remains only love for the State."[47] Undivided love for the State will at last enable utopians—including New Left and feminist activists—to effect social changes long prevented by competing loyalties to parents, children, and spouse.[48]

But allowing the State to cannibalize the family has not recommended itself as prudent strategy to all political theorists. The sixteenth-century philosopher Jean Bodin, in fact, poured scorn on the utopian notion that an ideal regime would have no need for nongovernmental associations, among which the family has always come first. "The societies of men," he reminded his utopian adversaries, "...have sprung from the love which was betwixt man and wife: from them have flowed the mutual love betwixt parents and their children; then the love of brothers and sisters toward one another; and after them the friendship between cousins and other kinsmen; and last of all the love and good will which is betwixt men joined in alliance." It is foolishness, he cautioned, to suppose "that a commonweale can be maintained and upholden without love and amity, without which the world itself cannot long stand."[49] Far more recently, Ohio State ethicist Andrew Oldenquist has stressed that "the family is our most ancient society" and that the larger society very much needs "the different species of love that bind families together." The love and loyalty which inspire us to "work and sacrifice for our families," he argues, help cement "a moral community." Thus, "small tribes are beautiful" because they provide "the emotional foundation of our capacity to feel a larger national loyalty."[50]

Family Decline…Civic Disorder

But quite aside from the theorizing, we have ample empirical evidence—discussed briefly in chapter 1—indicating that civic order suffers when families decline. Sociologist Robert Sampson reports, for example, that a high divorce rate is a strong predictor not only of a high crime rate, but also of "low rates of participation in community politics, recreation (e.g., YMCA), and educational activities...Married persons are likelier to participate in formal organizations than are divorced and unmarried people."[51] One reason that divorce drives down civic participation surfaces in another study revealing that "adolescents from broken homes are more likely to show a high level of distrust of other people" than are peers from intact families.[52]

The folly of anti-family utopianism appears more evident with every passing year. For it is not selfless public spiritedness that manifests itself when the family disintegrates; rather, it is cynicism and opportunism. Just as Tocqueville warned, Americans turn away from the demands of public life to pursue "immediate convenience" when "family feeling" becomes an "indeterminate, uncertain conception."

True, any number of opportunistic politicians—Republican and Democratic—have advanced their own careers by currying favor with environmentalists, feminists, senior citizens, and profiteering corporations and other groups pushing agendas harmful to the family. True, too, recent surveys do indicate that millions of young Americans who no longer have strong family ties have "shift[ed] allegiance increasingly to themselves and to the State."[53] But because these young citizens have never learned the moral selflessness which the family instills, their allegiance to the State is very fickle, vanishing whenever it conflicts with self-interest. Deprived of the civic nurturance of the family, atomized citizens cling to the State simply to extract benefits, not to offer the services of selfless patriotism.

Anti-family activists may bring a burst of energy to public life (of the sort Americans have seen among the homosexual zealots whose support some politicians have all too willingly sought).[54] But the long-term effect of this activism is always civic malaise, not health.

At a time when "activist" counts as a term of praise in most media commentary while "patriot" connotes xenophobia and violence, we ought to keep in mind research showing that the activists of the 1960s have had a decidedly elevated divorce rate.[55] Since we know that crime and cynicism go up and civic involvement goes down in divorce-prone communities, what kind of national future can such activists give America?

Inevitably, political movements borne of self-assertion produce citizens who regard the government as a benefits-machine which exists to fill their individual needs (even at the expense of other citizens). They do not view the government (as Americans traditionally have) as the authorized defender of families, which–being more important than the individual–can require the individual to make sacrifices for the common good. The American family may teach Americans to echo the words of Nathan Hale; the special-interest group never will. The political agendas of the National Organization for Women, of the American Association of Retired Persons, and of the National Chamber of Commerce reveal much about what such groups expect to receive from their country; they are quite silent about the sacrifices they are prepared to make on its behalf.[56] Indeed, the kind of self-centeredness encouraged by such movements will in the long run consume not only the family and the country but finally the movements themselves. It should have come as no surprise, for example, to hear prominent commentators lamenting in recent years that feminism was "falling victim to individualism" as "independent-minded women ensconced on the fast track to fame and fortune" refused to make sacrifices for the sake of other women.[57]

Of course, millions of strong American families have survived the transformation of the American government into a benefits-machine serving special-interest groups. But many of these families now regard their government with far greater suspicion than strong families did in the past and manifest far less willingness to make sacrifices on its behalf. Because (in the words of one traditionalist scholar) "opponents of liberal doctrines are increasingly treated as outlaws,"[58] many American citizens with strong family commitments feel profoundly alienated from their government. Millions have quietly withdrawn their willingness to sacrifice for a government they now regard as subversive of their moral principles.

Many enemies of the family have congratulated themselves on their remarkable success in reducing the political influence of its defenders.[59] Perhaps they should have been reflecting more seriously on the dismal experience of the ideologues who waged war against the family in the former Soviet Union. As the historians Becky Glass and Margaret Stolee point out, the founders of the Soviet Empire made an assault on the family central to their effort to erect a communist utopia. They thus enacted new family codes providing for "collectivized upbringing of children," legitimating "broad definitions of what constituted a family," facilitating easy divorce, abolishing the distinction between legitimate and illegitimate birth, enforcing child support, and giving women greater economic rights in marriage. Contrary to the ideologues' expectations, these laws created not a healthier and stronger country, but rather "social and internal confusion." The relevance of the Soviet ideologues' failure should be obvious to anyone who has recognized with Glass and Stolee that "many of the provisions in the earliest Soviet family law codes are the same issues . . . currently being discussed by [American] legal professionals, family scholars, and legislators."[60]

A Tottering Political Culture

The social and internal confusion caused by anti-family policies may not disturb America's leaders during periods of peace and prosperity. But recent difficulties in military recruiting portend a true crisis in times of deep national distress—and only those hopelessly ignorant of history can suppose that such times will not come. The nation's anti-family politics have produced millions of deracinated Americans totally incapable of selfless sacrifice. Their loyalty to America will last only as long as the stream of government benefits continues. On the other hand, among those Americans whose strong family ties still give them the power to make selfless sacrifice, many now feel profoundly estranged from a government which has waged undeclared war against the family for more than three decades. Who then will step forward in, say, 2020, to risk life and fortune for a beleaguered America?

Fortunately, the civic and political consequences of anti-family policies are attracting the attention not only of traditionalists, but also of many liberal statists who are belatedly realizing that in destroying the family, they have also been unintentionally destroying the State. Thus, many neo-liberal statists have banded together in a coalition calling itself the Communitarian Movement, led by former President Carter's domestic policy advisor, Amitai Etzioni. "Our political culture is in very bad shape," one of Etzioni's lieutenants has conceded, ". . . [W]e have not attended to what citizenship is all about. As long as we allow people to refer to themselves as 'taxpayers' and to think that their relationship to government is they pay the bills and get the service, then alienation will steadily get worse." As part of their effort to "heal a sick political culture" by contracting Americans' bloated sense of entitlements, communitarians have finally started challenging a regime of "easy divorce," while "encouraging families to stay together."[61]

To be sure, communitarians have very far to go in rolling back decades of anti-family governance. Nor should anyone underestimate the difficulty of effecting a true reversal in the government's posture toward the family, especially since the political background of most communitarians makes it very difficult for them to speak candidly about radical feminism or the welfare state. Real candor on such topics is essential, however, if communitarians are sincere about healing a political culture infected by anti-family pathogens. If the communitarians cannot help cure the contagion, then America may find very few defenders when the next crisis arises. But if communitarians can join with other Americans in restoring to national governance a commitment to defending the family, then America's next great trial will bring forth an army of patriots willing to make sacrifices on her behalf.

Notes

1.   David Brooks, "Politics and Patriotism: From Teddy Roosevelt to John McCain," *Weekly Standard* 26 April 1999: 16.
2.   Cynthia Crossen, "Patriotism Warms Americans' Hearts," *Wall Street Journal* 28 June 1998: 2A.
3.   Quoted in Brooks, op. cit.
4.   Scott McLean, "Land That I Love: Feelings Toward Country at Century's End," *Public Perspective* April 1999: 21.
5.   Jehan Sadat, "Preservation of Family Is Promotion of Peace," World Congress of Families II, Geneva, 16 November 1999, http://worldcongress.org/gen99_speakers/gen99_sadat.htm
6.   Owen Flanigan and Kathryn Jackson, "Justice, Care, and Gender: the Kohlberg-Gilligan Debate Revisited," *Ethics* 97(1997): 630.
7.   Marjorie A. Pett et al., "Paths of Influence of Divorce on Preschool Children's Psychosocial Adjustment," *Journal of Family Psychology* 13(1999): 145-164.
8.   Jeanne M. Hilton and Ester L. Devall, "Comparison of Parenting and Children's Behavior in Single-Mother, Single-Father, and Intact Families," *Journal of Divorce & Remarriage* 29.3/4 (1998): 23-50.
9.   Cicero, *De Legibus.*
10.   George Washington, Farewell Address, 19 Sept. 1796,www.virginia.edu/gwpapers/farewell/ fwatran.htm.

11. Quoted in Harrison Clark, *All Cloudless Glory: The Life of George Washington* (Washington, DC: Regnery, 1995), 1: 9.
12. Quoted in Carl Sandburg, *Abraham Lincoln*, one-volume ed. (New York: Harcourt, Brace, 1954), 111.
13. Lincoln, *Speeches to the One Hundred Sixty-fourth and One Hundred Sixty-sixth Ohio Regiments*, 18 August 1864, www.hetins.net/showcase/creative/lincoln/speeches/ohio.htm.
14. Lincoln, Letter to Mary Speed, 27 September 1841, *Abraham Lincoln: His Speeches and Writings*, ed. Roy P. Basker (Cleveland, OH: World, 1946), 121.
15. Kenneth S. Davis, *Soldier of Democracy: A Biography of Dwight Eisenhower* (Garden City, NY: Doubleday, 1945), 46, 472.
16. Susan D. Holloway, Kathleen S. Gorman, and Bruce Fuller, "Child-Rearing Beliefs Within Diverse Social Structures," *International Journal of Psychology* 23 (1988): 303-317.
17. Belsky remark at a consultation on "The Risks of Day Care," sponsored by The Rockford Institute, 6 December 1988.
18. Allan C. Carlson, Family Questions: Reflections on the American Social Crisis (New Brunswick, NJ: Transaction Publishers, 1988), 162-163.
19. Alexis de Tocqueville, *Democracy in America* (1848), trans. George Lawrence, ed. J.P. Mayer (New York: Harper & Row, 1969), 53.
20. Carlson, op. cit., 111-113.
21. Associated Press, "Young Men's Earnings Fall by Nearly One-Third," *Rockford Register Star*, 12 June 1987: 6A.
22. George A. Akerlof, Janet L. Yeller, and Michael L. Katz, "An Analysis of Out-of-Wedlock Childbearing in the United States," *Quarterly Journal of Economics* 111 (1996): 277-317.
23. Cf. Irwin Unger, *The Best of Intentions: The Triumph and Failure of the Great Society Under Kennedy, Johnson, and Nixon* (New York: Doubleday, 1996), 256-258.
24. Randall D. Day and Wade C. Mackey, "Children as Resources: A Cultural Analysis," *Family Perspective* 20 (1986): 258-262.
25. David Popenoe, *Disturbing the Nest: Family Change and Decline in Modern Societies* (New York: Aldine de Gruyter, 1988), 72.
26. Cf. Mary Baker and Elaine Fersh, "A Welfare Reform Necessity: More and Better Child Care," *Boston Globe* 29 July 1998: A19.
27. Cf. L. Feldman, "Clinton's $21 Billion Day-Care Gambit," *Christian Science Monitor* 8 Jan. 1998: 1.
28. Barbara D. Whitehead and David Blankenhorn, "Man, Woman, and Public Policy," An Institute for American Values Working Paper, Publication No. WP3, Feb. 1991.
29. Steven L. Varnis, "Broken Vows, Therapeutic Sentiments, Legal Sanctions," *Society* Nov.-Dec. 1997: 32.
30. Edward A. Wynne, "The Great Tradition in Education: Transmitting Moral Values," *Educational Leadership* Dec. '85/ Jan. '86: 8.
31. Cf. Paul Vitz, *Censorship: Evidence of Bias in Our Children's Textbooks* (Ann Arbor, MI: Servant, 1986), 37-38.
32. Kingsley Davis, "Population Policy and the Theory of Reproductive Motivation," *Economic Development and Cultural Change*, 25 Supp.(1987): 176.
33. Cf. Eric Schmitt, "Officer Who Wouldn't Fly With Women in Combat Is Retained," *New York Times* 20 Aug. '95: 23.
34. Robert H. Bork, *Slouching Toward Gomorrah: Modern Liberalism and American Decline* (New York: Regan Books, 1997), 223, emphasis added.

35.   Cf. Judy Jones, "Military Loses Ground in Mountain Recruiting," *The Courier-Journal* 4 April 1999: 1A; see also Mark Mueller, "Armed Services Recruiting Misses the Target," *Boston Herald* 24 Oct., 1999: 12; Frank James, "Military Recruiters Find Reluctance Over Combat Hinders Duty," *Knight Ridder Tribune News Service* 10 Jan. 2005: 1.

36.   Wesley Pruden, "No Jiggling, Please, We're Very Military," *Washington Times* 19 November 1999: A4.

37.   Bork, op. cit., 223.

38.   David G. Myers, *The American Paradox: Spiritual Hunger in an Age of Plenty* (New Haven, CT: Yale University, 2000), 175-180.

39.   Cf. United Press International, "The President's Summit Concludes," 29 April 1997, BC Cycle; see also Michael S. McPherson and Morton O. Schapiro, "What Price Patriotism?" *New York Times* 3 June 1993: 23A.

40.   Cf. Timothy W. Maier and Michael Rust, "A Decline in Crime?" *Insight* 27 April 1998: 8.

41.   David T. Courtwright, *Violent Land: Single Men and Social Disorder from the Frontier to the Inner City* (Cambridge, MA: Harvard University, 1996), 275.

42.   Cf. John J. Dilulio, Jr., "How to Deal with the Youth Crime Wave," *Weekly Standard* 16 September 1996: 30.

43.   Cf. David C. Johnston, "The Old Tax Dodge," *The New York Times* 15 April 1998: D1; cf. also Larry Van Dyne, "Tax Games People Play," *Washingtonian* April 1997: 74.

44.   Cf. Carolyn Kleiner, "The Cheating Game," *U.S. News & World Report* 22 Nov. 1999: 55.

45.   Cf. Basil Mitchell, *Why Public Policy Cannot Be Morally Neutral: The Current Confusion About Pluralism,* The Social Affairs Unit, 1989.

46.   Jacques Barzun, *From Dawn to Decadence: 500 Years of Western Cultural Life* (New York: HarperCollins, 2000), 783.

47.   Thomas Campanella, *City of the Sun*, trans. Thomas Halliday, in Ideal Commonwealths, rev. ed. (Port Washington: Kennikat, 1968), 147-156.

48.   Bryce Christensen, *Utopia Against the Family: The Problems and Politics of the American Family* (San Francisco, CA: Ignatius, 1990), 4.

49.   Quoted in Robert Nisbet, *The Quest for Community: A Study in the Ethics of Order & Freedom* (1953; rpt. San Francisco, CA: ICS, 1990), 114.

50.   Andrew Oldenquist, *The Non-Suicidal Society* (Bloomington: Indiana University, 1986), 120, 139, 196.

51.   Robert J. Sampson, "Crime in Cities: The Effects of Formal and Informal Social Control," in *Communities and Crime*, eds. Albert J. Reiss Jr. and Michael Tonry, Vol. 8 in Crime and Justice, eds. Michael Tonry and Norvel Morris (Chicago: University of Chicago, 1987), 271-307.

52.   Cf. Christina Giuliani et al., "Peer-Group and Romantic Relationships in Adolescents from Intact and Separated Families," *Contemporary Family Therapy* 20 (1998): 93-106.

53.   Cf. Paul C. Glick, "The Family Life Cycle and Social Change," *Family Relations* 38(1989): 123-189.

54.   Cf. William Goldshlag, "Gore Gets Nod From Gay Group, Backs Benefits," *Daily News* (New York) 17 Feb. 2000: 28.

55.   Doug McAdam, "The Biographical Consequences of Activism," *American Sociological Review* 54 (1989): 744-760.

56.   Cf. "NOW's Political Agenda" (Editorial), Boston Herald 24 April 1998: 28; see also "A Matter of Fairness. AARP's Agenda" (Editorial), *Union Leader* 29 June 1995; see also Jeffrey H. Birnbaum, "A Quiet Revolution in Business

Lobbying. Chamber of Commerce Helps Bush Agenda," *Washington Post* 5 Feb. 2005: A1.

57.   Cf. Pat Swift, "Is Feminism Falling Victim to Individualism?" *Buffalo News* 10 June 1995: 7C.

58.   Cf. George A. Panichas, *Growing Wings to Overcome Gravity: Criticism as the Pursuit of Virtue* (Macon, GA: Mercer University, 1999), 37.

59.   Cf. Ronald Dworkin, *Sovereign Virtue: The Theory and the Practice of Equality* (Cambridge, MA: Harvard University, 2000), 462-469.

60.   Cf. Becky L. Glass and Margaret K. Stolee, "Family Law in Soviet Russia 1917-1945," *Journal of Marriage and the Family* 49(1987): 893-901.

61.   See Rob Gurwitt, "Communitarianism: You Can Try It At Home," *Governing Magazine*, August 1993.

8

A New "Fable of the Bees": America's Family-Failure Economy

Unhealthy family life makes it hard for Army recruiters to earn a living, especially in wartime. But such social unhealthiness actually opens new economic opportunities for certain groups. To understand why this it is so, Americans might consider the economic effects of ordinary physical illness.

Illness puts money in the pockets of doctors and other health-care providers. Everyone understands this, and few object. After all, most physicians bring to their fight against disease an admirable professionalism that puts the health of their patients far ahead of their own desire for income. But only the naïve would suppose that financial incentives never cause medical professionals to commit medical fraud, to recommend unnecessary surgeries, or to return dubious diagnoses.

Indeed, a disturbing body of evidence implicates an enterprising but unethical minority of health professionals in the dubious practice of "disease mongering." "Disease mongering," as one investigator has explained, can take many forms—including unnecessary surgery and overly aggressive treatment—but it always amounts to "a strategy employed by the health care industry in exploiting patients to maximize profits."[1] For instance, pharmaceutical advertising often persuades those with minor or vague symptoms to purchase unnecessary medicines, so stretching "the boundaries of treatable illness ... to extend the markets for new medical products." These disease-mongers work at "making healthy people feel sick" even as they promote costly new cures for their "sponsored" illness.[2]

For good reason, leading medical authorities have criticized colleagues for resorting to propagandists' ruses in "selling sickness." Some medical professionals, these critics allege, form "informal alliances" with others who share their economic interests and then "target the news media with stories designed to create fears about [some] condition or disease and draw attention to the latest treatment." Media manipulation of this sort often involves the use of "disease prevalence estimates framed to maximize the size of a medical problem" and may include a "medical education plan" that amounts to no more than camouflaged "marketing strategy."[3]

More alarming yet is the disease mongering that takes place when health-care professionals take in huge sums by subjecting patients to invasive procedures not warranted by any real medical condition. One cardiac-surgery unit in California, for instance, was implicated in 2003 with having raked in over $90 million by performing hundreds of unnecessary open-heart surgeries.[4] Similarly, in 2001, authorities in New York investigated doctors accused of performing "needless and inappropriate prostate surgery for mentally ill patients" subjected to "assembly line" procedures.[5]

Sensational circumstances made the California and New York cases headline news, but medical analysts suspect that physicians actually perform hundreds of thousands of unnecessary surgeries every year outside of media scrutiny. One study of myringotomies (insertions in the ear of tiny tubes to prevent infections) concluded that "well over half" of such operations were performed for "equivocal or inappropriate reasons"—including "desire for profits."[6] Even more disturbing was a 2003 study finding that in 75 percent of the 600,000 hysterectomies performed each year, this highly invasive procedure has been "inappropriately recommended." Further analysis suggests that the physicians making such inappropriate recommendations are responding to a payment schedule that financially discourages "less invasive methods to treat female pain and bleeding" and "encourages jumping to hysterectomy because it will pay more."[7]

Profiting from Disease

Given that disease-mongers sometimes use the media to persuade the insecure and gullible to view "personal problems as medical," it is hardly surprising that many patients actively seek out inappropriate medical procedures.[8] However, while ethical health professionals help these misguided patients understand why they should not undergo the sought-for treatment, medical profiteers do not. Such profiteering may indeed be discerned behind the reports of thousands of cases of unnecessary and potentially dangerous plastic surgery, usually performed on affluent urban women suffering from "a body image disorder" not cured with a scalpel.[9] Sufferers from the man-made disease of obesity likewise turn their personal problems into opportunities for medical profiteering when they resort to the surgeon: experts estimate that five million Americans are likely to have their stomach "surgically altered so as to keep food from being digested." Surgeons who perform such operations report "long waiting lists."[10]

Disease mongering not only fills Americans with misguided hopes and shrouds them in ill-founded fears, but it also imposes tremendous financial costs. In the mid-nineties, when the nation's total annual health care bill was already approaching a trillion dollars ($400 billion of it paid by the taxpayer), the RAND corporation concluded that fully "one-fourth to one-third of medical care is unwarranted or of debatable value."[11]

The fraud and malpractice in the health-care industry should not blind Americans to the high quality of care that health-care professionals usually render. However, the documented and widely publicized abuses should remind Americans of the temptations likely to emerge in any situation in which one man's illness swells another man's income. And these temptations frequently show up far from the hospital and doctor's office.

Does the profitability of pathology explain, for instance, why the United States now has the highest incarceration rate and the costliest prison system in the world? Many observers wonder.

Though much of the criticism of what has been dubbed the "Prison-Industrial Complex" has come from American leftists, all Americans have good reason to ask why in 2000 the prison industry was the second-fastest growing industry in the country (trailing only the gambling industry in its growth rate). Why does a country inhabited by only 5 percent of the globe's population account for fully 25 percent of the world's prisoners?[12]

Something does indeed seem askew in a country that in the nineties spent an average of $7 billion a year in building prisons and that by 2000 employed 523,000 of its citizens in building, guarding, or otherwise serving the prisons that have now become the compulsory home of more than two million inmates.[13]

To be sure, the nation's critics of the Prison-Industrial Complex too often ignore the real social perils let loose by the cultural firestorm of the sixties. Still, just like the critics of medical disease mongering, the critics of the Prison-Industrial Complex raise legitimate questions about the profits derived from social illness.

By characterizing the nation's correctional system as "the Prison-Industrial Complex," critics have identified a starting point for questions, for this characterization purposefully echoes President Dwight D. Eisenhower's famous 1961 remarks about a "conjunction of an immense military establishment and a large arms industry" which was then "new in the American experience." Because this conjunction posed the risk of a "disastrous rise of misplaced power," Eisenhower urged Americans to "guard against the acquisition of unwarranted influence, whether sought or unsought by the military-industrial complex."[14] Eisenhower issued this warning at a time when defense contractors and their military, congressional, and media allies were fanning public fears of a "missile gap" supposedly giving the Soviet Union a perilous advantage over the Untied States. But Eisenhower knew from intelligence reports that no such gap existed and that those fostering groundless fears about it were simply trying to win profits or career advancement from an unnecessary enlargement of the military-industrial complex.[15] In other words, Eisenhower saw professionals tied to the military engaging in the same kinds of dubious tactics deployed by disease-mongering professionals in the health-care industry: both groups seeking to justify costly (and profitable) responses to an exaggerated threat.

Critics of the nation's Prison-Industrial Complex invoke Eisenhower's cautionary analysis to buttress their own assertions that "the lure of big money is corrupting the nation's criminal-justice system."[16] Like Eisenhower, such critics limn a problematic "conjunction" of political and economic interests and a real danger of "misplaced power." These critics view with concern the way small-town mayors have "sought out prisons as economic saviors" and then have grown "anxious to fill the beds of their bars-and-concrete growth strategy."[17] These critics view with particular concern the establishment of 100 for-profit prisons in twenty-seven states.[18] Even defenders of the for-profit prisons acknowledge that many Americans wonder "whether it is seemly to make money from incarcerating fellow citizens."[19] But, of course, correctional system money flows to recipients other than the owners of for-profit prisons. As *Atlantic Monthly* writer Eric Schlosser remarks, "The prison-industrial complex includes some of the nation's largest architecture and construction firms, Wall Street investment banks, and companies that sell everything from security cameras to padded cells available in a vast 'color selection.'"[20]

The smell of leftist ideology hangs over the assertion that "money motivates the United States to keep millions behind bars, regardless of the crimes committed, regardless of the inhumanity, and regardless of the overall damage to entire communities." [21] But the remarkable profitability of a Prison-Industrial Complex now incarcerating a record number of Americans should give pause even to Americans generally resistant to leftist doctrines. After all, if medical professionals—widely (and usually justly) regarded as models of integrity—sometimes allow financial incentives to lead them into inappropriate health-care decisions, how can Americans intelligently suppose that those associated with the nation's correctional system are always immune to the influence of such incentives?

What is more, the Prison-Industrial Complex offers its supporters more than money; it also offers them many non-pecuniary but very real political and career rewards. Thus, critics of the complex see politicians (of both parties) whose electoral success reflects their success in currying favor with constituents who profit from a growing Prison-Industrial Complex and in winning votes from constituents whose fears of crime make them supportive of "tough on crime" legislation. Critics also see many bureaucrats whose "fiefdoms have expanded along with the inmate population."[22] Thus, while one of the more thoughtful critics acknowledges that "the prison-industrial complex is not a conspiracy, guiding criminal-justice policy behind closed doors," he can still plausibly describe it as a troubling "confluence of special interests" sufficiently powerful to give "prison construction in the United Sates a seemingly unstoppable momentum."[23]

Defenders of the Prison-Industrial Complex argue that it was precisely the expansion of this complex in the nineties that pushed crime rates down during that decade. But after an exhaustive review of the data, two leading criminologists have concluded that although it appears to have succeeded in reducing property crime, America's aggressive "incarceration explosion" of the nineties merits no better than "a Gentleman's C" in suppressing violent crime and that "even a D minus" would be "generous" in evaluating its effects on drug use and distribution.[24] Critics of that complex also adduce evidence that its growth has been inordinate by pointing to Canada, which also saw its crime rates fall in the nineties (down by 1998 to their lowest levels since 1969) with almost no expansion in its prison system.[25] Indeed, since imprisonment is widely believed to harden young offenders, American citizens may have realized no more real benefit from an overly aggressive prison-building policy than American patients have realized from the overly aggressive medical practices that have accompanied disease-mongering.

More cynical defenders of the Prison-Industrial Complex might acknowledge that it has grown beyond any bounds defined by the public's legitimate need to control crime, yet insist that such growth has still benefited the nation by stimulating the economy. Particularly in rural areas, some Americans do indeed now regard "a surfeit of prisons" as "integral to [the country's] economy"[26] This kind of thinking echoes in strange ways the 18th-century argument advanced by Bernard Mandeville in *The Fable of the Bees: or Private Vices, Public Benefits* (1714). Arguing that "it would be utterly impossible, either to raise any multitudes into a populous, rich and flourishing nature, or when so raised to keep and maintain them in that condition, without the assistance of what we call evil both natural and moral," Mandeville viewed "vice ... [as] the very wheel that turned ... trade."[27] As a modern Enlightenment scholar has explained, Mandeville believed "it was greed, vanity and amour proper which actually kept the social merry-go-round turning —they provided work and created wealth."[28] "Bare virtue," Mandeville asserted, "can't make nations live in splendor" since "few virtues employ any hands," while "plagues and monsters" provide "livelihood to the vast multitudes."[29]

Mandeville's logic does indeed sound like a justification for the kind of profit-from-pathology social dynamics that have given America a burgeoning Prison-Industrial system. Mandeville truly sounds like an advisor to a small-town, twenty-first-century mayor lobbying for the construction of a prison in his community when he reasons that "private vices by the dexterous management of a skillful politician may be turned into public benefits." Moreover, he sounds even more like an apologist for twenty-first-century disease mongers when he rationalizes away the offenses of "physicians [who] valued fame and wealth above the drooping patient's health" and who worried less about "their own skill" than about "the apothecary's favour."[30] But as useful as they might prove to prison-builders or disease-mongers, Mandeville's cynically opportunistic views on building a social economy out of vice provide an even better gloss on the morally dubious but financially and politically remunerative activities of the profiteers who have made the decay of the American family "the very wheel" that turns their diverse enterprises.

At one time, American family life offered almost no opening for Mandevillian enterprise. Living in nearly-complete economic autonomy, a nineteenth-century agrarian family satisfied most of its needs through the labors of family members, so staying clear of the money economy in which Mandeville saw vice serving as an indispensable stimulant.[31] By the mid-twentieth century, though, the typical urban American family found itself fully enmeshed in the cash nexus so dear to Mandeville's calculating heart. By that time, most American families relied heavily on factories for clothing, automobiles, and household goods; public schools for their children's education; banks for financial services; and Hollywood and television for entertainment. Writing in the 1950s, the Harvard sociologist Pitirim Sorokin expressed dismay that the American home had lost so many of its productive functions that it was fast becoming "a mere incidental parking place."[32] Somewhere the shade of Mandeville must have been smiling.

Nonetheless, the average American family of the fifties or sixties resisted the gravitational pull of a fully Mandevillian world by safeguarding certain family loyalties and honoring certain domestic obligations. Most mothers still cooked family meals rather than relying on restaurants or take-out; many still sewed some of their husbands' and children's clothing. Almost all mothers cared for their own young children rather than turning this task over to a paid surrogate. Fathers not only provided for their wives and children financially but also performed many home repair and maintenance tasks. Though it had surrendered much, the American family still retained a residual core of its traditional autonomy and self-reliance.

During the last three decades, however, the nation's shrewdest Mandevillians have gone to work in turning family disintegration into a vast new opportunity to turn pathology into profit—with all the skill of the best disease-monger or prison-builder.

Liberating Mothers

Long the heart of a healthy home, the homemaking mother came under strong attack in the sixties and seventies by Mandevillians who recognized how much ready cash they could pocket if they could only take over the tasks that the homemaker did without monetary compensation. Of course, to some degree, advertisers had been busy for decades coaxing mothers out of "the handcraft age" in which they satisfied many of the household's needs for food and clothing through their own productive labors and enticing them into a modern era in which they served chiefly as a household purchasing agent. As discussed in chapter 5, the considerable success of this advertising threatened to make homemakers little more than the parking-lot attendant for the "mere incidental parking space" which the home was fast becoming. Largely blind to the cultural perils of unfettered capitalism, many Americans have been very slow to acknowledge the subversive influence of consumer capitalism and its advertising agents. But consumer capitalism and its agents helped to undermine homemaking in ways that created what one seventies analyst called "the festering contradiction of modern womanhood."[33] Social physicians could have prescribed a curative restoration of productive activities to the home and so renewed a homemaker's pride in her crafts. But where was the profit in that? No, the new Mandevillians recommended a radical but quite unnecessary kind of social surgery. It is time, they said, to cut the mother out of the home.

Like their distant cousins in disease-mongering medicine, these masters of social malpractice have understood very well the art of "making healthy people feel sick"; they have understood how to forge "informal alliances" with others who share their economic and political interests; and they have understood how to "target the news media with stories designed to create fears about [some] condition" that they can then promise to treat. By the early 1970s, potent anti-family coalitions were honing their ideological rhetoric. Consequently, Americans were softened up to the idea of allowing their home to go under the scalpel for a mother-ectomy by a relentless bombardment from media commentators and feminist intellectuals. These well-placed disease-mongers explained to a bewildered public that instead of being the very center of a normal social life, the home was rather a "prison of domesticity," "patriarchy's chief institution," and a horrible dead-end for enlightened women seeking "equality with men in the world of jobs and careers."[34]

At first, the new Mandevillians in education and the media establishments sought to persuade American families to submit to mother-ectomies voluntarily—like insecure women who seek out plastic surgeons or obese patients who ask doctors for a stomach stapling. But over time, Mandevillians won powerful allies in government and adopted more coercive tactics; avoiding a mother-ectomy became more and more difficult as policymakers removed the tax protections previously afforded young families and utterly destroyed the traditional "family wage" regime which had given a married man enough income to support his homemaking wife and his children.[35]

And just as the new Mandevillians anticipated, as mothers surrendered the previously unremunerated task of caring for their children to paid surrogates, rivers of new money began to flow. By 1997, the nation's nearly 44,000 child-care establishments were reporting total income of $8.4 billion with total annual payroll of just under $4 billion going to 389,000 employees.[36] New money—public and private—has likewise flowed into after-school programs and summer camps serving families whose homemaking mother has been surgically excised in a social operation even more unnecessary than most hysterectomies and myringotomies. However, in the social merry-go-round, the new Mandevillians set turning, neither are day-care providers, nor summer-camp operators, nor their political allies were complaining: they were too busy counting their profits. When these profits took the form of corporate earnings, even self-identified conservatives typically turned a blind eye. Thus, few conservatives perceived the harm in the profiteering food-service companies joy–riding on the Mandevillian social merry-go-round set spinning by family disintegration that helped these companies increase their income rise to almost $90 billion in 2002 as they faced less and less competition from unpaid homemakers cooking meals at home.[37] And because the cash nexus is also the tax nexus, liberal and leftist activists were quite happy to see the Internal Revenue Service benefiting from the increasingly frenetic whirling of the Mandevillian social merry-go-round: when money changes hands for childcare or meal preparation, the taxman collects revenues that were unavailable so long as homemaking mothers performed the tasks. The new tax money has helped to pay the army of new government workers licensing and supervising the new day-care centers and restaurants.

But as profitable as mother-ectomies for them, the new Mandevillians saw even bigger money in an even-more radical social surgery—the father-ectomy, more commonly called a divorce.

Naturally, just as they did done in promoting the mother-ectomy, the new Mandevillians have done some very successful diseasemongering in "making healthy people feel sick," forging "informal alliances" with others who share their economic and political interests, and "target[ing] the news media with stories designed to create fears about [some] condition" that they could then promise to treat. In the late sixties and seventies, just as they filled the media with screeds about the awfulness of homemaking, progressive disease-mongers began to characterize wedlock as an outmoded institution, sexually repressive, professionally hobbling, and psychologically suffocating. "I wouldn't say that marriage and self-actualization are necessarily mutually exclusive," explained Laura Singer, president of the American Association for Marriage and Family Therapy during the seventies, "But they are difficult to achieve together."[38] Some of the more aggressive disease-mongering advocates of father-ectomies began to warn of the dangers of domestic violence inherent in marital relationships, even describing the marriage license as "a hitting license."[39]

Mandevillian legislators in every state soon enacted "no-fault" divorce statutes that made the state—as one legal analyst noted—an ally of "the spouse who wants to get divorced."[40] And by the early eighties, a profitable new industry was in high gear, raking in professional fees with every turn of the disintegrative social merry-go-round. Profiteering attorneys found high salaries through employment in a Mandevillian system described by one observer as "'a divorce industry' ... of professional meddlers who make millions of dollars every year off marital turmoil, much of which they have a hand in creating themselves."[41] Indeed, although the sponsors of "no fault" divorce statutes promised that their passage would reduce adversarial litigation, legal analysts have seen an increase in property-division and child-custody litigation under "no fault," an increase which caused one commentator to wonder "whether the legal profession has not been the major beneficiary of the no-fault divorce reforms."[42]

But as any well-versed Mandevillian could explain, the divorce industry churns out economic benefits for many besides the courtroom lawyers. Therapists and psychologists have also turned divorce into an economically rewarding opportunity as they help "a dissolving couple system ... [to] achieve a constructive divorce."[43] Real-estate agents likewise punch their tickets on the divorce gravy train, since a divorcing family now needs two residences rather than just one. Even advertisers see new opportunities in making their consumer pitches to "a post marital society."[44]

But in the true spirit of Bernard Mandeville, the divorce industry has created a particularly lucrative opportunity for those who perform a service that intact families simply do not need: collecting child-support from the non-custodial parent (almost always the father) and delivering it to the custodial parent (almost always the mother).[45] In 2001, government agencies, divorce attorneys, and private collection agencies collected $19 billion in child support.[46] Fathers, of course, would have earned that money for their families even if they had never been divorced. But only divorce creates a profit for those who collect and deliver that money. So profitable is this enterprise that, just as America's incarceration boom has produced private for-profit prisons, even so, America's divorce revolution has produced private for-profit child-support collection agencies. A single such company, Supportkids, has already claimed $40 million as its commission for collecting $120 million in child support. The size of such commissions has prompted a few journalists to ask, "Do [such] companies ... profit children or mainly themselves?" But defenders of such companies have responded by arguing that "the bounty-hunting industry might not exist if the government were more competent. The state is supposed to collect child support free of charge."[47]

But then only the hopeless naïve supposes that the state has ever done anything "free of charge." American taxpayers are now paying a great deal to fund the government sector of the Mandevillian child-support system. Government officials must spend approximately one tax dollar for every four child-support dollars collected, amounting to nearly $5 billion a year.[48] Of course, neither the family-court judges, nor the collections officers and accountants, nor the child-support computer analysts, nor their vendors are complaining about this expenditure. Since the federal government now offers incentive fees to states to collect child support, state officials are particularly unlikely to express dismay at how the child-support system is burdening the taxpayer.

It is not necessary to see anything conspiratorial in the child-support network to recognize that, just as in the Prison-Industrial Complex, this network has created a dubious "confluence of special interests." Political scientist Stephen Baskerville has aptly pointed out, "Fatherlessness and the judicial bureaucratic machinery connected with it have grown up together." And within that Mandevillian machinery, "full-time lawyers, judges, child support enforcement agents, and representatives of other organizations ... have a vested interest in both removing children from their fathers and making the fathers' support obligations as burdensome as possible."[49] Even a defender of that system acknowledges that "if all children lived with both of their biological parents in the same household, every civil servant who works in a child-support agency would be out of a job."[50] Since the government jobs of these civil servants usually pay well and offer good benefits—unlike the low-pay, no-benefit jobs multiplying in the post-family service sector—it is hard not to wonder if such civil servants do not share with Bernard Mandeville a certain distaste for social virtue. But then, as discussed in chapter 7, civic as well as social virtues tend to disappear when families disintegrate.

However, the divorce industry generates profits from pathology for many besides its direct employees. Compared to children raised in intact families, children of divorced parents are much more likely to give work to pediatric and adolescent psychiatrists, juvenile detention and probation officers, social workers, and remedial teachers.[51] Divorce even drives up the incidence of the domestic violence falsely associated with wedlock by the disease-mongering propagandists promoting the surgical dismembering of families.[52]

No one need suppose anything conspiratorial or even anything consciously Mandevillian in the growth of enterprises that profit from marital and family failure. But just as in the explosive growth of the Prison Industrial Complex and in the suspicious rise in doctors' reliance on certain costly surgeries, Americans must wonder about a disturbingly Mandevillian confluence of special interests. Indeed, even if they trusted those employed in the divorce industry and its spin-offs as much as they trust physicians, Americans would still have reason to believe that this industry has performed unnecessary father-ectomies for profit at least as often as doctors have performed unnecessary hysterectomies and myringotomies for profit. And since many Americans actually regard the professionals at the very heart of the divorce industry—that is, lawyers and therapists—with considerable wariness,[53] they might well wonder if the number of unnecessary father-ectomies performed for Mandevillian profits does not actually run far higher.

Even if those who profit from family failure do not deliberately subvert marriage and family life, only rare virtue could keep their behavior entirely unaffected by a vague awareness of how family disintegration enlarges their bank accounts and increases their political power. At a minimum, such an awareness fosters quiet acquiescence in policies that undermine wedlock and family life. Such awareness also weakens support for policies that reinforce marriage and family life.

Family Failure and Economic Growth

But even evidence that many Americans now actively subvert wedlock for monetary and political profit would not horrify obdurate Mandevillians. Rehabilitating the arguments that Mandeville himself put forward almost three hundred years ago, these theorists would insist that, like other vices, family failure stimulates the economy. They could even plausibly assert that the success of all American marriages and families would mean unemployment for an army of convenience-goods makers and marketers, of day-care providers, of after-school program employees, of divorce court judges and attorneys, of child-support collection officers, and feminist-cause lobbyists. Similarly, they might warn that a strong resurgence in family life would throw tens of thousands of prison workers, detox specialists, pediatricians and abortion doctors, psychologists and therapists, juvenile court judges and officers out of work. These new Mandevillians might even characterize weak family life as an absolute necessity for sustaining the nation's economy.

Still, Americans who look closely at the new economy of family failure will give little credence to Mandevillian justifications for its growth. In the first place, this dubious economy generates dollars only parasitically. When Americans spend their money on divorce proceedings, on collecting child support, or on giving therapy to children traumatized by family disintegration, they are producing nothing of positive value—not computers, not cars, not books, not steel or oil. They are instead consuming dollars produced in truly value-added enterprises. When a state legislator recently complained that money spent on building prisons was "just money down a rat hole" because it was money unavailable for genuinely productive pursuits,[54] he might just as well be looking at the burgeoning family-failure industry. For building new divorce courts does no more to enrich society than does building more prisons. In fact, the multiplication of divorce courts inevitably presages the multiplication of prisons.

Even the convenience foods, day care, and second homes that Americans buy when family life weakens or fails look like very poor purchases. How many fast-food meals compare to a lovingly prepared home-cooked meal? How many day-care-center workers will ever give the children in their care the kind of affection an at-home mother can? And how can a split family ever hope to maintain in two homes the same level of physical or emotional comfort that they could attain with comparable resources if living in just one home?

Nevertheless, of course, what is lost as the family-failure industry grows cannot be measured monetarily because so much of it cannot be purchased at any price. Maternal love is not for sale in any day-care center. None of the collection agencies chasing down child-support dollars offers paternal devotion. And the carnal services sold as a pathetically incomplete substitute for spousal love bear the name of prostitution.

Also beyond price, civic health declines when family life disintegrates. The great nineteenth-century French economist Frederic Le Play understood the indispensability of strong family life to a harmonious society. As one of his disciples has explained, Le Play's economics made "moral and social harmony ... of paramount importance; for without these wealth itself may be merely [an inducement] to feud, pride, bad blood, and envy, if not an instrument of positive oppression." Rather than attending solely to the flow of money, Le Play made the family "the touchstone by which [he] test[ed] institutions" and economic arrangements. Wiser than Mandeville, Le Play viewed the strength of family life as a protection for ordinary citizens, who he felt needed to be "shielded ... from being blown about by every breath of economic influence."[55] The twenty-first-century Stanford economist Jennifer Roback Morse is thus updating Le Play's style of economics when she asserts that "the loving family is surely the foundation of the moral and cultural [element] of a free society." "A limited government and free market," she explains, "cannot exist without a substantial component of self-restraint among the citizenry. This internalized ethic cannot come into existence in the absence of loving families taking personal care of their own children."[56]

Hence, while family failure may generate huge political and monetary profits for shrewd Mandevillians, it eventually bankrupts society. For good reason, even among the zealots and profiteers most deeply involved in the family-failure industry, most keep the Mandevillian justification for their enterprises out of view, a dirty little secret confessed only under duress. Many even avoid any self-scrutiny that would entail sober reflection on what they are doing and why. But just as government investigators and media reporters have managed to expose the Mandevillian excesses of disease mongering and prison-building, public-spirited government leaders and honest journalists need to start asking hard questions about America's Mandevillian family-failure industry. Because those reaping some of the biggest profits from that industry now control many government offices and media forums, posing those questions will require persistence and resolution. But the reasons for asking those questions are no less urgent than those for inquiring into the Mandevillian dynamics behind disease mongering and prison-building. Asked to comment on a coronary surgery which subsequent investigation revealed to have been performed for profit and not for legitimate medical reasons, one patient remarked only that such surgery "hurts like hell."[57] Millions of Americans who have seen their families dismembered by Mandevillian profiteers could speak with the same voice.

Notes

1.   Lynn Payer, "How to Protect Yourself Against Disease-Mongering," *Health Confidential* July 1993: 7-8.
2.   "Disease Mongering Is A Marketing Ploy," *Pharmaceutical Journal* 20 April 2002.
3.   Ray Moynihan, Iona Heath, and David Henry, "Selling Sickness: The Pharmaceutical Industry and Disease Mongering," *BMJ: British Medical Journal* 324 (2002): 886-890.
4.   John Blackstone, "Unnecessary Open-Heart Surgeries Performed at Redding Medical Center in California on Hundreds of People," *CBS Morning News*, CBS News Transcripts, 7 May 2003.
5.   Clifford J. Levy and Sarah Kershaw, "Inquiry Finds Mentally Ill Patients Endured 'Assembly Line' Surgery," *New York Times* 18 March 2001: A1.
6.   "Needless surgery, Needless Drugs," *Consumer Reports* March 1998: 1-4.
7.   Elizabeth Vargas, "Unnecessary Surgery Hysterectomies," *World News Tonight With Peter Jennings*, ABC News Transcripts, 22 August 2003.
8.   "Disease mongering," op. cit.
9.   J. Conant and J. Gordan, "Scalpel Slaves Just Can't Quit," *Newsweek* 11 January 1988: 58-59.
10.   Anne Chisholm, "The Land of the Fat American Is Eating its Way to an Early Grave," *Sunday Telegraph* (London) 22 June 2003: 10.
11.   Edmund Faltermayer and Rosalind Klein Berlin, "Why Health Costs Can Keep Slowing," *Fortune* 24 January 1994: 76-81.
12.   Andrew Hartman, "U.$. Prisons Mean Money," *Humanist* November/December: 6-10.
13.   "Prisons Fuel Profits," *New Internationalist* May 2000: 8-15.
14.   Eisenhower quoted in Chalmers Johnson, *The Sorrows of Empire: Militarism, Secrecy, and the End of the Republic* (New York: Metropolitan Books, 2004), 39.
15.   Cf. Eric Schlosser, "The Prison-Industrial Complex," *Atlantic Monthly* December 1998: 51-77.
16.   Ibid.
17.   Douglas Clement, "Big House on the Prairie," *Fedgazette* (Minneapolis) January 2002: 2-7.

18.   "Prisons Fuel Profits," op. cit.
19.   Cait Murphy, "Don't Lock Out Private Prisons," *Fortune* 11 June 2001: 54-58.
20.   Schlosser, op. cit.
21.   Hartman, op. cit.
22.   Schlosser, op cit.
23.   Ibid.
24.   Henry Ruth and Kevin R. Reitz, *The Challenge of Crime: Rethinking Our Response* (Cambridge, MA: Harvard University Press, 2003), 102.
25.   Schlosser, op. cit.
26.   Jerome G. Miller, "The American Gulag," *Yes! A Journal of Positive Futures* Fall 2000: 12-17.
27.   Bernard Mandeville, *The Fable of the Bees: Or Private Vices, Public Benefits* (1714), in *Eighteenth-Century Poetry and Prose*, ed. Louis I. Bredvold et al. (New York: Ronald, 1973), 324-356.
28.   Roy Porter, *Flesh in the Age of Reason* (New York: W.W. Norton, 2004), 143.
29.   Mandeville, op. cit.
30.   Ibid.
31.   Allan Carlson, *From Cottage to Work Station: The Family's Search for Social Harmony in the Industrial Age* (San Francisco, CA: Ignatius, 1993).
32.   Pitirim A. Sorokin, *Social and Cultural Dynamics: A Study of Change in Major Systems of Art, Truth, Ethics, Law, and Social Relationships*, Rev. and abridged ed. (1957; rpt. New Brunswick, NJ: Transaction Publishers, 1985), 700.
33.   Stuart Ewan, *Captains of Consciousness: Advertising and the Social Roots of the Consumer Culture* (New York: McGraw-Hill, 1976), 164-166.
34.   Cf. Germaine Greer, *The Female Eunuch* (New York: McGraw-Hill, 1971), 216-220; Kate Millett, *Sexual Politics* (Garden City, NY: Doubleday, 1970), 33, 126-127; and Christopher Lasch, *Haven in a Heartless World* (New York: Basic Books, 1977), xvi.
35.   Cf. Allan Carlson, *Family Questions: Reflections on the American Social Crisis* (New Brunswick, NJ: Transaction Publishers, 1988), 116-125.
36.   U.S. Census Bureau, *Statistical Abstract of the United States: 2002* (Washington, DC: U.S. Government Printing Office, 2002), Table 546.
37.   Ibid.
38.   Singer quoted in Martha Weinman Lear, "Staying Together," *Ladies' Home Journal* September 1991: 60-64.
39.   Jan E. Stets and Murray A. Straus, "The Marriage License as a Hitting License: A Comparison of Assaults in Dating, Cohabiting, and Married Couples," paper presented at the annual meeting of the American Sociological Association, 8 July 1988.
40.   Lenore Weitzman, *The Divorce Revolution: The Unexpected Social and Economic Consequences for Women and Children in America* (New York: The Free Press, 1985), ix.
41.   Charles Edgley and Dennis Brissett, "A Nation of Meddlers," *Society* May/June 1995:36.
42.   Cf. Lynn D. Wardle, "No-Fault Divorce and the Divorce Conundrum," *Brigham Young University Law Review* 1 (1991): 79-142.
43.   Cf. Barbara F. Okun and Louis J. Rappaport, *Working With Families: An Introduction to Family Therapy* (North Scituate, MA: Duxbury, 1980), 202.
44.   See Martha Farnsworth Riche, "The Postmarital Society," *American Demographics* November 1988: 23-26, 60.
45.   Over 90% of those ordered to pay child support are fathers. See U.S. Bureau of the Census, op. cit., Table 539.

46. Ibid.
47. Cf. Nadya Labi and Deirdre van Dyk, "Deadbeat Profiteers," *Time* 2 September 2002: 43-44.
48. Cf. Bryce Christensen, "The Strange Politics of Child Support," *Society* November/December 2002: 69.
49. Stephen Baskerville, "The Politics of Fatherhood," *PS: Political Science and Politics* 35 (2002): 695-697.
50. See Jo Michelle Beld, "Revisiting the 'Politics of Fatherhood,'" *PS: Political Science and Politics* 36 (2003): 714.
51. See Bryce J. Christensen, ed., *When Families Fail ... The Social Costs* (Lanham, MD: University Press of America, 1991).
52. See Christopher J. O'Donnell, Angie Smith, and Jeanne R. Madison, "Using Demographic Risk Factors to Explain Variations in the Incidence of Violence Against Women," *Journal of Interpersonal Violence* 17 (2002): 1239-1262; see also Martin Daly and Margo Wilson, "Child Abuse and Other Risks of Not Living With Both Parents," *Ethology and Sociobiology* 6 (1985): 197-209.
53. See Howard Troxler, "Lawyer Jokes Won't Vanish with A Mere PR Cmpaign," *St. Petersburg Times* 8 July 2002: 1B; see also Philip Rieff, *The Triumph of the Therapeutic* (Chicago: University of Chicago Press, 1966), 243-261.
54. Quoted in Clement, op. cit.
55. See H. Higgs, "Frederic Le Play," *Quarterly Journal of Economics* 4 (1890): 412, 419, 422.
56. Jennifer Roback Morse, *Love & Economics: Why the Laissez-Faire Family Doesn't Work* (Dallas, TX: Spence, 2001), 229-231.
57. Quoted in Blackstone, op. cit.

9

Taking off the Rose-Colored Glasses: Post-9/11 Sobriety as a Basis for Healthier Family Life

The nightmarish attacks of 9/11/01 prompted a wide variety of emotional responses: grief at the loss of those whose lives were so cruelly snuffed out, pride in the united national response in helping those harmed and in standing up to those who threaten further outrages, hatred of the murderous perpetrators and their allies, fear and anxiety about an uncertain future. These responses briefly forged a new patriotic theme in political forums but also created a climate of nervous volatility in many of the nation's financial markets. However, perhaps no response to the tragedy of 9/11 mattered more or held more promise for the country's future cultural health than that of the renewed sense of moral sobriety evident in the lives of Americans rediscovering the critical importance in their own lives of marriage and family.

Bombarded with myriads of reports of how 9/11 affected national attitudes toward everything from sports to immigration, Americans may not have noticed the few, but signally important, reports of how reflection upon the events of 9/11 stirred a new appreciation for wedlock and family.

"The terrorist attacks shook me up," confessed Antal Voros of Elmer, New Jersey, who decided shortly after the attacks that it was time to tie the knot with his New York City sweetheart. "I was really worried about her," he explained. "This made me think, maybe I shouldn't wait as long." His fiancée, Darcy Rowan, employed similar language in commenting on her decision to accept Voros's proposal of marriage. "I felt so disconnected. I heard all of those stories about people losing their loved ones. It made him seem more important." Nor is the Voros-Rowan union peculiar. Associated Press correspondent Anne D'Innocenzio reported a national "surge" in weddings in the weeks after 9/11, which she characterized as a "pleasant surprise" for the bridal industry. David's Bridal, a national chain of 144 stores, reported "a tremendous increase in bridal registries," with a significant number of clients moving wedding dates up from 2004 and 2003 to 2002. Wedding World, Inc. reported that sales for the fall of 2001 ran 22 percent higher than they had the year before, while a number of jewelers reported a comparable post-9/11 bump of 20 to 25 percent in sales of engagement rings. "The Sept. 11 event is giving the business more momentum," remarked one Wedding World, Inc. executive.[1]

Without doubt, a certain odor of crass commercialism adheres to pronouncements that convert the tragedy of 9/11 into a business opportunity for merchants in bridal goods. But Americans can distinguish between the commercialism of the merchants and the renewed appreciation for family ties among the couples who–like Antal Voros and Darcy Rowan–have given those merchants business as they have headed to the altar in the post-9/11 world. For the future of the nation ultimately depends far less upon the success of any of its business enterprises, far less even upon the power and number of its anti-terrorist weapons or soldiers, than upon its citizens' commitments to marriage and family. For that reason, it was profoundly encouraging when one commentator on the prevailing attitudes among young couples remarked, "I think that since September 11 people are putting more weight into weddings."[2] A second observer added, "Love, home, hearth–these have been consistent themes since Sept. 11 and nowhere more so than for young couples planning weddings and a life together."[3] Indeed, social psychologists began predicting that the shifts in attitude effected by 9/11 would produce not only more weddings, but also more babies in the New York area.[4]

No doubt some of the marital unions created in the aftermath of 9/11–as well as some of the pregnancies subsequently initiated–sprang from nothing but a short-lived emotionalism (which probably explains why the social psychologists who predicted a surge in post-9/11 marriages and births also predicted a rise in divorces). But among those prompted by 9/11 to who rediscover wedlock and childbearing, Americans might have glimpsed a return of moral sobriety, the kind of sobriety that transcends the cheery-mindedness generated both by capitalist commercialism and New Left ideology and so makes marital and family ties our most reliable and important protection against the shocks of adversity.

Of course, marital and family ties had shown their power to shield and protect life long before 9/11. Consider, for example, how family ties helped preserve family life even in the grim circumstances faced by the nineteenth-century Donner Party. So severe were the privations visited upon the ninety pioneers who took the Hasting's Cutoff to California in the fall of 1846 and subsequently found themselves trapped by a November blizzard in the Sierra Nevada Mountains that the mere mention of the Donner Party now evokes a chill of horror. Yet forty-eight members of this ill-fated group did survive the cruel snows and the months of starvation. Why were some able to pull through while others perished? Epidemiologist Stephen A. McCurdy of the University of California-Davis highlights the importance of family connections: of those Donner Party members who were traveling without other family members, 83 percent died; of party members who were traveling with family members, only 38 percent died. McCurdy explains this disparity by suggesting that "members of family groups formed strong support networks, saving food and other provisions for their members rather than sharing them with the group," while "persons traveling alone did not have the benefit of these networks." Indeed although some Donner Party members survived by resorting to cannibalism, McCurdy stresses that family ties made such ghoulish measures unnecessary: "the two family groups with the highest survival rates (the Breens and the Reeds, all of whose snowbound members survived) are considered not to have engaged in this cannibalism."[5]

For McCurdy, the Donner disaster still retains "contemporary significance"; since "family structure was an important determinant of mortality" for the Donner Party, he suggests, modern Americans may be able to "improve survival" in the face of contemporary disasters through "measures to keep family groups intact." Professor Curdy's remarks—written before 9/11—now carry an even greater cogency. In fact, only because of the horrors of that day have some Americans belatedly surrendered an illusion of invulnerability that for too long obscured the importance of marriage and family. Before 9/11, far too few Americans recognized in their family ties a priceless safeguard against catastrophe, precisely because far too few Americans supposed that catastrophe could ever puncture their optimistic dreams. And since marital family ties often require sacrifice and impose bur-

dens, cheery pre-9/11 Americans often simply avoided or severed
them.

Not that the invincible pre-9/11 optimists paid any more attention
to them than to the Donner Party's wintry trial, but the man-made
disasters of the twentieth century also provided dire episodes illustrating the power of family ties in extremis. During the Great Depression of the 1930s, for example, sometimes only the bonds of
family kept children from starvation. Social worker Lillian Wald reported seeing Depression-era parents who had "starved themselves
for weeks so that their children might not go hungry."[6] Similarly,
when Nazi and Communist tyranny plunged Europe into darkness,
it was often only family loyalties which offered a ray of hope, sometimes by saving life, sometimes simply by defying death. Historian
Paul Johnson recounts the harrowing case of the Russian woman
who died at the hands of Stalinist torturers rather than betray her
husband to the executioners by accusing him of treason.[7] Similar
acts of family heroism repeat themselves with astonishing regularity
in French scholar Tzevtan Todorov's *Facing the Extreme*, a probing
inquiry into the morality of prisoners in the Soviet gulag and the
Nazi concentration camp. Todorov recounts numerous cases of family
solidarity in the face of murderous barbarism: a nurse sacrificing her
life by giving her daughter her own government pass to prevent her
deportation to a death camp; a daughter racing to catch up to her
mother so that she could join her on the train that she knew would
take both of them to their deaths at Treblinka; an able-bodied father
voluntarily joining his exhausted son in death in a labor camp; a
husband protecting his wife's belly from a German rifle by putting
his hand over the barrel and having it blown off; a mother dying in
the gas chamber with her infant son rather than surviving without
him.[8]

To be sure, in his research on Soviet and Nazi camps, Todorov
uncovers instances of exceptional concern shown on behalf of non-
family members and even complete strangers. Yet he concludes that
"most often, the beneficiary of such concern was a family member–a
mother or daughter, brother or sister, husband or wife." "Some human
relationships," Todorov explains, "especially those between close family members, are more apt to inspire caring than others." Todorov
especially underscores the importance of "the maternal attitude" in
the camps, with "the figure of the mother t[aking] on special importance for the inmates." "He writes from Salonika to Auschwitz, from

Moscow to Magadan, in the cattle cars that carried them to the concentration camps and the gulags, mothers continued to nurse their babies and did their best to keep them in dry diapers. ...[E]ven in the gas chambers, mothers stroked the hair of their children to calm them." But for all the importance of the mother-child bond in the camps, "other family ties were also likely to elicit caring responses," with camp survivors remembering acts of great caring performed on behalf not only of immediate family members, but even on behalf of cousins and grandparents.[9]

America's pre-9/11 optimists could easily persuade themselves that they did not need family ties of the sort that counted for so much during the Depression in America and in the concentration camps of Eurasia, because they were sure they would never experience a Depression nor be imprisoned in a concentration camp. But family ties have shown their life-affirming power not just against particular historical catastrophes, but also against the generic afflictions of disease, poverty, and distress. If only they had been listening, America's pre-9/11 optimists could have heard a chorus of epidemiologists extolling the power of family ties to shield men, women, and children from illness and to help them survive when sickness does strike. Princeton scholars looking at data from around the world have concluded that "in developed countries, married persons of both sexes experience a marked mortality advantage relative to single individuals." Their research further demonstrates that "for the majority of countries [investigated]...as well as for both genders, the excess mortality of each unmarried state (relative to married persons) has increased over the past two to three decades."[10]

The Fortress of Marriage

Epidemiological research has further shown that an intact marriage safeguards the health not only of the husband and wife but of the children as well. "Marital status," remarks a research team writing in *Family Relations*, "is related to the health status of all the family members, including both parents and children."[11] A 1995 study, in fact, determined that experiencing parental divorce before age twenty-one is "associated with a forty-four percent increase in mortality risk," shortening the life of a white male or female by an average of 4.5 years.[12] And even when illness does strike, medical researchers have amassed substantial evidence indicating that the "long term commitment and face-to-face contact" of family members helps sufferers to survive their affliction.[13] Thus, while researchers for the Michigan Cancer Foundation could find no consistent evidence that an intact marriage helps prevent cancer, they did find that "marriage influences survivorship among cancer patients." "The decreases in survival associated with being unmarried," the Michigan scholars wrote, were "not trivial."[14]

A fortress for the mind as well as for the body, family ties help adults and children survive extreme stress and shock without plunging into psychological illness. Researcher Robert Coombs of the UCLA Medical School has underscored the "therapeutic benefit of marriage" in his argument that rates for alcoholism, suicide, schizophrenia, and other psychiatric problems run lower among married men and women than among their unmarried peers because the married man or woman enjoys "continuous companionship with a spouse who provides interpersonal closeness, emotional gratification, and support in dealing with daily stress."[15] An intact marriage apparently offers therapeutic benefit to children as well as spouses; in a study published in 2000 by scholars at the University of Southern California, researchers established that, even after adolescence, adults reared in broken homes suffer from a "significantly lower level of general psychological well-being" than peers reared in intact families.[16] Not surprisingly, then, the ultimate act of adolescent despair–suicide–occurs disproportionately among teens from broken homes: a 1988 study of teen suicides in California found that in over half (52 percent) of the cases investigated, the decedent's parents were divorced or separated.[17]

The psychological solace provided by the family extends even into the final hours of lives not cut short in despair. Sociologist Clive Seale reports that adults who are married and have children are much more likely to have "emotional accompaniment" at their death bed than are the unmarried and childless, who often find themselves exposed to "abandonment and isolation" in their final hours.[18] It would thus appear that those with family ties will find it much easier than those without them to share in the poet John Donne's famous reflection, inspired by a church bell tolling out a death knell, that "no man is an island, entire of itself."[19]

Yet despite their power to shield and protect, to ward off illness and death in many instances, to comfort the sufferer in others, pre-9/11 America was in full retreat from family ties. The marriage rate, already at an all-time low in the United States, drifted lower and lower in the late twentieth century. Total American fertility languished below the replacement level from the early 1970s through the end of the twentieth century, with births to unmarried women accounting for a third of the depressed total by century's end. And although the divorce rate, which skyrocketed in the 1960s and 1970s, moderated slightly in the 1980s and 1990s, it remained high by historical standards.[20]

While the retreat from family life reflected many social and economic developments, the emergence of a pervasive and insistent American optimism deserves scrutiny as an important but too-little-noticed cultural force in weakening family life. For to the degree that pre-9/11 Americans believed that no harm could befall them, to that degree they discounted their need for family ties to help them to endure or survive such harm.

The ebullient optimism characteristic of pre-9/11 Americans did indeed draw critical comment from a number of prominent Americans not specifically looking at its effects on family life. Surveying postwar America, rhetorician Richard Weaver saw a nation carried away in "hysterical optimism," a nation which could not "admit the existence of tragedy."[21] Polish poet and Nobel laureate Czeslaw Milosz likewise decried the callow optimism of twentieth-century Americans who knew of "the distress of [their] distant fellowmen only from movies and newspapers" and who betrayed an "appalling" lack of imagination in their inability to conceive of a world in which they themselves would experience "fire, hunger, and the sword."[22] In his famous Harvard Address of 1978, Russian Nobel laureate Aleksandr Solzhenitsyn warned that America was teetering on the brink of "the abyss of human decadence" in part because American youth were growing up complacently taking for granted their right to "physical health, happiness, the possession of material goods, money, and leisure...almost unlimited freedom in the choice of pleasures."[23] And in their landmark 1980s study, Robert Bellah and company detected the rise of a characteristically American optimism that transcended mere consumer complacency, as millions of Americans who came of age in the sixties (the Woodstock Generation sure that they were seeing the dawning of the Age of Aquarius) "saw a dream...had a vision [and]... had a belief that things could be much better, on many levels" than they had been during the previous centuries of America's history.[24]

Post-World War II America provided an ideal incubator for optimism of both the complacent and vaunting types. After all, Americans who had (as Milosz pointed out) never experienced the devastation that reduced much of Europe and Japan to rubble had experienced material prosperity of a sort beyond the dreams of other times and places. Postwar prosperity, as writer Alan Thein Durning observed, sparked "the Great American Boom," a "fifty-year shopping spree" which created a "new morality" which did "not consist in saving but in expanding consumption." "We act," Durning wrote, "as if the sales days will last forever."[25]

Helping to create not merely an economy, but almost an entire culture based on consumer confidence, ad men bombarded the American public with decades of happy slogans. In a culture suffused with advertising, complained semanticist S.I. Hayakawa, hucksters deployed "poetic language...constantly and relentlessly for the purpose of salesmanship." And having lost their traditional vocabulary to the advertisers, serious poets–those who might, like Shakespeare, Marlowe, or Milton, have dealt with tragic or serious themes–were reduced to "unintelligibility" and "frustration."[26] As one of those feeling the frustration of having been relegated to that status of "a suffering, complaining, helplessly nonconforming poet-or-artist-of-a-sort, far off at the obsolescent rear of things," poet Randall Jarrell raged against the way advertisers and businessmen contaminated the American imagination with a soulless vision of consumption, "a child's dream before Christmas," complete with "station wagon, swimming pool, power cruiser, sports car, tape recorder, television sets, cameras, power lawn mower, garden tractor, lathe, barbeque set, sporting equipment, domestic appliances."[27]

Jarrell saw as one of the worst consequences of this cheerful but frenetic American consumption the emergence of a new cultural rootlessness, in which Americans who constantly watched "new products and fashions replace the old" came to believe that the mere fact that new things do replace old ones constituted "proof enough of their superiority." Such thinking, Jarrell feared, had made American culture "essentially periodical: we believe that all that is deserves to perish and to have something else put in its place...The present is better and more interesting, more real, than the past; the future will be better and more interesting, more real, than the present."[28]

Not surprisingly, the American commercial machine sponsored as its typical entertainment the laugh-track situation comedy, not the classical tragedy. America's pampered optimists simply did not want the challenge of serious drama; they wanted merely the pleasant diversion of pointless farce. In a perceptive evaluation of the nation's first $1 billion sit-com (*Seinfeld*), one critic suggested that in this "emblem of American comedic values," viewers were watching a show "about nothing," a show in which "nothing counts...nothing has consequences." This critic further asserted that the success of this vapid program indicated not so much how well *Seinfeld* reflected American society, but rather how fully "society has been reconfigured as a milieu for commenting on *Seinfeld*."[29]

And unfortunately, beyond *Seinfeld* reruns, mass entertainment offered little to engage the sober or serious auditor. The world of pre-9/11 commercial television, asserted critic Todd Gitlin, was one that was "relentlessly upbeat...and materialistic." Gitlin elaborated:

> The sumptuous and brightly lit settings of most series amount to advertisements for a consumption-centered version of the good life, and this doesn't even take into consideration the incessant commercials, which convey the idea that human aspirations for liberty, pleasure, accomplishment, and status can be fulfilled in the realm of consumption. The relentless background hum of prime time is the packaged good life.[30]

Though consumer optimism fostered by the constant contemplation of the packaged good life portrayed on TV has been profoundly subversive of family life, many Americans who regard themselves as politically conservative have not noticed. Preoccupied with the pursuit of their share of this packaged good life and reassured by Republican leaders about the unfailing beneficence of capitalism, many self-identified conservatives have simply not noticed how radically unfettered consumerism clashes with the moral and religious traditions that sustain strong family life. Too few Americans of any political persuasion have noticed that consumer optimism in the market economy differs very much from the optimism that Americans have traditionally derived from their religious faith. Such religious faith has traditionally inspired Americans with a profound hope that God could turn all things to good for those who worship and serve him (cf., for instance, Romans 8: 35-39). But this optimistic hope has always entailed the restraints of divine commandments (cf. Heb. 5:9) and has been informed by a profound consciousness of human suffering and guilt (cf., for example, Job 30: 15-19 and Isaiah 53: 3-8).

Nine-Eleven may have helped some Americans rediscover some of the sterner elements of their religious faith, but for many Americans, it has been exceedingly difficult to see in the terrorist attacks a reminder of stern but abiding truth. More than a few Americans belong to mainstream denominations that have in recent decades drifted away from scriptural truths about repentance and self-denial and toward "a liberalized religion" celebrating "the power of human choice and the possibility of self-acceptance." [31] Contemporary American religion, all too often, is a religion of happy psychological adjustment, religion without tears, without doctrinal rigor.

Recovering metaphysical sobriety in the wake of 9/11 was even harder for the relatively few but prominent and influential Americans who profess no faith whatever in the God of Scripture nor in the promise of heaven. Their metaphysical poverty and their vulnerability to false optimism is well explained by George Orwell (himself an agnostic), who once remarked that as Christian faith waned, and with it the promise of heavenly joy, the "pessimistic view of life" lost credibility, making it "easier to comfort yourself with some kind of optimistic lie."[32]

Optimistic Lies

Some appealing optimistic lies surrounded pre-9/11 Americans because of the deceptive labors of the advertiser, labors that rarely came in for negative scrutiny in a complacent America. However, other forms of optimism flourished because of the regnant political ideologies. To be sure, even the brand of politics called *conservative* in America shares with the brand of politics called *liberal* elements of fundamental optimism. Thus, in her analysis of how liberalism became "a national creed" pervading the social and political culture, historian Joyce Appleby of UCLA could as easily be talking about Ronald Reagan as Franklin Delano Roosevelt when she stresses that "liberalism forcefully projected its optimistic vision of the possible onto the future," forever creating "robust images that stilled anxieties of possible disasters." Instead of sobering citizens with reminders of past catastrophes (such as the Depression), liberalism persuaded Americans that "society...[is] always poised at the threshold of accomplishments, turning collective life into a kind of perpetual adolescence." The stiffer and darker heritage of Puritans and traditionalist Catholics has traditionally provided some check on liberalism, but in general, the hegemony of liberalism has fostered an "expectation of positive improvement in the future [which has] denigrated both past and present," as "the past lost its attraction and the present became a mere springboard for the future." Under liberalism's tutelage, no one has feared the future as "the dreaded unknown," but rather all have welcomed it as a blank slate on which they could write "human potential" in a sprawling script.[33]

Inevitably, the liberal impulse has lent support to the utopian project of building heaven on earth through political engineering. Edward Bellamy, Charlotte Perkins Gilman, B.F. Skinner, and others found large American audiences for their visions of a glorious utopian future. And an astoundingly large part of their fantasies was actually translated into American public policy–freeing mothers from economic dependence upon the fathers of their children, liberating aging parents from dependence upon their children, seeing children free from dependence upon their parents. In the 1946 preface to his prophetic *Brave New World*, Aldous Huxley marveled that Utopia was "far closer to us than anyone... could have predicted" when his novel was published fifteen years earlier.[34] And in a 1963 study, political theorist George Kateb judged "antiutopian positions on the nature of government" to be "out of touch with what had already become part of the political life of the United States."[35]

Because, as Naomi Blivin remarks, "in all modern societies, the road to Utopia runs through the classroom,"[36] modern liberalism has relied heavily on the public schools to inculcate in young citizens a glowing, politicized optimism toward the future. Sobering lessons about honor and duty, about obligations to those who have gone before, were shoved aside in pre-9/11 America in favor of upbeat slogans priming students for personal and political fulfillment. Instead of institutions which made students self-effacing and conscientious, schools became "centers radiating the values and the motives" for effecting "enormous social progress."[37] "Self-esteem" and "emancipation" emerged as the buzz words for educators who saw themselves as having "Promethean roles as change-agents and leaders of empowering education."[38] These pre-9/11 Prometheans helped students to develop a new "capacity for autonomy" by smashing a "wide range of social and institutional constraints, from religious doctrine to racism."[39] Such teachers had little time for the purgative and chastening works of classical tragedy by Shakespeare, Marlowe, or Euripides, being far too intent on what one critic has called the "moralistic cartoons" used to inculcate a happy multiculturalism.[40]

But beyond the support it drew from liberal politics–in the legislative chamber and in the classroom–pre-9/11 utopianism derived strength from the advancements of modern science. A thoroughgoing scientific outlook might actually have fostered a deep pessimism since the latest cosmology predicts a far distant but inescapable and universal "heat death," with solitary decaying atoms finally floating in a frozen void.[41] But for most pre-9/11 Americans, science still meant what it meant for its greatest propagandist, Francis Bacon, who declared that through science, "human life [would] be endowed with new discoveries and powers."[42] With good reason, the nineteenth-century German philosopher Friedrich Nietzsche worried that "the optimism of science" would banish the sterner and darker "tragic view of things."[43] So successfully did scientists spread their disciplinary optimism, that many pre-9/11 Americans, living in history's most scientifically sophisticated society, saw every human dilemma as amenable to a scientific solution.

So thoroughly did this technocratic optimism insinuate itself into pre-9/11 American thought that cultural historian Philippe Aries suggested that Americans (and citizens of other technologically advanced countries) had started to indulge in illusions of immortality. "Technology," Aries wrote, "erodes the domain of death until one has the illusion that death has been abolished." Aries observed further that "with the advancements in therapeutics and surgery, it has become increasingly more difficult to be certain that a serious illness is fatal; the chances of recovery have increased so much.... Everyone acts as though medicine is the answer to everything. Caesar must die one day, [but] there is absolutely no reason for oneself to die."[44]

Born of many linked causes—including the commercial exuberance and political utopianism—the boundless optimism of pre-9/11 America helped catalyze a new and extreme individualism. Weaver rightly diagnosed "egotism and shallow optimism" as linked cultural diseases.[45] So the spread of an immature optimism could be expected to entail a rise in egotism. And so it did. Though he traced a thread of individualism running through all of American history, sociologist David Popenoe detected a troubling "shift toward radical individualism" in late-twentieth-century America. "America," he asserted, "seems to be spiraling towards an ever more unencumbered individualism," while "the authority of institutions withers."[46] Bellah and colleagues lamented a widespread repudiation of "the old normative expectations of what makes life worth living." This repudiation of our cultural heritage incubated a "modern individualism in which the self ha[d] become the main form of reality" and from which all the traditional republican and biblical virtues were disappearing.[47]

Not surprisingly, the family fared poorly in this atmosphere of heady individualism and overheated optimism. Given that the liberal-utopian state and the unmoored self emerged as the prime carriers of the virus of optimism, it was entirely predictable that sociologist Paul Glick would report that young adults in pre-9/11 America "shift[ed] their allegiance increasingly to themselves and the State" and away from their spouses and families.[48] Likewise predictable in the current cultural milieu were the findings of another pre-9/11 study indicating that many Americans naively (and very optimistically) supposed that they could live a fulfilling and meaningful life without making personal sacrifices for anything.[49]

For the pre-9/11 adolescent who anticipated a life of unbroken triumphs and satisfactions, a life without tears, the demands and constraints of wedlock and family life would likely look unappealing. As the institutional embodiment of utopian optimism, the modern welfare state could serve as a spouse-surrogate for the unmarried mother, parent-surrogate for the employed mother, and child-surrogate for the elderly non-parent–all without the lifestyle restraints of traditional marriage and family life. As Popenoe has wisely remarked, "the inherent character of the welfare state by its very existence help[ed] to undermine family values or familism–the belief in a strong sense of family identification and loyalty, mutual assistance among family members, and a concern for the perpetuation of the family unit."[50]

Besides building the welfare state, a pervasive American pre-9/11 liberalism undermined family life by ensnaring many Americans in what Appleby perceptively labeled "perpetual adolescence." No wonder that the pre-9/11 milieu fostered the rise of a Peter Pan generation who refused to grow up: whereas Americans previously assumed their adult identities in the community while still in their early twenties, sociologists in the late twentieth century reported that Americans commonly found themselves "in their late twenties or early thirties before they [had] any sense of who they [were] or where they [were] going in life."[51] A Peter-Pan-like relish for childish irresponsibility even manifested itself among many affluent middle-aged men who reverted to adolescent fantasies by dumping their first wives and finding some young, beautiful trophy wife as a replacement.[52]

Peter Pan never pondered his own mortality. Neither did his rein-carnation in the optimistic pre-9/11 America. Indeed, the widespread illusion of immortality in pre-9/11 America may owe as much to prolonged emotional adolescence as to the faith in scientific medi-cine which Aries highlighted. This illusion of immortality prevented many pre-9/11 Americans from reflecting seriously on their rela-tionship to departed forebears. Yet without such reflection, family life lost moral depth. The point literary critic Joseph Schwartz made in stressing "the force of memento mori in formulating a belief and an ethic"[53] finds its interpretation in the family context in Weaver's logic: "Those who have no concern for their ancestors will, by simple application of the same rule, have none for their descendants."[54] To explain three decades of below-replacement fertility in the United States, we might well start by looking at why young pre-9/11 Ameri-cans so seldom visited cemeteries and at why so many answered completely to Orwell's description of "a race of enlightened sun-bathers, whose sole topic of conversation [was] their own superior-ity to their ancestors."[55]

For a great many influential Americans, however, neither the de-cay in family life nor the prevalence of hysterical optimism consti-tuted a problem in the years preceding 9/11. For a few prominent commentators, the disintegration of the family actually constituted yet another reason for optimism. "Good riddance to the family," said sociologist Judith Stacey, who saw a future of wonderful new possibilities in gender roles in the family's decline.[56] Sociologist Stephanie Coontz likewise gladly welcomed the breakup of the tra-ditional family, interpreting it as a wonderful opening for "expanded tolerance for alternative family forms and reproductive arrange-ments."[57] Yet even before 9/11, many Americans tried to resist such ebullient anti-family sophistry and recognized in the decline of the family the cause of widespread and needless suffering, especially among children. And in the aftershock of 9/11, many more–with Antal Voros and Darcy Rowan–have regained a strong appreciation for the family ties derided by modern ideologues.

A Chastened Society?

As he brooded over the retreat from family life he saw unfolding in the twentieth century, the distinguished Harvard sociologist Pitirim Sorokin grimly predicted that only "tragedy, suffering, and crucifix-ion" would sufficiently chasten and humble society to effect a renewal in the values which inform family life.[58] Is it possible that in the terrible wound America sustained on 9/11 we see the purgative event Sorokin anticipated, the event that will help Americans jettison the perilously optimistic illusions that helped weaken marriage and family life in late-twentieth-century America? In the months that followed that great tragedy, some trends appeared promising. The upsurge in post-9/11 weddings looked like a possible indication that Americans had finally reversed America's giddy flight from marital and family obligations, that we had recovered enough sober realism to make and keep family commitments.

Unfortunately, very soon some observers detected a slide back into dubious pre-9/11 attitudes. At a conference convened in New York City in May 2002, emergency officials who responded to the September 11 attack warned that "complacency was creeping back into society."[59] National Public Radio commentator Mark Hertsgaard has even wondered if a "return to normalcy" is not making "the newly inquiring mood after September 11...a mere blip." Hertsgaard cites polling data indicating that "attitudes of average Americans have not changed much since the September 11 attacks," with little movement discernible in public responses to questions about "religion, government, civil liberties, and other issues."[60]

The remarkable post-9/11 upsurge in engagements and weddings may thus signify only a limited and temporary puncturing of the complacency that previously kept many Americans from making wedding commitments. It may not signal a real or widespread shift in American culture, one that brings us back to home truths forgotten during decades of heedless pre-9/11 optimism. It can only vex Americans who care about the future of family that for many of their fellow citizens, the deeply painful lessons of 9/11 quickly evaporated in yet more of the same antifamily hysteria that infected so much of the late twentieth century. Americans may well fear that if the horrors of 9/11 were not enough of a calamity to inculcate the moral lessons that Sorokin thought only tragedy and suffering could teach and if the post-9/11 upsurge in weddings prove only a short-lived pause in the national retreat from wedlock and family life, we may anticipate an even more grievous national tutorial in moral sobriety and family commitment. If 9/11 has not dispelled the commercial hype and the political ideology that together hide the preciousness of marital and family ties, all of America may have to learn of that preciousness in the prolonged privations of another Great Depression or in hardships of a truly calamitous war.

Notes

1. Anne D'Innocenzio, "Engagements on the Rise? Bridal Retailers Report A Sales Surge after Sept. 11," *Associated Press State and Local Wire* 20 Nov. '01, BC cycle.
2. See Jacqueline Rivkin, "Still in Style: They May Be Cozier, but Weddings Are Still Lavish, Even After 9/11," *Newsday* 9 June '02: F8.
3. Ibid.
4. See Richard Morin, "A 9/11 Baby Boom?" *Washington Post* 31 March '02: B5.
5. Stephen A. McCurdy, "Epidemiology of Disaster: The Donner Party (1846-1847)," *Western Journal of Medicine* 160(1994): 338-342.
6. Wald quoted in William Manchester, *The Glory and the Dream: A Narrative History of America, 1932-1972* (Boston: Little, Brown, 1973), 1:48.
7. See Paul Johnson, *Modern Times: The World from the Twenties to the Nineties*, Rev. Ed. (New York: HarperCollins, 1983), 303-304.
8. Tzvetan Todorov, *Facing the Extreme: Moral Life in the Concentration Camps*, trans. by Arthur Denner and Abigail Pollak (New York: Henry Holt, 1996), 18, 70.
9. Ibid., 76-77.
10. Yuaureng Hu and Noreen Goldman, "Mortality Differentials by Marital Status: An International Comparison," *Demography* 27(1990): 233-250.
11. John Guidubaldi and Helen Cleminshaw, "Divorce, Family Health, and Child Adjustment," *Family Relations* 34(1985): 35-41.
12. Joseph E. Schwartz et al., "Sociodemographic and Psychosocial Factors in Childhood as Predictors of Adult Mortality," *American Journal of Public Health* (1995): 1237-1245.
13. See Eugene Litwak et al., "Organizational Theory, Social Support, and Mortality Rates: A Theoretical Convergence," *American Sociological Review* 54(1989): 49-66.
14. James S. Goodwin et al., "The Effect of Marital Status on Stage, Treatment, and Survival of Cancer Patients," *Journal of the American Medical Association* 258(1987): 3125-3130.
15. Robert H. Coombs, "Marital Status and Personal Well-Being," *Family Relations* 40(1991): 97-102.
16. Timothy J. Biblarz and Greg Gottainer, "Family Structure and Children's Success: A Comparison of Widowed and Divorced Single-Mother Families," *Journal of Marriage and the Family* 62(2000): 533-548.
17. See Franklyn L. Nelson, "Youth Suicide in California: A Study of Perceived Causes and Interventions," *Community Mental Health* 24(1988): 31-42.
18. Clive Seale, "Dying Alone," *Sociology of Health and Illness* 17(1995): 376-392.
19. John Donne, *Devotions Upon Emergent Occasions* (1624), XVII.
20. See *U.S. Census Bureau, Statistical Abstract of the United States: 2001,* Tables 82, 85, and 144; http://www.census.gov/prod/2001pubs/statab/sec.02.pdf
21. Richard M. Weaver, *Ideas Have Consequences* (Chicago: University of Chicago Press, 1984 [1948]), 11.
22. Czeslaw Milosz, "American Ignorance of War" (1951), in Janice Neuleib et al., *The Mercury Reader* (Boston: Pearson, 2001), 170-173.
23. Aleksandr I. Solzhenitsyn, *A World Split Apart: Commencement Address Delivered at Harvard University, June 8, 1978,* trans. by Irina Ilovayskaya Alberti (New York: Harper & Row, 1978): 15, 21.

24. Robert N. Bellah et al., *Habits of the Heart: Individualism and Commitment in American Life* (Berkeley: University of California Press, 1985), 17.

25. Alan Thein Durning, "American Excess," *E Magazine* (Jan./Feb. 1993): 26-35.

26. S.I. Hayakawa, *Language in Thought in Action*, 3rd ed. (New York: Harcourt, Brace, Jovanovich, 1972): 223-225.

27. Randall Jarrell, "A Sad Heart at the Supermarket," in Norman Jacobs, ed., *Culture for the Millions? Mass Media in Modern Society* (Boston: Beacon, 1964), 97-100.

28. Ibid.

29. Geoffrey O'Brien, "Sein of the Times," *New York Review of Books* (14 August 1997): 12-14.

30. Gitlin quoted in Bellah, op cit., 279-280.

31. Ibid., 63-64.

32. George Orwell, review of *Tropic of Cancer* by Henry Miller, in *An Age Like This, 1920-1940*, Vol. 1 of *The Collected Essays, Journalism and Letters of George Orwell*, ed. Sonia Orwell and Ian Angus (New York: Harcourt, Brace & World, 1968): 155.

33. Joyce Appleby, "Liberal Education in a Postliberal World," *Liberal Education* 79.3 (1993): 18-24.

34. Aldous Huxley, *Brave New World* (New York: Harper & Row, 1969 [1932]): xiii.

35. George Kateb, *Utopia and Its Enemies* (London: Free Press, 1963): 209, 232.

36. Bliven quoted in Appleby, op. cit.

37. Howard R. Bowen, "What's Ahead for Higher Education? Opportunities for Optimism," *Change* Nov./Dec. 1994: 36-40.

38. Ira Shor, *Empowering Education: Critical Teaching for Social Change* (Chicago: University of Chicago Press, 1992), 236, 263.

39. Scott Fletcher, *Education and Emancipation: Theory and Practice in a New Constellation* (New York: Teachers College Press, 2000), 186-187.

40. See Jeffrey Hart, *Smiling Through Cultural Catastrophe* (New Haven, CT: Yale University Press, 2001), 246-248.

41. Cf Lawrence M Krauss, *Atom: An Odyssey from the Big Bang to Life on Earth . . . and Beyond* (Boston: Little, Brown, 2001), 280-283.

42. Francis Bacon, *Novum Organum* (1620), I.lxxxi and I.xcii.

43. Friedrich Nietzsche, *The Birth of Tragedy from the Spirit of Music*, Volume I in *The Complete Works of Friedrich Nietzsche*, ed. Oscar Levy (London: Allen & Unwin, 1909), 131.

44. See Philippe Aries, *The Hour of Our Death*, trans. Helen Weaver (New York: Alfred A. Knopf, 1981), 591-595; see also Philippe Aries, "The Reversal of Death: Changes in Attitudes Toward Death in Western Societies," in Philippe Aries et al., *Death in America* (Philadelphia: University of Pennsylvania Press, 1975), 151.

45. Weaver, Ideas, p. 177.

46. David Popenoe, *Life Without Father* (New York: Martin Kessler Books/Free Press, 1996), 46-48.

47. See Bellah, Habits, pp. 55-84, 142-163.

48. Paul C. Glick, "The Family Life Cycle and Social Change," *Family Relations* 38(1989): 123-149.

49. Howard M. Bahr and Kathleen S. Bahr, "Families and Self-Sacrifice: Alternative Models and Meanings for Family Theory," *Social Forces* 79(2001): 1231-1258.

50. David Popenoe, *Disturbing the Nest: Family Change and Decline in Modern Societies* (New York: Aldine de Gruyter, 1988), 196-239.

51. See Susan Littwin, *The Postponed Generation: Why American Youth Are Growing Up Later* (New York: William Morrow, 1986), 17, 245-248.

52. Cf. Cynthia Tucker, "Barbie and Life," *New Orleans Times-Picayune* 24 November 1997: B5.

53. Joseph Schwartz, "Life and Death in The Last Gentleman," *Renascence* 40(1988): 125.

54. Weaver, Ideas, p. 30.

55. Orwell quoted by Ivan Illich and Barry Sanders, *The Alphabetization of the Popular Mind* (San Francisco, CA: North Point, 1988): 109.

56. Judith Stacey, "Good Riddance to the Family: A Response to David Popenoe," *Journal of Marriage and the Family* 55 (1993): 545-546.

57. Stephanie Coontz, *The Way We Never Were: American Families and the Nostalgia Trap* (New York: Basic Books, 1992), 1-3, 225.

58. Pitirim A. Sorokin, *Social and Cultural Dynamics: A Study of Change in Major Systems of Art, Truth, Ethics, Law, and Social Relationships*, Rev. and abridged ed. (New Brunswick, NJ: Transaction Publishers, 1985), 701-702.

59. See Al Baker, "For Emergency Officials Touched by 9/11's Horrors, Fears of Creeping Complacency," *New York Times* 21 May '02: A17.

60. Mark Hertsgaard, *The Eagle's Shadow: Why America Fascinates and Infuriates the World* (New York: Farrar, Straus, and Giroux, 2002), 14, 202.

10

Turning Back the Clock: Should America Try to Recover Lost Family Strengths?

Though family failure may put money in the pockets of twenty-first-century Mandevillians, its consequences trouble most ordinary Americans. Children–abused, depressed, sick, suicidal, mired in poverty, addicted to drugs, seduced by crime. Women–abused, depressed, sick, mired in poverty, stressed, fearful of crime. Men–alienated, angry and confused, sick, suicidal, addicted to drugs, prone to violence and crime. The catalogue of Americans trapped in pathologies traceable to the national retreat from family life has grown long and sobering. And unfortunately, that retreat from family life continues. Marriage and marital fertility rates have fallen to historic lows while rates for illegitimacy, divorce, and cohabitation are running very high. Most Americans see the destructive dynamic at work, one responsible for ever more distress and heartache. However, whenever serious discussion begins about how to halt or even reverse this destructive dynamic, a peremptory metaphor intrudes, cutting off the discussion and fostering a sense of resignation and fatalism.

This paralyzing metaphor is nearly ubiquitous. It showed up, for instance, in a 1993 analysis by *Money* magazine editor Denise M. Topolnicki of how the incidence of poverty of children has shot up in recent decades and of how "changes in family structure" are implicated in this malign trend. "If somehow," Topolnicki acknowledged, "all families stayed together, the child poverty rate would plummet by about a third." A helpful and sober observation. But then comes the immobilizing metaphor, as Topolnicki despairs of "turning back the clock on divorce and illegitimacy," and turns to political and financial palliatives.[1]

This same unhelpful metaphor provided the rhetorical focus for sociologist Constance Ahrons's 1996 screed against "the traditionalists [who] bemoan the demise of The Family." "That isn't to say that families aren't in trouble; indeed they are," Ahrons conceded. But "trying to turn back the clock won't meet the needs of families" in a society characterized by a growing number of "single-parent, dual-worker, bi-nuclear, remarried and homosexual" households. As a social scientist who understood the futility and foolishness of trying to turn back the clock of family change, Ahrons urged her readers to reject the "outdated ideal of the traditional nuclear family." What readers needed to do instead was to work for "reforms to mitigate the greater societal problems that undermine the quality of life for all of America's families," regardless of their structure.[2]

Though the clock metaphor hides more than it reveals–perhaps *because* it hides more than it reveals–politicians invoke it at least as frequently as journalists or academics. Thus, in a 2001 attack on President Bush's attempt to cut federal subsidies for day care centers, Senator Hillary Rodham Clinton accused the President of trying to "turn back the clock," of "attempting to reverse the last eight years of progress."[3] Senator Clinton did not bother to consider the psychological or epidemiological problems associated with the centers taxpayers are forced to support. But then a distracting metaphor can help the shrewd rhetorician by keeping listeners from even thinking of such considerations.

Far too many Americans have, in fact, unthinkingly accepted the metaphor of a clock of social change, a clock which only the naïve or senseless would try to push back. But when any metaphor comes to bear great weight in the rhetoric surrounding important issues, it deserves to be interrogated. No balanced understanding of the Kennedy administration, for example, is possible so long as the metaphor of Camelot remains unscrutinized, just as no good analysis of America's Vietnam policies can leave the metaphorical Domino Theory unexamined. Even so, the metaphor of a clock of family change cries out for thoughtful investigation. Such an investigation will quickly expose this as a metaphor lacking substance and meaning. And those who carry out such an investigation will quickly discard the metaphor as an impediment to honest discussion about America's social trajectory and about the ways that trajectory might be changed.

Implicit in the rhetoric of commentators warning against attempts to turn the clock back on social change is the belief that social history ineluctably unfolds along a one-directional axis, just like the hours and minutes marked out by the cesium-isotope clocks which set the standard for modern time measurement. The gradual transmutation of radioactive cesium that drives a modern clock can neither be retarded nor reversed. Neither, so the hidden argument runs, can the gradual transmutation of family patterns. The argument well needs to stay hidden. For it cannot bear the light of day. Social historians can supply ample evidence of the difficulty of extrapolating trends in family life into the future. The social scientists who based their predictions about marriage and family life in the 1950s on trends away from marriage and child-bearing discernible in the preceding decades were profoundly surprised by the reversal of those trends during a decade which saw marriage and fertility rates soar and divorce rates fall. "Social observers," remarks historian Allan Carlson, "were astonished at the time, and in retrospect we can appreciate their surprise."[4] Making deliberate but unexpected choices, American men and women reversed what many scholars supposed were irreversible social tides. Those who crave a chronological metaphor are confronted in the 1950s with a clock that ran backward for a decade. Or was the clock actually moving forward in the 1950s and backward in the preceding decades? Who can with confidence say which way this fictive clock might move in future decades?

But it is not simply the unpredictability of its movements which makes the clock metaphor problematic. Far worse is the way in which optimistic rhetoricians and zealous ideologues have made the forward movement of the clock a guarantee of social and cultural progress. Investing the clock metaphor with this kind of metaphysical value has the perhaps not unintended consequence of making those who try to turn it backward appear not simply foolish but positively evil.

Inevitable Progress?

The hope that time will bring social progress is in itself a humane hope, one to be cherished. The trouble comes when that humane hope hardens into a doctrine, an ideology, declaring that time will bring social progress, that time must bring social progress, that whatever time does bring constitutes social progress. And unfortunately, this rigid doctrine (discussed briefly in chapter 9) has pervasively insinuated itself into American cultural life, making our clock metaphors genuinely dangerous.

The danger springs from largely discredited assumptions about the nature of history. For when Americans embrace the view that the forward movement of time ensures social progress, they are—whether knowingly or not—accepting a highly fallacious philosophy of history. It is in fact because of skepticism about the view that the passage of time guarantees progress that the Whig school of historians, a school widely regarded as one the earliest proponents of this historical optimism, is widely viewed with suspicion. As one of the leading exponents of the Whig perspective on history, the nineteenth-century British statesman Thomas Babington Macaulay articulated the school's guiding theme in writing history as "the history of physical, of moral, and of intellectual improvement."[5]

Elsewhere Macaulay enlarges on this theme as he exults in the way the British, once a "wretched and degraded race," have progressed to become

> ... the greatest and most highly civilized people that ever the world saw ... [a people who] have carried the science of healing, the means of locomotion and correspondence, every mechanical art, every manufacture, everything that promotes the convenience of life, to a perfection which our ancestors would have thought magical, have produced a literature which may boast of works not inferior to the noblest which Greece has bequested to us, have discovered the laws which regulate the heavenly bodies, have speculated with exquisite subtlety on the operations of the human mind, have been acknowledged leaders in the career of political improvement.[6]

Many Americans today see nothing wrong with Macaulay's approach to history. To the degree that they think about history at all, they think about it in the upward-and-better way that Macaulay did. Indeed, were the Whig understanding of history not so widely accepted among contemporary Americans, the illusory clock metaphor so often invoked in discussion of trends in family life would carry little force.

But the kind of history Whig philosophy gives us (and which gives power to the ever-present clock metaphor) comes in for sharp criticism from the distinguished historian Herbert Butterfield, who understands the historical blindness it can easily induce as its self-congratulatory writers massage the evidence into "a story which is the ratification if not the glorification of the present."[7] More recently, the accomplished American historian Christopher Lasch has singled out the dean of the Whig school of historiography for criticism, commenting perceptively that "Macaulay's complacency was in no way

qualified by the conventional reminder that his own age–since the
process of accumulation continues without any foreseeable end–
would appear to future ages just as primitive ... as earlier ages appeared to him and his contemporaries."[8]

As part of an extended critique of the concept of progress so dear
to Whigs, Lasch points back to "the eighteenth century, when the
founders of modern liberalism began to argue that human wants,
being insatiable, required an indefinite expansion of the productive
forces necessary to satisfy them." The progressive credo of modern
liberalism has fostered an "easy optimism," Lasch complains, seeing in that optimism nothing that would serve as "an effective an-
tidote to despair." In place of the shallow optimism of modern
liberalism, Lasch asserts that what Americans need is the traditional virtue of hope. "Hope," he writes, "does not demand a
belief in progress... Hope implies a deep-seated trust in life...It rests
on confidence not so much in the future as in the past. It derives
from early memories...in which the experience of order and content-
ment was so intense that subsequent disillusionments cannot dis-
lodge it." Those who can "distinguish hopefulness from the more
conventional attitude known today as optimism," Lasch avers, can
"see why it serves us better, in steering troubled waters ahead, than
a belief in progress."[9]

The Need for a Past

But developing an authentic sense of hope, rooted (as Lasch rightly
insists) in the past, is particularly difficult in contemporary America.
For the dominant American political philosophy–that is, liberalism–
rests upon progressive premises (discussed in chapter 9) that cut us
off from our past. In her analysis of how liberalism became "a national creed" pervading the social and political culture, historian Joyce
Appleby of UCLA stresses that "liberalism forcefully projected its
optimistic vision of the possible onto the future," so persuading
Americans that "society...[was] always poised at the threshold of accomplishments, turning collective life into a kind of perpetual adolescence." The hegemony of liberalism thus fostered an "expectation of positive improvement in the future [which] denigrated both
past and present," as "the past lost its attraction and the present became a mere springboard for the future."[10]

Speaking in similar tones, Barzun decries "the 20th C[entury]
dogma that latest is best," a dogma he traces to "a false analogy with

science," within which the doctrine of progress is less problematic and equivocal than it is in philosophy, art, and politics. It is this misleading dogma that Barzun blames for the absence of historical consciousness in "Modernist Man," a being who always "looks forward, a born future-ist, thus reversing the old presumption about ancestral wisdom and the value of prudent conservation. It follows that whatever is old is obsolete, wrong, dull, or all three."[11]

American poet Randall Jarrell has similar things to say as the practitioner of a literary art within which the doctrine of progress does not comfortably fit (note that in his catalogue of nineteenth-century British attainments, even Macualay invokes the standard of ancient Greek classics). Speaking from the "far off at the obsolescent rear of things," Jarrell diagnoses a dangerous rootlessness induced by progressive thinking and living. Americans who constantly watch "new products and fashions replace the old," Jarrell warns, come to see in the mere fact that new things replace old ones "proof enough of their superiority." Such thinking has made American culture "essentially periodical: we believe that all that is deserves to perish and to have something else put in its place...The present is better and more interesting, more real, than the past; the future will be better and more interesting, more real, than the present."[12]

If Americans wish to avoid the kind of historical blindness induced by the complacent theory of progress (and to overcome the attendant vulnerability to the mendacious metaphor of the clock now so often invoked in discussion of trends in family life), they will need to look to sources other than Whig ideologues and liberal political theorists for richer and more promising perspectives on history. They could do far worse than to start with the sophisticated cyclical vision of history advanced in the early eighteenth century by the Italian scholar Giambattista Vico. In limning the *corsi* and *ricorsi* by which barbarian races advance to become great civilizations and then degrade themselves into new barbarism, Vico offers a compelling alternative to the simplistic linear view of history later propounded by the Whigs, an alternative that has stimulated the minds of such thinkers as Goethe, Coleridge, Hegel, Michelet, and De Sanctis.[13] A modern Vico scholar acknowledges the real "temptation to...progressivism" to which Vico was exposed, but explains that Vico was "restrained from succumbing, in the first place, by the profound sense of the ever-imminent tragedy of human history and even more, by his insight into the roots of tragedy, resident in the very definition of man which he has advanced."[14]   The unsentimental honesty with which Vico defined man enabled him to realize that, in the words of another modern student of Vico, "the second barbarism that engulfs civilization after it has reached its summit is worse than the first." For while the original barbarians possess such virtues as "modesty, duty to the family, and virile courage," the new barbarians "have none left."[15]

But contemporary Americans need not look back to eighteenth-century Italy to find strong arguments against the facile Whiggery responsible for the popularity of deceptive clock metaphors. In 1880, the American author Henry George protested in his *Progress and Poverty* against the "hopeful fatalism" embraced by many Americans according to which "progress is the result of forces which work slowly, steadily, and remorselessly, for the elevation of man." Against the simple faith that "progress would be continuous–that advance would lead to advance, and civilization develop into higher civilization–" George argued that "the universal rule is the reverse of this. The earth is the tomb of dead empires, no less than of dead men. Instead of progress fitting men for greater progress, every civilization that was in its own time as vigorous and advancing as ours is now, has of itself come to a stop. Over and over again, art has declined, learning sunk, power waned, population become sparse, until... [there remained] only a remnant of squalid barbarians, who had lost even the memory of what their ancestors had done." A true theory of history must "account for retrogression as well as for progression," George insisted, calling for sober inquiry, for "as society develops, there arise tendencies which check development."[16]

George's call for an inquiry into those forces which put society into retrogression was answered a few years later by the maverick scholar Brooks Adams in *The Law of Civilization and Decay* (1896). Advancing a cyclical vision of history that contradicts Whig history's premise of unending progress, Adams reasoned that the primal religious, military, and artistic energies of a society tend to "dissipate" once economic centralization and economic competition become its dominant imperatives. Cultural decay accelerates when "the waste of energetic material is so great that the martial and imaginative stocks fail to reproduce themselves." Finally, when "the energy of the race has been exhausted," the previously "highly centralized society disintegrates" and "must probably remain inert until supplied with fresh energetic material by the infusion of barbarian blood."[17]

Sorokin and the Sensate Culture

For a twentieth-century version of cyclical history that challenges Whig complacency and its misleading clock metaphors, however, Americans may consult *Social and Cultural Dynamics*, first published in 1937-41 by the distinguished Harvard sociologist Pitirim Sorokin. Based on exhaustive study of ancient and modern cultures around the world, Sorokin's *Dynamics* posited the alternation of Ideational and Sensate eras, with the first governed by transcendent values, the second by materialism. It troubled Sorokin that he seemed to detect the impending disintegration of our own Sensate era, signaled by "the 'blackout' of culture" and the disintegration of "the family as a sacred union." Yet Sorokin still hoped for the appearance of "new Saint Pauls, Saint Augustines, and religious and ethical leaders" who could bring society "back to reason, and to eternal, lasting, and absolute values."[18]

Of course, contemporary Americans may justly protest that a cyclical view of history can be just as deterministic as the Whigs' linear view. And if conceived of deterministically, a cyclical view of history may induce a fatalism as harmful to the spirit as the shallow complacency of the Whigs. Indeed, a clock metaphor with daylight hours and nighttime hours can quickly be contrived to serve cyclical determinists. And its proponents can argue as stridently as today's Whiggish progressives that we cannot push back the clock but must passively wait for it to cycle back.

But the study of cyclical visions of history need not induce fatalism and paralysis. Such versions of history *can* shake us out of shallow optimism about continuous progress. And they *can* make us vigilant against the loss of cultural strengths that prevent us from relapsing into barbarism. They *can* even awaken us to the need to recover lost strengths that made our culture stronger in the past.

Indeed, in saying that modern America needs to be brought back to eternal and lasting values, the cyclical-thinking Sorokin clearly directs our attention to the past, just as he does by naming great religious leaders of the past as the type of what we need now. Likewise, in analyzing the reasons that our culture is currently trapped in decadence, sterility, and confusion, Barzun predicts renewal only when daring cultural leaders rediscover in history "the record of a fuller life." Having "found a past" they will have what must be "used to create a new present."[19] And it will be recalled that Lasch insists that a hope deeper than progressive optimism "rests on confidence not so much in the future as in the past."

But it is the past that is denied to us who shut off debates about family life with a clock metaphor. Ahrons, for instance, ridicules the very notion that contemporary Americans would look to the past for cues as to how to improve family life. We must, she says, get rid of "a destructive mythology" spread by "traditionalists [who] plead for a return to the family of yesteryear." And when it comes to scorning the past as a source of inspiration for improving family life, Ahrons has numerous academic allies. Historian Stephanie Coontz attacks "conservative writers" such as George Gilder, Allan Bloom, and Allan Carlson who "want to return to a traditional family" of bygone eras. Such appeals, she warns, are premised upon "nostalgic notions about 'the way things used to be'" and not upon a realistic understanding that "the past was not all it's cracked up to be." Rather than fret about "the doomsday scenario" which focuses on family disintegration, Americans ought to rejoice in the "undeniable gains associated with the democratization of family relations, the expansion of women's options outside the family and men's responsibilities within it, the erosion of ethnocentric and moralistic norms about what a proper family must be and do, and the new tolerance for unconventional family relations."[20]

Koontz admits that America does face difficult social problems. But she is adamant in arguing that "we will not solve these problems by looking backward. It's time, as anthropologist Jennifer James puts it, to start 'thinking in the future tense.'"[21] Sociologist Edward L. Kain speaks in a similar vein when he dismisses the "prophets of doom" responsible for spreading "the myth of family decline—the notion that families in the past were stable and happy and that recent decades have seen a rapid decay of family life." The reality hidden by the myth, Kain asserts, is that "the family is not dying; it is changing," as "the structure and content of family life [becomes] different for each cohort as individuals and families adapt to a world of rapid social change." Today's Americans, Kain urges, should overcome their "tendency to romanticize the past" and begin to "wield the power to shape the direction of the future of families in the United States."[22]

Given this pervasive bias against the past among intellectuals eager to validate contemporary family life and discount the family life of the past, it is easy to understand why it was a serious study of "changing patterns of family life" that caused Lasch to have doubts about his "friends on the left." Because, Lasch began to realize, these progressive friends regarded themselves as "the party of the future," they had become "unbearably smug and superior" in their "confidence in being on the winning side of history."[23] Before they join the smug party of the future with regard to family issues, perhaps more Americans should contemplate the sobering warning of Spanish writer Jose Ortega y Gasset, who underscored the loss of the past as a deplorable aspect of "the radical demoralisation of humanity" in a modern world intoxicated with the "possibility of limitless progress":

> This grave dissociation of past and present is the generic fact of our time and the cause of the suspicion, more or less vague, which gives rise to the confusion characteristic of our present-day existence. We feel that we [present-day] men have suddenly been left alone on the earth; that the dead did not die in appearance only but effectively; that they can no longer help us. Any remains of the traditional spirit have evaporated. Models, norms, standards are of no use to us. We have to solve our problems without any active collaboration of the past, in full actuality, be they problems of art, science, or politics. The [modern] European [or American] stands alone, without any living ghosts by his side.[24]

But contemporary Americans have more than a few reasons to want living ghosts by our sides to guide us in renewing family life. For despite the ubiquity of a metaphorical clock which cannot be turned back, despite the Panglossian cheery-mindedness of intellectuals who assure us that past family life was never very good and that the future will be a wonderland of diversity, tolerance, and progress, Americans have strong reason to believe that the families of the past could teach the families of today valuable lessons.

Strong Families

Evidence of the superiority of family life in the past over family life today abounds. Consider, for example, the strong evidence that intact parental marriages and at-home mothers protected the mental health of children in the past in ways that it is not protected in our time of divorce, illegitimacy, and maternal employment. In a 2000 study, social psychologist Jean M. Twenge documented a remarkable shift "toward substantially higher levels of anxiety and neuroticism" among American children and young adults. This shift was "so large that by the 1980s normal child samples were scoring higher [in anxiety] than child psychiatric patients from the 1950s." Twenge dismissed "economic conditions" as a plausible explanation of the sharp rise in mental distress, while emphasizing that "changes in the divorce rate, the birth rate, and the crime rate are all highly correlated with children's anxiety."[25]   Similarly, in a study conducted in 2000 at the Pittsburgh School of Medicine, pediatric specialists traced a parallel between the rising incidence of mental-health problems among children and the rising number of single-parent families. "Children from single-parent households," they pointed out, "were roughly twice as likely to be identified with psychosocial problems" as peers in intact families.[26]

But illegitimacy and divorce are not the only adverse family trends causing psychological distress among the nation's children. Maternal employment figures as a cause as well since such employment often takes children out of the home and puts them in day-care centers. University of Minnesota psychologists report "anxious and withdrawn behavior" and elevated blood cortisol levels among day-care children.[27]   Even some day-care center operators have acknowledged seeing "how children in day care suffer from separation, anxiety, and depression despite competent staff."[28] Scholars at Penn State and the University of Michigan warn that day care can compromise healthy psychological development in another way, too: by facilitating the spread of chronic otitis media, a type of ear infection which often causes "mild hearing loss," day care produces "hard of hearing children [who] exhibit social problems characterized by less acceptance by their peers, a tendency to be more aggressive in their behavior, and serious difficulty in making friends."[29] Lingering psychological effects of day care may help to explain why when researchers at the University of California–Irvine looked at school-aged children, they found that "as mothers worked more hours...children displayed less resilience, resourcefulness, and adaptability in the classroom." The poorer work habits and lower grades among children of mothers working full-time may, the California–Irvine scholars suggest, be "consequences of maternal absence on children."[30]

In far too many cases, though, recent changes in family life have left children vulnerable to more than just psychological distress and academic failure. For one of the most horrific consequences of recent family disintegration has been the sharp rise in child abuse. Whereas authorities received just ten reports of child maltreatment per 1,000 children in 1976 (and even fewer in the decades before that), they received forty-two such reports per 1,000 children in

1997.[31] Reluctant to admit the superiority of family life in the past, some commentators have argued that this sharp increase in reports of child abuse actually reflects a kind of progress in exposing a social problem that was always there but simply covered up and denied. Their argument, in fact, gives contemporary Americans a reason for self-congratulation for being more honest about a problem that that was just as bad in the past but was hidden from view. Unfortunately for those who advance such arguments, careful research discredits them as specious. In the first place, we have abundant empirical research on abuse implicating the very family forms that have grown more numerous in recent decades. Again and again, researchers have established that the abuse of children is much more likely to occur in single-parent and step-families than in intact families. Sociobiologists Martin Daly and Margo Wilson have calculated that "preschoolers living with one natural and one stepparent were forty times more likely to become child abuse cases than were likeaged children living with two natural parents."[32] David G. Gil, author of *Violence Against Children*, discerns in the available data "an association between physical abuse of children and deviance from normative family structure, which seems especially strong for non-white children."[33]

Safer Children

Further discrediting the sophistry of those arguing that child abuse was just as common in the past as it is today is the historical scholarship of John Demos. In his investigation of American colonial life, Demos finds no justification for the "consensus view" that "children have always been abused" in America. Rather, Demos diagnoses child abuse as a uniquely modern phenomenon caused by urbanization, on-the-job alienation, and the collapse of "the 'providential' world-view of our forebears–their belief that all things, no matter how surprising and inscrutable, must be ascribed to God's overarching will."[34]

Given the linkage between family disintegration on the one hand and distress and abuse among children on the other, it should surprise no one that during the decades when divorce and illegitimacy rates were soaring, so too were adolescent suicide rates. In a 1989 study of the epidemic in teen suicide, John Wodarski and Pamela Harris blamed "turmoil in American families" for the grim problem.[35] And more recent investigations have only confirmed their analysis, with a 1998 study diagnosing suicidal characteristics in 38 percent of adolescents in stepfamilies and in 20 percent of adolescents in single-parent homes, compared to just 9 percent of adolescents in intact families.[36]

But not all of the violence caused by family disintegration happens within the home. America witnessed an unprecedented surge in violent street crime, particularly in the inner city, during the latter half of the twentieth century, and the retreat from family life looms large as a reason. In his groundbreaking study *Violent Land*, social historian David Courtwright remarks that "the root cause of the wave of black inner-city male violence that began building during the 1960s and 1970s and rose again in the late 1980s and early 1990s was the decline of stable two-parent families and the institution of marriage in the context of an entrenched culture of poverty in an isolated, youthful subsociety with diminishing employment opportunities and a chronically low gender ratio." Because of the "breakdown in the familial mechanisms for controlling young men," Courtwright sees in the modern inner city the very same social pathology which once made America's Western mining camps and cowtowns "the most tumultuous region of the expanding nation." But whereas family life finally came to and pacified the Western frontier, it seems to be disappearing from "the riptide of modern history."[37]

If Americans hope to rescue American children from this riptide, it would appear imperative to recover strengths once found in American marriages and families. And let no one suppose that turning to the past is a mere indulgence in nostalgia. Even skeptical empiricists are finding evidence that past generations did a better job of making marriage and family life work. In a 2001 study of marital happiness conducted at Penn State and the University of Nebraska-Lincoln, sociologists uncovered an unexpected pattern showing that "older marriage cohorts experience[d] higher levels of marital happiness than younger marriage cohorts." The authors of the new study infer from their findings the likelihood that the older couples had "strengths that allow them to maintain high levels of marital happiness over the long haul." Such strengths were conspicuously absent among younger couples.[38]

Explaining survey data showing a decline since the early 1970s in the number of couples who report "marital happiness," sociologist Norval Glenn reasons that the problem is precisely that the increasingly pervasive fear of divorce has fostered a new and disturbing reluctance to "commit fully" in making marital commitments.[39] And when psychologist Mihaly Csikszentmihalyi puzzles over data indicating that American dependence upon psychotropic drugs has increased in recent decades even as household income has increased, he implicates the malign influence of an economic rationality within which "the opportunity costs of playing with one's child, reading poetry, or attending a family reunion become too high, and so one stops doing such irrational things."[40] Somewhere, the shade of Brooks Adams is nodding in agreement.

Confronted by empirical studies showing us the relative strength of family life in the past, progressive intellectuals may still smile wryly as they invoke their favorite metaphor: like it or not, we cannot turn back the clock. Why is it that many of these intellectuals adopt a very different attitude towards the same kind of chronological metaphor when it is invoked in environmental discussions? That is, when the issue is polluted air, dirty water, or endangered species, progressive intellectuals are more than willing to turn back the clock. Why is it that no prominent pundit accused environmental activist Kelly Evans of nostalgia or atavism when he recently urged "government, business, and individuals to make a real difference when it comes to turning back the clock on global warming"?[41] Why is it that the progressive intellectuals who cry out in horror against any attempt to turn back the clock on family patterns are the same ones we see loudly applauding an aggressive environmentalist plan in Florida to "turn back time and give the Everglades back to nature"?[42] Why do commentators who lecture us on the impossibility of turning the clock back on divorce or illegitimacy speak in such different tones when "Britain turns back the clock on cars" with commuting rules that cut air pollution? [43]

Rebuilding Families

Of course, chronology cannot be reversed. Americans cannot put Dwight Eisenhower, Teddy Roosevelt, or Abraham Lincoln back in the White House. Hoary trees cannot be turned into the saplings they were when Lewis and Clark explored the Missouri, and aged men and women can be guided to no Fountain of Youth. But environmentalists are perfectly right when they insist that some aspects of the past can be recovered. Species now endangered can be brought back from the brink of extinction. Lakes and rivers now befouled with pollutants can be returned to something like their purity of decades ago. And air filled with smoke can be restored to the cleanliness of times long past. Why can Americans not look at family life in the past–and only shallow analysts will fasten on the family life of the fifties, since the germs of many of today's family diseases were already strong and spreading at that time–to identify desirable patterns to be recovered? We need, of course, to heed Barzun's warning against idealizing any period as a golden age, since every era is to some degree "an Age of Troubles."[44] But it is not blind nostalgia but careful research that assures us that family life in the past–imperfect as it was–was significantly stronger than it is today. And in the strengths of the past we can find goals for the future. If we can turn the clock back for alligators or cranes, why not for intact families and maternal child care?

Given the severity of the problems caused by family decay, Americans need to recognize not only that they *can* turn back the clock on such decay, but also that they *must* turn back the clock. In this context, perhaps the clock metaphor that Americans need to start thinking about is the one developed by the editors of *The Bulletin of Atomic Scientists* published at the University of Chicago. On this metaphorical Doomsday Clock, midnight represents nuclear apocalypse. Periodically, the editors of this newsletter move the minute hand on this clock, forward (closer to midnight) when yet another country announces the testing of a nuclear weapon or when tensions between nuclear powers increase, backward (farther from midnight) when nuclear powers slash their arsenals or agree upon new arms-control treaties. [45] On this clock, as on the environmentalists', moving the clock backward renews hope and safeguards life.

Perhaps it is time that Americans started to worry about the nightmarish midnight of complete family meltdown. Perhaps we should start to worry not just about nuclear Armageddon but social Armageddon, the Armageddon which threatens us when the last couple to bother with a marriage ceremony has divorced; when the last child not to be aborted has been dropped off at the daycare center by his unwed careerist mother; when the last grandmother ever to tell a grandchild her life story has chucked her family Bible on her way to a gated retirement community in Arizona. Perhaps if we honestly and soberly contemplate such a midnight, we will join atomic scientists in an earnest search for ways to turn back the clock.

Notes

1. Denise M. Topolnicki, "The American Dream: Economic Myths and Realities," *Current* May 1993: 4-9.
2. Constance Ahrons, "Should Government's Bias Against Marriage Be Reversed?" *Insight on the News* 15 April 1996: 25.
3. See Maki Becker, "Hil Blasts W's Policies to Upstaters," *New York Daily News* 25 March 2001: 2.
4. Allan C. Carlson, *Family Questions: Reflections on the American Social Crisis* (New Brunswick, NJ: Transaction Publishers, 1988), xvii.
5. Thomas B. Macaulay, *The History of England from the Accession of James the Second* (London, 1849), 1: 3.
6. Macaulay quoted in John Clive, *Macaulay: The Shaping of the Historian* (New York: Alfred A. Knopf, 1973), 422.
7. Herbert Butterfield, *The Whig Interpretation of History* (1931; rpt. New York, 1965), v.
8. Christopher Lasch, *The True and Only Heaven: Progress and Its Critics* (New York: W.W. Norton, 1991), 58.
9. Lasch, op. cit., 13, 81.
10. Joyce Appleby, "Liberal Education in a Postliberal World," *Liberal Education* 79.3 (Summer '93): 18-24.
11. Jacques Barzun, *From Dawn to Decadence: 1500 to the Present* (New York: HarperCollins, 2000), 714.
12. Randall Jarrell, "A Sad Heart at the Supermarket," in Norman Jacobs, ed., *Culture for the Millions? Mass Media in Modern Society* (Boston: Beacon, 1964), 97-100.
13. See A. Robert Caponigri, *Time and Idea: The Theory of History in Giambattista Vico* (Notre Dame, IN: University of Notre Dame Press, 1953).
14. Ibid., 92.
15. See Barzun, op. cit., 315.
16. Henry George, *Progress and Poverty* (1880; rpt. New York: Robert Schalkenbach, 1955), 480-515.
17. Brooks Adams, *The Law of Civilization and Decay* (1896; rpt. New York: Vintage, 1955), 6-7.
18. Pitirim A. Sorokin, *Social and Cultural Dynamics*, Rev. and abridged ed. (1957; rpt. New Brunswick, NJ: Transaction Publishers, 1985), 695 - 702.
19. Barzun, op. cit., 801.
20. Stephanie Coontz, *The Way We Never Were: American Families and the Nostalgia Trap* (New York: Basic Books, 1992), 2-4, 42-43.
21. Stephanie Coontz, *The Way We Really Are: Coming to Terms With America's Changing Families* (New York: Basic Books, 1997), 177.
22. Edward Kain, *The Myth of Family Decline: Understanding Families in a World of Rapid Social Change* (Lexington, MA: Lexington Books, 1990), 9-11, 149-151.
23. Lasch, op. cit., 31, 35-37.
24. Jose Ortega y Gasset, *The Revolt of the Masses* (1932; rpt. New York: W.W. Norton, 1957), 36,107, 125.
25. Jean M. Twenge, "The Ago of Anxiety? Birth Cohort Change in Anxiety and Neuroticism, 1952-1993," *Journal of Personality and Social Psychology* 79(2000): 1007-1021.)
26. Kelly J. Kelleher et al., "Increasing Identification of Psychosocial Problems: 1979-1996," *Pediatrics* 105 (2000): 1313-1321.
27. Kathryn Tout et al., "Social Behavior Correlates of Cortisol Activity in Child Care," *Child Development* 69 (1998): 1247-1262.

28. See Edward L. Levine, "Day Care: Cons, Costs, Kids," *Chicago Tribune* 18 September 1984: 15.

29. Lynne Vernon-Feagans et al., "Otitis Media and the Social Behavior of Day-Care Attending Children," *Child Development* 67 (1996): 1528-1539.

30. Wendy A. Goldberg et al., "Employment and Achievement: Mothers' Work Involvement in Relation to Children's Achievement Behaviors and Mothers' Parenting Behaviors," *Child Development* 67 (1996): 1512-1527.

31. Crimes Against Children Research Center, David Finkelhor, Director, University of New Hampshire, 3 January 2002 http://www.unh.edu/ccrc/factsheet.html

32. Martin Daly and Margo Wilson, "Child Abuse and Other Risks of Not Living With Both Parents," *Ethology and Sociobiology* 3 (1982): 197-209.

33. David G. Gil, "Violence Against Children," in *Child Abuse: A Reader and Source Book*, ed. Constance M. Leck (Abingdon: Open University Press, 1978), 49.

34. John Demos, *Past, Present, and Personal: The Family and the Life Course in American History* (New York: Oxford University Press, 1986), 68-91.

35. John S. Wodarski and Pamela Harris, "Adolescent Suicide: A Review of Influences and the Means for Prevention," *Social Work* 32 (1989): 477-484.

36. Judith L. Rubenstein et al., "Suicidal Behavior in Adolescents: Stress and Protection in Different Family Contexts," *American Journal of Orthopsychiatry* 68 (1998): 274-284.

37. David T. Courtwright, *Violent Land: Single Men and Social Disorder from the Frontier to the Inner City* (Cambridge, MA: Harvard University Press, 1996), 242, 272, 280.

38. John VanLaningham et al., "Marital Happiness, Marital Duration, and the U-Shaped Curve," *Social Forces* 78 (2001): 1313-1341.

39. Norval D. Glenn, "The Recent Trend in Marital Success in the United States," *Journal of Marriage and the Family* 53 (1991): 261-270.

40. Mihaly Csikszentmihalyi, "If We Are So Rich, Why Aren't We Happy?" *American Psychologist* 54 (1999): 821-827.

41. Kelly Evans, "Earth Day 2000," *Solar Today* March/April 2000: 24-27.

42. See Kirk Brown, "The Everglades: Reversing Man's Mistakes," *Palm Beach Post* 11 April 1993: Spec. Sec., 1-8.

43. See Nick Nuttall, "Britain Turns Back the Clock on Cars," *Times* (London) 15 January 1994: Home News Section.

44. Barzun, op. cit., 655.

45. See Debbie Howlett, "Nuclear Clock Ticks Closer to Doomsday," *USA Today* 12 June 1998: 4A.

Index